16. 5

Publisher's Comment

As Florida evolves toward the megastate, Al Burt roves it clocking the changes. His work reflects a kind of running history of the state, but less of the blood-and-guts events that make headlines than of the common joys and dilemmas that in sum help explain how it is for the ordinary Floridian during these times.

Burt goes to each part of the state, to both the cities and the villages, mingling with the powerful and the powerless, exploring how these individual struggles bring new character and direction. He gives us some of those elusive common flavors of life that too often get lost in press conferences and board meetings and sidewalk protests.

He tells us something of the shock of change, of customs and traditions lost in payment for new ambitions raised, of the disorientation and gradual reformation that takes place when a state doubles its population within 20 years not because Floridians mass-produced babies but because people from other regions and other lands wanted to live in Florida.

Occasionally he stops and thinks out loud, commenting on how it all digests, questioning the herd instincts, reminding us that even during the computer age the answers still begin with the reasoning and resolve of individuals.

Becalmed

in the

Mullet Latitudes

Al Burt's Florida

Mugil curema Valenciennes

Becalmed In The Mullet Latitudes

Al Burt's Florida

by

Al Burt

With an Introduction by Ernest Lyons,
retired Editor of the Stuart (Fla.) News

Florida Classics Library

Library of Congress Catalog Card Number 83-81677

Paperbound ISBN 0-912451-10-6
Clothbound ISBN 0-912451-11-4

Becalmed In The Mullet Latitudes
Al Burt's Florida

Published in cooperation with the editors
of

The Sunday Magazine of The Miami Herald

Typesetting by

Typographic Expressions
Stuart, Fla. 33494

Published by

Florida Classics Library
P.O. Box 1657
Port Salerno, Fla. 33492-1657

Printed in the U.S.A. by Southeastern Printing Company, Inc.
Stuart, Florida 33495

for Gloria and Biddy

Cover Design by Florida Classics Library

The Seven Little Florida's Awash In the Mullet Latitudes

Table of Contents

Floridiana

Places

People

Reflections

Home

Preface

The Mullet Latitudes are an imaginary place, but real. They exist in the shade of the condos, between the rows of orange trees, among the mangrove-lined bays and inlets, in big cities and small.

They are the spiritual homeplace for every person who loves Florida, a personal vision that blends what the state is, was and ought to be. They combine the appreciation of place with the sense of identification and belonging.

They can be found anywhere on the peninsula, for they come out of individual intuition, and by any person enchanted by the mystique of Florida, whether native Cracker, volunteer resident or tourist.

This book, bit by bit, unfolds my findings about their people, places and things. All of these essays, except for minor alterations to indicate the time they were written or to combine recurring thoughts on a single subject, appeared in The Miami Herald, most of them in its Sunday magazine Tropic, and are collected here with The Herald's blessing.

— Al Burt

Additional Books by Al Burt
PAPA DOC (with Bernard Diederich)
FLORIDA A PLACE IN THE SUN

Ernest Lyons and Pudge with fresh caught bass

Photo by Ezelle Lyons

Eternal Discovery
an introduction
by *Ernest Lyons
Retired Editor, The Stuart News

Floridians come in waves from all over. Each must discover a personal Florida, shaped by his own concepts.

Used to be there was plenty of time to do this, when it took generations to produce Cracker Floridians and decades to make Floridians out of real estate breeches boom-and-busters, tin can tourists, military personnel that trained here and returned and even tourists.

They all came, saw, were captured by Florida's magic, put down roots and made their discoveries. We have always needed writers like Al Burt to tell us what Florida is like, its interesting places, unique Floridiana and fascinating people — but now there's an urgency about it. We're getting instant Floridians.

They just buy a condominium and are eligible for homestead exemption. You can't be more Floridian than that.

We all are fortunate in The Miami Herald's choice of Al as its roving columnist on Florida. The paper has been blessed by having had Steve Trumbull and Nixon Smiley in that slot before him. As a retired small town newspaper editor, and a reporter for fifty years, I have been privileged to know all three as friends. Each shares the distinction of being a "habit-forming" writer. The term is highly complimentary. It means that the writer gets the public in the habit of buying the paper — so they won't miss anything he has to say.

No one knows the magic formula that makes readers swing to certain writers like iron filings behind a magnet. My theory is that this type of writer likes what he is doing, takes joy in his work, and some of his fun rubs off on the reader. All we know, however, is that all of a sudden readers begin saying: "This guy is good." They clip his pieces and send them to friends. They write him: "I feel the same way you do."

With all these new instant Floridians about, this book could not be more timely. The need to experience Florida in all its forms is greater than it has ever been. Many of us, even old mossback Floridians, will visit some of these places Al writes about, and will personally meet some of these people we first met vicariously here. Thus he will become a part of us.

You've got to watch Al or he will trap you into thinking when you don't suspect there's a thought around in crouching distance. Happened to me when I was sitting peacefully half-dreaming in my garden reading his essay on old-fashioned scarecrows and how modern men still need the beauty and miracle of a garden to scare away the black thoughts of nuclear war, old age and all that junk. Suddenly, I heard the flapping of their wings, the crows, buzzards and pterodactyls of new, old and primordial fears.

Al's beat is all Florida, more than 700 miles from Key West to the Panhandle. He plans his coverage so that each section will be fairly represented. Based at quiet Melrose in Central Florida, he and his lovely wife Gloria fan out from there to run down leads from Chipley to Immokalee. His writing maintains an unwavering standard of excellence.

His job is to supply the background that all Floridians hunger for. They are "family" now, all of them; this is home no matter where they came from, magically turned into Floridians, wave after wave.

While there were ripples before them, the first wave came mostly from the South and their descendants are known as Crackers. For a long time they claimed to be the only real Floridians. They farmed, ranched, fished and kept stores. They worked. Even their dogs worked, slow-trailing deer, catching wild hogs by the ears and treeing coons. When a Cracker asked anyone "What does your dog do?" he expected a straight answer.

Crackers believed intensely that they were the only rightful Floridians by virtue of living here year around while the mosquitoes drained them white and their blood was thinned by the savage summer sun. They believed they served a purpose in the scheme of things, telling newcomers what to do if they got snake-bit and warning them never to build on the ocean beaches. Now Crackers are an endangered species because mosquito control and air-conditioning have so changed their environment that hordes of competing species have rushed in.

They deserve our sympathy. They are utterly confounded by the walls of condominiums facing the surf and it is a little too much to expect them to believe that all those cubicles in the sky are inhabited by new Floridians.

The Cracker has always been friendly; now he is frustrated. When he meets a lady with blue hair being led by a prancing poodle of the same hue, it is natural to want to ask "What does your dog do?" but he doesn't, just standing mute and staring, not really being sure that it is a dog.

There's one last thing. Before the Crackers go bye-bye, they would like Al, on his mission of eternal discovery, to find out how grownups can live in caves in the sky without any kids around, live and live well just playing around without working a lick. Just answer that and he can skip telling what their dogs do, if they are dogs.

*Lyons is author of MY FLORIDA and
THE LAST CRACKER BARREL.

The Author

Floridiana

Becalmed in the
Mullet Latitudes

Where is the real Florida? People always ask that. Sometimes they call it the forgotten Florida, or the other Florida, but whatever they call it they mean the remnants of Florida That Used To Be.

That Florida is lost in the mullet latitudes. It is less a place now than a certain time at a certain place. It reveals itself like a ghost that stalks spitefully in the halls of the disbelievers during quiet times.

That Florida lies wholly within the mythical Tropic of Cracker, a few degrees north of the Tropic of Cancer and hiding like the pea in a con game, under one shell or another.

But under which shell? That is the question they keep asking. Where?

Sometimes, it is everywhere; sometimes, nowhere. Like happiness, it lives in your head and must be coaxed out. Maybe for me it will appear during November in Miami, a conglomerate of small places, or during summer at my hometown Melrose, a miniature large place.

Real Florida comes on like a mood, inspired by little catch-hooks, by the preseasonal budding and blossoming of a place just before it comes to full flower and invites its own consumption.

A suspended condition calls it up, like the eye of a hurricane when a fugitive calm seems a powerful presence because the renewed uproar is anticipated. The moments have a quality of challenging mental digestion, the kind of thing that occurs when someone plants a seed and tries to articulate why miraculous life will follow.

To conjure up that Florida requires as much philosophy as literal search. Think of that Florida as a reverse mirage: When the reality was here, we did not understand it, but with time it retreats; it is painted with nostalgia and the anxiety is removed. We like that kind of reality.

The real Florida hovers around Sanibel Island and the Keys during September and October, when the tourist tide ebbs for the hurricane season. It shows up during January and February at Panama City and Destin, those cities of summer, when icy winds hollow them out and they resemble the villages of old wearing clothing that is too large for them.

It stays alive in small towns all over Florida, those places meant to be lived in, not visited, peculiarly blessed by an ugly duckling aura that steers the growth cyclone away.

Smatterings of it can be detected in the big cities along the South Florida coasts in summer, when the height of the high-rises seems surpassed by the Fahrenheit and sweat inspires pause, contemplation and visits to the mountains.

Some of it is suggested in the cities' shopping mall clusters that have become small towns with everything in them but homes — communities populated by an ever-changing roster of urban Crackers with rural insides. So many of them, it seems, yearn nostalgically for the days of grace and courtesy in public places.

All of these, and more, make up the mullet latitudes — Florida's version of those becalming horse latitudes that encircle the earth between the tradewinds and the prevailing westerlies — and they are the spiritual home of the real Florida.

The mullet latitudes come and go like moody apparitions. They are Florida's blackberry winter or Indian summer, except that they are much more than a span of weather enchantingly out of season. They encompass place and time and memory and call up visions and emotions like those that occur when you study pictures of your childhood home.

In Florida, the budding megastate, they nourish a strain of rusticity even as the population centers spread and line up, fastening one to the other like so many oysters.

Oddly, it exists in the cities as much as it does in the countryside.

The villages still have the hulls of old Florida — the rusting tin roofs, the weather-darkened frame homes, the quaint churches — like working museum pieces, but they are being taken over to a surprising degree by the city folk with the rural insides.

The multiple effects of population movement — a mammoth immigration primarily to South Florida cities, coupled with a small counter tide of urbanites and retirees moving to the North and to the interior seeking the beauties of the past and the places where they still might be found, or at least imagined — make the mullet latitudes a potent if unearthly influence.

A surprising percentage of the legitimate country folk, whose numbers are few and dwindling in Florida today, still dream feverishly of converting pastures into parking lots, filling up messy old swamps with clean asphalt, abandoning the old farm for what they innocently perceive as the gentle life in a condo.

It is not surprising to go into a small town today and discover that the folk who are agitating to keep things the way they always have been are the ones that moved in from the city not too long ago.

A lot of the good ole boys are going to town, or at least want to, and a lot of the urban slickers are following their dream into the country. The spiritual heirs of the real Florida may be the ones who know the least about it. The children who grew up on streets and sidewalks are the backward revolutionaries who truly keep the real Florida alive.

Not enough of the native noble-Indian types are left in the Tropic of Cracker, protecting the old homestead from being remodeled, worshipping the wetlands, fretting about the purity of the rivers and lakes, musing about Real Florida with the sadness of a miser reconstructing the terrors of inflation.

Today, when you find that fine old piece of Floridiana, chances are you can thank some fellow from Michigan or Miami who got becalmed in the mullet latitudes.

The Seven Little Floridas

Within Florida, there are many little Floridas, casual fiefdoms where subleties of geographic difference nourish cultural identities. The result is a puzzling, pleasing mosaic.

Every four years, when Presidential politics picks out some handsome heads and finely tuned images to rear, the little Floridas take on unreal importance.

Heavy thinkers leave Washington in advance of the candidates and dutifully come out into the provinces to grope with reality. We are a microcosm of the nation, they say, especially if the winter is cold, and that gives them exploratory rights.

The thinkers ought to understand that there are seven Floridas, not one, and that it is hard to throw a single piece of wisdom over all seven without some important things sticking out the sides.

We begin with *Floribama,* the Florida of the Northwest, the one with the panhandle shape. This is mullet and collard green country. Floribamans tend toward fundamentalism in all things, and they contend that they live in the only real Florida. But, as a matter of fact, Floribamans so resemble Alabamans that it is almost impossible to tell them apart. The capital is Panama City, sometimes known as Alabama Heaven.

Florgia comes next. It extends from Floribama to the Atlantic Coast, and then south below Ocala. Florgia is a de-Georgiaizing zone that enables travelers to pass between Georgia and Florida gently and without excessive trauma.

It looks like Georgia, sounds like Georgia, and sometimes even acts like Georgia. So thorough is the intermingling that Jacksonville long has been known as the largest city in South Georgia.

On ambience, the capital should be Starke.

Florgia was the Cracker motherlode, the heartland of old Florida. For much of the first half of the 20th century, it dominated the state. It produced the most powerful politicians, shaped the attitudes, until the southern half of the state attracted enough population to muscle away the leadership.

No road signs mark Florgia and the geographical changes are subtle, a kind of harmonious smoothing down of the Georgia hills and blanching of the clay and lowering of sea-level until finally you are among the sinkholes and sand.

Something about this Little Florida always was magical to Georgians. So many saw the act of growing up and going to Florida as an essential step in finding that world where farm boys become presidents and tycoons.

There has been a sharing of customs, intermarriage, the creating of an accent a shade less broad than Georgia's yet distinctively Southern, the emergence of Florgia Creoles whose blood and heritage override formal borders.

Crudities have developed in the dispute over whether Florgia was mongrelized or Superbred. Former U.S. Sen. Herman Talmadge (D., Ga.) defined that situation with a verbal two-by-four. He blessed the persistent migration of Georgians to Florida as a boon that raised the level of intelligence in both states.

Next comes New Miami, which in the 21st century will be to Florida what Florgia was in the first half of the 20th. New Miami is shaped like a squat H. It covers a belt across the middle of the State, and spreads a short way north and south on each coast.

New Miami, powered by migration toward Disney World, revels in boom growth and strangers' dollars. Here in this magic land, it is said, anything is possible and nothing ever rusts or needs painting. Some compare it to a mermaid: beautiful, but missing some practical parts. The capital is Disney World; the soul symbol, Goofy.

Below New Miami, down the center of the state, is *The Ridge,* a highlands spine traversed by U.S. 27, where oranges grow robustly and where the residents treasure a gentler life than can be had on the coasts. Many here sniff and wrinkle their noses at the goings-on in New Miami.

The capital is Lake Wales, and for soul advisor I would nominate a committee from the Florida League Against Progress (FLAP), whose distinctive public service includes the annual issuance of a Florida Calamity Calendar that details disasters and inconveniences, arranged to make prospective residents pause.

Below The Ridge is the state of *Okeechobee,* the only other little Florida that is landlocked. Not until the 1920s boom did the world fully penetrate Okeechobee, and there is divided opinion whether this was progress. Okeechobee has the same attractive flavor of Old Florida as Floribama, without the disadvantage of having so many Alabamans.

Okeechobee is round, clustered around the great lake that gives it distinction, and has pioneer character. Okeechobee City is the capital and the soul symbol is embodied in a live-and-let-live woodsman named Rod Chandler, an Audubon Society warden who blends perfectly with the people and the environment.

At the bottom of the peninsula, shaped like a *U,* is the longtime champion, the richest and most hugely populated of the little Floridas. We call it *The Colonized Coast* for pilgrims from the Northeast have peopled its Atlantic side and from the Midwest, its Gulf side. Settled in the bottom of the cup are a mix of pilgrims from everywhere, including a large portion from the Caribbean. On sentiment, the capital is Miami Beach.

Finally, there is the famed *Conch Republic,* a Florida unto itself, the beautiful and unique Florida Keys. The Keys are at a political riptide between the old ways that consume its natural physical identity and restrictive new ones that try to preserve what is left.

These are The Seven Little Floridas, each worthy and lovable and peculiar, just like a family. With the fabled election year 1984 coming up, that nightmare time forecast by George Orwell, we want the wizards to have every bit of help possible. Consider this a preliminary scorecard.

What to call these lucky seven? The field is open. How about, The United Flakes?

The Surreal Seasons of Florida

As a matter of pride, Floridians can strain at their calendars and construct a case that they have the traditional seasons — winter, spring, summer, fall — but the result is as graceful as a forced smile.

Others will explain that the seasons are confused in Florida, and that it is foolish to try to make sense of them, that the Florida seasons slide into one another like a telescope and cannot be separated. But that does not perfectly fit, either.

Marjorie Kinnan Rawlings, who wrote sensitively about rural Florida a half century ago, put it as poetically as any. "Here in Florida the seasons move in and out like nuns in soft clothing, making no rustle in their passing," she said.

However, neither Rawlings nor any of the other fine writers who have taken a swing at describing Florida's seasons did a full and thorough job. They insisted upon using the traditional framework and it warped their accuracy. The Florida seasons simply do not fit tradition.

To illustrate the awkwardness of the task, consider the following. Summer in South Florida lasts from late March to November. But in North Florida, it begins in May and continues until September.

Spring in South Florida usually stretches from about 5 o'clock on an April afternoon to sunset. In North Florida, spring is more elastic. At its best, it fills April.

In South Florida, fall occurs during the playing of the *Star Spangled Banner* before a University of Miami football game. In North Florida, by ancient tradition, it covers at least three University of Florida losses, all of them often in October.

Some winters, South Florida has no winter. In other years, it might happen on any Tuesday or Wednesday — never on a weekend

— during February and March. North Florida, by contrast, is vulnerable to a hit-run strike from winter at any time during December, January, February and March.

As you can see, this becomes a clumsy explanation. It gets even worse if you include the shadings of seasons in middle Florida. Better you should understand that Florida simply does not fit those traditional concepts of season. It has its own seasons, lots of them.

For example, the two basic seasons are Hot and Cool (spiced with several dashes of cold in the north). From those, the pattern breaks down into several subseasons, at least one of which is precipitated by foreign events.

A major South Florida cycle, one that requires the equivalent of storing up coal and firewood and keeping snow shovels handy, is the In-Law season. This nearly always coincides with snow and ice somewhere in the rest of the country.

Rather than coal and wood, though, this requires huge stores of expensive food and booze. The challenge, rather than frostbite, is crimped pocketbook and small-talk paralysis. Those deprived of mobile in-laws refer to this, less heatedly, as Snowbird Season.

Always too, there has been this rap against Florida that it has no colorful fall, none of the beautiful reds and golds that appear on the trees in the Georgia and Carolina mountains. Again, this is ignorance.

South Floridians love going up to the mountains — which are considered to be no more than upstairs Florida — to see the colors of the leaves. But if the rigors of the In-Law season have taken too much of a toll, they simply can wait until mid-Hot — say, July or August — and travel the shorter distance to Daytona Beach. On display there will be spectacular reds and golds on the backs of thousands of Georgia and Alabama Crackers in varying degrees of sunburn.

There is more. Twice a year, corresponding to traditional spring and fall, Florida has a Love-Bug season. This is marked by an erotic sideshow performed by little black insects that fly along the highway upside down and backwards, athletically making love all the while, so enthralled by their own performance that they happily accept a suicidal smash into the first auto that comes along. They produce stains that should be wiped off.

Some of the seasons coincide and overlap. For instance, Rainy, Mosquito and Hurricane seasons — though actually separate and distinct phenomena — occur in Hot.

During the first hints of Cool, Sandspur season begins. Sandspurs are little burrs, souvenirs actually, which collect on your socks if you mistakenly stray off the asphalt and concrete at any time.

Stonecrab season, Oyster season and Mullet season — are so-named for gourmet delights from the sea — crowd in on the calendar about the same time as the sandspurs mature.

There are so many. By accident of geography, Central and North Florida have a bonus period that South Florida does not share — Sinkhole Season. This sometimes occurs during traditional spring. Great holes suddenly appear in the earth. Anything resting upon the affected surface — houses, autos, people — involuntarily dives beneath the ground. This has not yet replaced scuba in popularity.

A very special season bears the name Retirees' Winter, the Florida version of Indian Summer. This transpires as a subdivision of Hot and requires at least 65 years of experience to be enjoyed. The participants can be detected wearing sweaters in August.

These are some of the real Florida seasons. Coleridge advised, "All seasons shall be sweet to thee," and that is how it is in Florida: Not traditional, not confused but — once you have cultivated the taste — oh so sweet.

Florida Time

Florida is a sunset state, but it has a sunrise soul. A special sense of time prevails. The standard measures do not apply. So many leave somewhere else and come here to glow but not to fade. Florida makes the blossoms last longer, lengthens the harvest season.

Florida is part of a brave extended world, spiritually fuelled by contrasting memories of Michigan and Illinois and New York and New Jersey, a place where people are born into old age with a license to forget it.

Daylight Savings Time is child's play. *Florida Time* operates on a clock that ticks by years, not seconds, and nobody listens. It gongs for parties. Florida Time does for life what DST does for daylight.

Every bum in America, every wage-slave, every tycoon — of whatever age — can come to Florida and be part of the sunset. That is the big, possible dream: To climb aboard this sandy rainbow. The illusion, the colors are wonderful. Nowhere else does the sunset so fire the imagination, so carry the hope if not the reality of a sunrise.

Everywhere else there is a proper time to mourn and a proper time to dance. Florida Time does away with that. Dance any time you feel like it; mourn never, if you choose. Where the inhibitions of age are concerned, Florida is devoutly libertine. It is an all-ages summer camp with a year-round summer.

"The nightingale, if she should sing by day, when every goose is cackling, would be thought no better a musician than a wren," wrote Shakespeare, apparently an old-fashioned man who believed in the conventions of time. But in Florida, if the nightingales and the geese duel vocally under the sun, it might as well be harmony. Cacophony is the Florida song. Sing along. Honk along.

10

The other states do not mind. The stage revolves. How many nurture the thought that perhaps one day they might live in Florida? Anyway, there is reciprocal propaganda at work. Never in South Dakota itself was South Dakota so genuine as in the memories of a Florida sunset citizen, though of course never so grand, either, as the new life. Never did Illinois or New York or New Jersey have such extraordinary qualities.

Those first Florida impressions on a newcomer have the aura of magic. Illusion induces giddiness. The low, flat terrain and the great sweep of sky introduce an extraordinary sense of unreality and suspension of time. Reality will resume sometime in the future at some other place. Imagination suggests that the cities sit at a crest of the horizon, miniaturized, silhouetted against that sunset. The effect is symphonic.

Florida is in the eye of the time hurricane. There is a touch of euphoria. Drudgery could wear out so frail a veil quickly; the huffing and puffing of regular labor can blow away the bemusing vapors. But tourists and retirees have little of that to worry about. They do not have to abuse Florida Time with work routines, plod upon it like a mule, treat it as they might in New Jersey or Michigan.

In Florida the rivers flow quietly; the lakes gleam like 30,000 earth-eyes; the ocean laps at both sides of the peninsula, scrubbing and cleansing it with saltwater waves. The body of Florida is sand over limestone, and the past leaches quickly through. Do not bring up the future; humidity will mildew it. All is present.

For newcomers, and the pleasurably idle, it is one long happy hour. Booze permitted, but not necessary. Daybreak does not come hard, like more new ground to be broken; it does not require zealotry to face it gladly, or cunning and stamina to survive it. The poetry of Florida moves that sunset ease up, spreads it around, and all the mornings have a Sunday morning quality. They begin with an end-of-the-day satisfaction.

Geography encourages it all. The long Florida sandbar is a poor divider of sunrise and sunset. When the sun rises above the Atlantic and rolls over to the gulf side, it does not seem so long a journey, or so significant a one.

At high noon over the middle, there is so noticeable a pause that not even the years seem to tick away. It is the time to seek shade and siesta, to sort out the next smile and get it ready.

In Florida, the search for shade is part of the pursuit of happiness, but the sunset qualities nourish a curious kind of courage. For only in the final moments of sunset, when the brilliant colors so soften that we look directly at them, do we dare to face it and really see it, alone and without help.

Ernie Lyons, a fine writer and one of the great decoders of life in Florida, once noted how even small, delicate flowers stare devotedly at the sun, but humans cover their eyes and turn away from it. "What frailty is in us that we cannot even look the sun directly in the eye?" he asked.

Sunset is the great liberator, and Florida is the sunset state. Nobody rides off into the sunset here. They live in it, silhouettes on the crest of a horizon that have shed the old inhibitions and have fitted their lives to the unrealities before them.

There are all sorts of time. There is waltz time, spare time, free time, good time, tax time, Christmas time and so many others. But none is so different as Florida Time, the sunset time that stretches that late glow and makes it last.

If it is all an illusion, the illusion for so many has become as real as their patio stones. Finally, they have come to a place where nobody demands that they quit dreaming. Florida Time permits unrealism.

No wonder they keep coming.

Dunnellon ★

The Healthy Appetites of Alligators

Ernest Jackman enjoyed swimming at night. His retirement home graced the high bank of an old phosphate pit that opened off the Rainbow River in Dunnellon. The river's clear blue waters had turned the pit into a deep, lovely lake ringed by greenery.

He could step off his front yard and swim in water that Tarzan would have admired. There were some alligators, but he was not afraid of them.

Once, for awhile, a little gator hung around the water by the house. Jackman and his wife imagined it enjoyed their company, but it would flee when Jackman swam toward it. Another time, while swimming on his back, a small gator crawled up on his chest. Jackman shoved it off and it came back. He had to splash water to scare it away.

For a retired Ford employee from Detroit, an active man, this flirtation with wildlife caused a certain exhilaration, especially because alligators were involved. Somehow, for newcomers to Florida, no wild animal has more fascination. "I never figured they would hurt anybody," Jackman said.

One July night after dark, he swam out to the middle where the water was maybe 30 feet deep. "Something grabbed my left arm," he said. "Hit me and held. When I resisted, it let go." It was a gator. Jackman, 67 then, suffered shock and it took 23 stitches to close the wounds. Even after three years, the scar still showed.

"After that, I didn't swim anymore at night, but I'd go every afternoon. I needed the exercise," he said.

At 7:30 one August evening 11 months after the attack, about

13

dusk, he swam only 20 feet offshore. "Something grabbed me around the head. Didn't see or hear anything. Don't know whether it came up behind me, under me or what. Suddenly it just had me. Clamped down on both sides of my head.

"I tried to pull away, and it let go of my head and grabbed my arm. It pulled me down under the water, maybe 6 feet. I was swirling around and being pulled down. Maybe it was twisting its head.

"Then it let go again and I came up. I could see it, maybe 15 feet away, a big one, the biggest I've ever seen. It didn't come at me again and I swam ashore."

"He walked in the door and said, 'It happened again,'" Mrs. Jackman recalled. "There was a hole in his head and blood was pouring out." It took 22 stitches to close the wounds this time. There was an operation to remove a piece of bone from his head. "It left me with two fingers that feel like they are asleep," he said.

After that, Jackman rarely swam and never at dusk or at night. His experience, 17 miles west of Ocala in North Central Florida, symbolizes much about the Florida dilemma with wildlife, particularly alligators. The animals serve a purpose in the natural environment, but there have been unprovoked alligator attacks on humans.

The problem by now is familiar: as Florida's population soars, human residences encroach on the wetlands alligator habitat. The alligator population, protected since 1962 when its numbers were thought to be dwindling, began to boom in the early 1970s after a federal law curbed poachers' interstate sales of hides.

During the 1970s, alligator attacks became more numerous and more serious in Florida. In 1973, an 11-foot gator killed a girl swimming in a state park; in 1978, a man clearing a lake shoreline was attacked by a 7-foot alligator, which clamped on his arm and began to twist. Loss of the arm resulted in shock and death. Also in 1978, a 15-year-old boy swimming in a canal was attacked and killed.

Most victims were in or near the water late on a summer day, had no fear of alligators and had no warning there was an alligator in the vicinity. The larger the gator, the larger the feeding prey he might choose.

Tommy C. Hines, alligator expert at the Florida Game and Fresh Water Fish Commission wildlife research laboratory in Gainesville, directed a program both to preserve alligators and to protect humans.

With current controls and nearly three million acres of gator habitat under government protection in Florida, alligator survival is not presently endangered. However, the future of the alligator in non-protected wetlands could be endangered.

In 1979, the commission received 5,000 alligator complaints (down from 10,000 in 1977) and "harvested" (killed) 1,679 nuisance gators. About half the complaints and half the kills came in South Florida and the Everglades. The hides and the meat were sold under controlled circumstances (hides to tanners at auction; the meat to restaurants) to pay the 60 Florida trappers licensed by the commission. It remains illegal for anyone else to kill an alligator.

Hines preached that common sense and caution can permit people and alligators to coexist in most situations. He tried to enlighten the public to a realistic fear without overreaction that could lead to demands for a harsher policy toward gators. But after a case study on attacks, he warned: ". . . large alligators will attack humans with the intent to eat them."

While Jackman's case was distinctive because he suffered two attacks, the examples are numerous and chilling. One 45-year-old man, while swimming, was attacked by an 11-foot gator. It clamped jaws on his chest and pulled him under the water twice. Going under a third time, the man pushed his hand down the alligator's throat. It released his chest and grabbed the wrist. The man's screams brought help and he lived.

A 34-year-old wildlife officer, standing in knee-deep water, saw no gator until he was knocked down, and then struck a second time. Its jaws clamped on his arm and shoulder and the alligator began to shake him. He pushed the animal's nose with his free hand and tore the other arm loose. He beat off a third attack, striking the gator with his hands and shouting. It was a 12-footer.

Some wildlife enthusiasts tend to minimize the dangers, but the experts know that among alligators there are no Bambis or Flippers who may be fed, petted and tamed. These powerful, primitive animals grow bolder as they become accustomed to humans in their environment. And when hungry enough, they will sneak up and try to eat one.

Gainesville

The Annual Sweet Anguish

The homogenization of Florida endangers all the proud, wild creatures. It blenderizes tradition. The chances to see the remaining wild ones, to let the old customs fluff up the psyche as though it were a feather pillow, dwindle.

Without patience and perfect timing, you have little chance now. At no time can you expect to spot a panther, rarely a bobcat and only at certain places and times see roseate spoonbills or sandhill cranes or wood storks.

Neither do you get many chances any more to attend such cultural events as hog-killings and cakewalks. But, with proper guidance, you still can refresh your assessments of humankind at family reunions, cemetery cleanings and covered dish church luncheons, in small towns across the Panhandle.

Fall offers another remarkable opportunity, one possibly about to vanish. You can witness the tradition of *the annual sweet anguish*. It begins each September for a special tribe of men. These temporarily wild ones will walk on the campus of the University of Florida on selected Saturdays for three months.

Some proudly wear orange and blue snapbrim hats, or monstrously snouted plastic alligator heads, or some other ridiculous costuming that does not embarrass them. Early in the day they smile beatifically, priest-like, and raise their hands in blessings upon all they meet.

By tradition most of these garishly festooned creatures display the confidence of monks, if not the manners, until the sun goes down. They quaff from bottled elixirs and grow flush with cheer. But at sunset they suffer the agonies of fallen men. That, too, is part of the tradition.

17

It has been that way, I know, at the Gainesville campus for most of a half-century. I have been writing of it periodically for a quarter century. The all-knowing fellows emerge when the leaves begin to turn brown and the air promises to turn thin and cool. Preening and saluting, they creep out of big and little towns all over Florida and head to Gainesville on Saturdays.

In other times and places, they appear normal. Their protective coloration is splendidly conventional. In the fall, however, the compulsion hits them — perhaps the kind of chemical thing that creates the migrating urge in birds and bugs — and they go briefly and happily mad. It is as peculiar a tradition as you ever will hope to see.

Their joy and their cups runneth over. The accents turn Cracker, the behavior boisterously beneficent, the feathering orange and blue. They huddle in coveys amid great murmuring, and occasionally a hand waving a flag or an elixir will shoot straight up into the air and there will be great whoops of positive thinking and self-congratulation.

These are the fall-blooming Gators, interesting anthropological subjects who follow the ritual, no matter how painful, of Florida football — *the annual sweet anguish*. They drink deeply of it, suffer horribly, and each fall come eagerly back for more.

Old Gators are the boys of September. Never champions, rarely bridesmaids, for them the taste of bittersweet is like Mama's cooking. In past years they have been the Who-all's Who-all of Florida, products of the days when Florida was the unchallenged king of the state universities, football aside.

They reach back into memory for Cracker accents and expressions that make it easier to laugh, easier during the fallow season to recover their spirit for another September.

Old grads and pickup truck alumni (the Gator version of Notre Dame's subway alumni) set the unofficial National Collegiate Athletic Association (NCAA) record during the 1940s for loudest cheering in the first half in support of the most inept football teams.

Old Gator fans always have appraised Florida football with the same optimism that Mark Twain determinedly maintained for classical music. Twain said classical music was better than it sounds. Old Gators swear that Florida football teams always are better than their performances.

Graybeard Gators come to the game for tailgate parties and ceremonies to sustain a kinship and to preserve a tradition. They celebrate a kind of middle-class and middle-aged mania that foreshadows for the students, representatives of a cooler age, how time will turn their present campus grumbles into good-old-days fantasies.

Periodically, a new coach arrives promising to introduce victories aplenty and championships. Usually, it takes three to five years to calm him down.

Every fall is a new challenge. There is a risk that victory could occur and start the dominos toppling. The entire schedule could go, according to the September view.

The hoots and hollers start. The proud, wild creatures unlimber and creep out. By sunset on the September Saturdays we know: The annual sweet anguish has begun again.

Apalachicola ★

The Oyster and Virility

Is it true what they say about oysters? A firmly plumpish, creamy-colored oyster lying bare on half a shell stimulates erotic ambition in some, but is it the oyster's fault?

According to old wives' tales, the oyster has a beneficial effect on virility. But are old wives the best source on this subject?

Any solemn, scientific consideration of the oyster must include these questions. The trick is to get answers rather than smirks.

Around Apalachicola Bay, they have reduced to bumper stickers and worn the tread off the old line, "Come to Florida and Live Longer, Eat Oysters And Love Longer." But Apalachicolans do not laugh at it. They only chuckle quietly and get thoughtful looks on their faces. They concede there is no laboratory proof that eating oysters makes love either more probable or more time-consuming. It is a ghost claim, a myth, a closet conviction. However, they do eat a lot of oysters.

The old salts around Apalachicola, the veteran fishermen and shuckers and gargantuan gourmands, treat it as a superstitition to avoid embarrassment. But they are not sure, "Couple years ago, I started testing this thing out," said one old timer. "I jest wanted to know. Did it work or not?"

Whenever all the proper ingredients for the experiment were available, he would eat a dozen raw oysters — just one dozen, never more — and await a message. "Ain't but very little to it," he concluded. "Nothing you can depend on. I can tell you that. There ain't been a time yet when more than one of them oysters worked."

The pioneer oyster scientist in Florida, Robert M. Ingle, lived in Apalachicola. He had been experimenting with oysters 30 years, and eating them even longer. His home was a 100-year-old frame house, porches all around, sitting on high ground looking toward the bay.

In outlining the basics of oysters, a primer course in why they are seasonal, Ingle did not dignify the virility myth with even a mention. However, to the hopeful, his explanations encouraged speculation.

Late in the spring, when the weather turns warm, the oyster starts to spawn, to reproduce, Ingle said. The details of that process do nothing for romance, and so we omit them. In fact, during warm weather the oyster spawns so enthusiastically that it burns out its energy, loses its appetite, does not even make a proper effort to get food. As a result, it loses weight, becomes thin, colorless and watery. In that state, it is not tasty.

But about November, when the weather begins to turn cold, the honeymoon is over. The oyster changes, like a bridegroom developing into a husband. As it cools off, appetite and energy return. Spawning less, it eats more. It fattens up, turns succulently creamy-colored and plump. At that point, it is full of something called glycogen, a stored starch, and becomes a delight to eat.

The encyclopedia, interestingly, defines glycogen as a stored animal starch. It notes that some attribute the phenomenon of "second wind," which occurs during violent exercise, to chemical activity caused by burning off glycogen. The myth grows muscles.

To sum up, then, in the summer months when the oyster is preoccupied with reproduction to the detriment of its health, it is a wan, puny thing not truly fit to eat. In cold weather, appetite replaces ardor and it plumpens with glycogen which makes it beautiful again.

Out of that cycle grew another old wives' tale, the one that says oysters should be eaten only in the months spelled with an "R." Ingle did not address this one directly, either, but his explanation clearly credited a common sense base. The "R" months are the cool ones. However, his explanation suggests that the wives might have underestimated the oyster's persistence in prolonging the summer frolics. In Florida, not until at least November have there been chills enough and time enough to change the oyster's disposition. Ingle, then, suggested May through October as the oyster's puny months.

Ingle knew more about the oyster than any other Floridian. He came to Apalachicola in 1949 with a fresh masters degree from the University of Miami, and opened an Oyster Culture Section for the state Board of Conservation (later to become the Florida Department of Natural Resources). In 1979, the state named a marine lab in St. Petersburg for him.

After retiring in 1972, Ingle formed the nonprofit Adelanto Corporation to determine if oysters could be made more edible in the summer months, an idea under study since 1962. Apalachicola, which produces 90 per cent of Florida's oysters and an annual haul of some $8 million, would be embarrassed for the world to know that some of its seafood dealers import oysters in the shell from Louisiana, Virginia and Maryland to keep business going during the summer.

Adelanto received a $360,000 grant from the U.S. Coastal Plains Commission to prove Ingle's contention and he opened an oyster feedlot operation. In it, summer oysters taken from the bay showed a 60 per cent increase in yield. It was not commercially feasible then, but might be important in the future.

Also important would be proof for the old wives' tale about oysters and virility. There seems no question that the oyster is a romantic little bivalve mollusk. Its summer performances prove that. But whether in winter that stored romantic starch transfers to the imbiber, that involves individual matters that transcend scientifically defined statistics. The scientists will continue to let the old wives answer that one.

Winter Park

The Sinkhole: Terra Infirma

The horror of a sinkhole is that it tampers with the place we always turn to for final safe haven. We call it mother earth, terra firma, home. It is our psychological base. If it collapses, the shocked psyche recoils and rests well in no other place.

As The Wandering Jew said, "The earth is all the home I have." We do not completely trust the sky even though it never has fallen, no matter what Chicken Little said. The water seems too insubstantial. All we have is the earth, a place to stand, a foundation.

Everything depends on the earth. It is our standard for security. If we feel it even flutter, or shiver, it is a moment of significance. In *For Whom The Bell Tolls,* Ernest Hemingway used the earth to illustrate the life-altering love affair between Roberto and Maria. "But did thee feel the earth move?" Roberto asked afterward. That defined the experience as nothing else could. It should not be surprising that a place where the earth failed us, the monster sinkhole in Winter Park, gathers spectators like cautious moths. They understand the horror of what happened, with no guarantees it will not happen again, but still they are lured by the need to see and wonder.

In the cool of the evening on the fifth of May, 1981, Mae Rose Owens went outside to feed her dog. She heard a swishing noise. A tall sycamore tree dropped into the ground and disappeared. The next day, her three-bedroom home fell into the same big hole that ate the tree. Half a city swimming pool followed, along with telephone poles, paved parking lots, cars, parts of business houses.

Finally, there was left only a monstrous, ugly hole, but about it there was an aura of something more. The monster was perceived to have a life of its own, a personality. It lay there in Winter Park like a captured animal, and the crowds began flocking as though to a zoo.

Parasitic commercial enterprises — sinkhole T-shirts, sinkhole pictures, merchants' sinkhole bargains — crusted around it, scab-like.

Winter Park encircled the hole with a chain link fence and put up a sign, "Viewing Area." The city posted policemen at hole-side in eight-hour shifts. For the officers' comfort, a tent was erected with bug netting on the sides, a fan, light, radio, a thermos, table and chairs inside. Nearby, a portable toilet stood like a telephone booth without windows.

"I'm here trying to keep people from jumping over the fence and doing idiotic things like running down in the sinkhole so they can say, 'I ran around the bottom of the sinkhole.' You'd be surprised at how many people try things like that," said Officer J.R. Kaschalk.

The monster was neither the first nor will it be the last of Florida's sinkholes. But, at approximately 400 feet wide and 75 feet deep, it has had the greatest impact on the public mind of any yet.

History and myth have many sinkhole stories. One of the early recorded ones came in 1830 as a group of hunters prowled through the woods at night on horseback. They heard a terrifying roar and fled. Next day, they discovered a half-acre sinkhole had swallowed up part of the forest.

Though usually there is time to escape, in the past some autos, hikers and horsemen have fallen in as pathways and highways and even railroad beds have collapsed.

In 1967, after 15 new sinkholes had occurred in the Lakeland area during a five-month period, state geologist Robert Vernon blamed it on a drop in the water table. A sinkhole collapses, the experts say, when the water level drops. This removes support from underground limestone caverns common in Central and North Florida. Vernon said the water had gone down 55 feet since 1920. Asked then what this might portend by the year 2000, he replied, "Frankly, it scares hell out of me."

Unfortunately, sinkholes are the kind of possibility few want to take seriously until they see or fall into one. The psychological hazard is too great. Henry J. Swanson, who lives in Winter Park, and retired as Orange County extension agent in 1978 after 30 years service, predicted Winter Park's monster nine years before it happened. Hardly anyone listened.

In the early 1960s, Swanson had become concerned. He had found that in peninsular Florida, south from a point in Marion County, rainfall was the sole source of water. He checked some figures and discovered the county was using more water than rainfall replenished. "I whooped and hollered about it but nobody listened," he said.

Jan. 25, 1972, he wrote a letter to the mayors of Orlando, Winter Park, Winter Garden, Ocoee, Maitland and Cocoa. "Gentlemen," he began, "I sincerely hope you won't think I'm a nut. . . ." He pointed out the water imbalance and predicted a variety of problems, but sinkholes in particular. He even went to the extent of citing the area of the 1981 monster sinkhole as especially vulnerable.

Hometown prophets never had it so easy. Even with the example of The Monster laying there, nobody seems unusually excited. Swanson cannot understand this. He asks, as Hemingway did, "But did thee feel the earth move?"

Pensacola

The Twilight of The Creoles

The remnants of a twilight society here, the Pensacola Creoles, are vanishing into the Florida melting pot because their young no longer care. After 200 years of struggling to maintain a separate identity, the Creoles will let it die with their old men.

The reasons involve a richly human history that testifies to the hypocrisy involved in prejudice.

Only a plaque nailed to the wall of a yellow-and-red frame house, just a half block from Old Seville Square, stands as public recognition of a once prominent ethnic group. It notes that the building, erected in 1895 by the St. Michael's Creole Benevolent Association, has been placed on the National Register of Historic Places.

There at 416 East Government St., the Pensacola Creoles, kissing cousins to the elitist Creoles of New Orleans and Mobile, held their last regular meetings. In 1972, they dissolved the organization. The membership of 19 older men decided that time and new ideas had passed them by. They sold the building and divided the proceeds.

"We still have identity, just no organization," said Harry Tuttle, the last president of the association. He and his wife lived next door at No. 420, a neat frame house built a century ago with pegs instead of nails.

Tuttle, retired from his job at the Naval Air Station here, was president of the association for 20 years and held its confidential records. He was a member of the Historic Pensacola Preservation Board, but differed strongly with historians on the definition of a Pensacola Creole. "I go by the dictionary definition," he said. "A Creole is a descendant of the French or Spanish. That's all."

There is room for disagreement because no thorough study of Pensacola's Creole history has been published, and because in practice the term has been applied generally and imprecisely. The Creoles sprang from the French and Spanish colonists who fought with each other and with Great Britain for control of West Florida from 1559 to 1821. They included all offspring of the colonists born in the New World, whether with slaves, Indians, other colonists or other free people of whatever origin. All were Creoles.

Not even the charter of the St. Michael's Creole Catholic Benevolent Association, first drawn up in 1888 and revised in 1897, defined the term more clearly. It simply said that each prospect for membership should state in writing his nationality, age and creed, and "must bring clear proofs of honesty, integrity and a name above slander." The charter added: "No application will be received from a non-Creole Roman Catholic...."

In the case of Pensacola, historians have taken their cue from a quotation in the 1939 *American Guide Series* book on Florida. It said: "The Pensacola Creoles are chiefly descendants of a much larger group, of Spanish and Negro admixture, who enjoyed prosperity before the War Between the States.... Although they hold themselves aloof from Negroes, they are not accepted on terms of social equality with the whites."

Other historical accounts describe them similarly. They tell the story of lonely colonists (Spanish law forbade or discouraged provincial marriages) giving children of mixed ancestry their freedom or the right to earn it, and the rise of a small group of Creoles to property and status which was honored after West Florida became U.S. territory in 1821. Creoles carried firearms and sat on juries with whites, for example. For two decades prior to the Civil War they lost this status but regained it during the 1870's, probably their time of greatest prominence. In 1878 a Creole, Salvador T. Pons, was elected mayor of Pensacola.

During the 1890's a strong white backlash began in the form of Jim Crow laws which legalized segregation (two Florida lynchings reinforced it illegally). The law at that time defined a Negro as any person with one-eighth Negro blood, and forbade mixing.

The Creoles were caught in the middle. Properly or not, they were denied association with whites, and in the climate of the times they chose to withdraw from association with blacks. They formed several fraternal and benevolent organizations (including the one that survived longest, the St. Michael's Creole Benevolent Association), to which they paid dues and in return received medical care, moral support, and participated in group social affairs.

In 1895, the city directory began identifying citizens as white, Creole, Mulatto or Negro. Some, depending upon color and pressures, were accorded one by one all four designations as they were discovered or thought to be passing in the wrong category. By 1910 feelings ran so high that all three non-white categories were lumped into one, Negro.

Not until the civil rights protests of the 1960's did things change significantly for the Creoles. The desegregation of the Pensacola public schools in 1969 brought the end of the Creoles as a separate society. A young Creole, for the first time in a century, could attempt social mobility — that is, cross racial lines — without fear of legal penalty.

By 1972, the St. Michael's Creole Benevolent Association reached the decision to dissolve. "We didn't have any more young members," Harry Tuttle explained. "The young people had different ideas. There have been a lot of lies and misunderstandings about Creoles."

After that, the Creoles began to fade away. The pragmatic underpinnings of their special society had been pulled. The young were willing to forget a history of anguish and uncertainty.

Two young Creoles — one light, one dark — explained, "A lot of higher-up people in this town are Creoles, but they don't like to be identified," said the first. "Their kids don't know and they're better off not to know. In New Orleans and Mobile, they're still proud of it. In Pensacola, Creoles consider it a disadvantage."

"My father was a Creole from Mobile," the second said. "He married my mother, who was black. He was a member of the association. I guess you could say I'm half-Creole, but I don't think I could have joined because I'm black. There never was a definition of what was Creole. It turned out to be that if you looked white you were Creole. But in the old days, the Creoles were a third race.

"I know of a Creole who went to New Orleans while he was young, passed for white, married a white lady, and now he has grandchildren. They know nothing of his past. The secret will die with him. But he can't tell his family anything about their roots.''

So the Pensacola Creoles, once a proud and culturally distinct group, are vanishing from Pensacola, but the irony remains. At a time when distinctive heritage attracts celebration, they have abandoned it. At a time when the government mandates reverse discrimination for minorities, many have given up being members of a minority.

When their old men die, the Creoles will be like everyone else. You have to wonder, looking at the special thing they had, how many generations will pass before the urge will come to reach back for that unique identity.

★ Key Largo

A Hurricane: Leaves Hit Like
A Boxer's Jabs

Capt. Calvin Albury knew about hurricanes. He rode out 11 in
the Florida Keys. He could tell you how the wind screams, and how
the pressure rises as though you are deep-sea diving. "It builds up
to a screaming pitch and your head feels like it's gonna explode,"
he said.

He could tell you about seeing the wind and water break three
corners of the foundations off a two-story house, how it swung
slowly around like a giant battleship and then disintegrated as
though a bomb had hit it. He could tell you of rising water, and
panic, and drownings that nearly wiped out entire families.

He had seen a fish house, made of bolted two-by-sixes, wrung off
its anchors and rolled across the island like a bowling ball. He had
seen six-inch pipe bent into an elbow without splitting.

Albury had raced his fishing boat ahead of the winds and had
mangrove leaves slap him in the face with the force of a boxer's jab
and the rain beat the backs of his ears and neck raw. He had seen
salt spray strip the side of a frame house as though it were sand-
blasted.

"Nobody can tell you about a hurricane. You have to see it. You
won't believe the things that happen unless you see them," Albury
said.

Albury, born in 1914 in Key West of a Bahamian father, could
stand flatfooted and reach his fryingpan-sized hands eight feet into
the air. He was a trim, powerful, independent, proud man. He
listened to hurricane warnings. He had found beds so high in trees
he could not reach them, had seen trees snapped off at ground-level

and chunks torn out of the ground mass itself, had seen the tidal surge make debris of docks and houses and watched that debris turn into junk-weapons pounded against other buildings. "In high wind, a garbage can lid can be as dangerous as dynamite, just as destructive," he said.

Capt. Albury, a bonefish guide, worked out of a base near his Key Largo home until his death in 1981. "The next one that comes," he always said, "we're evacuating. I'm not afraid of them, but I respect them. We haven't had a bad one in a long time, but if one comes it could be worse than anything anybody ever saw before."

Albury reasoned that 75 per cent of the people living or visiting in the Florida Keys have never seen a hurricane before. Of those, perhaps 90 per cent have only seen the fringe effects. He doubted whether newcomers would heed the warnings, and feared that ignorance would multiply the possibilties of disaster.

Water does the worst damage. Hurricane experts say that winds of 155 miles per hour bring a tidal surge up to 18 feet. A storm in the Keys like the one which hit Sept. 2, 1935 — with winds estimated as high as 250 miles per hour (after the anemometers blew away), and 20-foot tides — could flood all Keys land areas. In that one, 405 died and the population then was only a fraction of what it is now.

"If another hurricane hit as large as the one in '35, it would be disastrous," said Richard Urbanek, chief meterologist for the National Weather Service in Key West. The experts have the difficult job of convincing people of the dangers without seeming alarmist. In fact, even a medium-sized hurricane could be disastrous.

A 'hurricane watch' is set up when a storm moves within 36 hours of land. A 'hurricane warning' goes into effect when it is expected to hit land within 12 to 18 hours. Time is important, and short.

Houses must be boarded or shuttered, loose objects tied down, hurricane shelter or high ground sought. Only 700 cars an hour can be evacuated from the Keys. Experts recommend that no one below Marathon even try to get out, rather than risk being caught in the open when the highway between Homestead and the Keys floods, as it will, and becomes impassable.

There are some 11,000 mobile homes in the Keys and experts rate their chances poor. For other homes, quality of construction will be decisive. High-level homes, built with hurricanes in mind, can survive. But risks remain great after the hurricane for injury and sickness during the period of being without power and telephones, when there is limited fresh water and food.

"What you haven't done before the hurricane hits, you're not gonna do," said Albury, the expert. "When I was younger, I was as strong as anybody around here, and I can tell you that when you get into one, you're helpless. You're not gonna do anything. You just don't walk up against that wind and rain."

The 1935 hurricane ended the Overseas Railroad and temporarily ended growth on the Keys. There have been no significant reminders in the Keys since Hurricane Betsy in 1965. "I can imagine what Hiroshima looked like after the atomic bomb by remembering what that 1935 hurricane did to Islamorada and Matecumbe," Albury said. "For miles and miles you looked down there where the railroad used to be and there was absolutely nothing. No houses, nothing. You wondered how anybody at all survived. There's still pieces of railroad iron 20 miles out in the bay. They found automobiles and house trailers and one thing and another like that for 15 years afterward. Some of the cars had bones in them.

"I hope we never see another one," he said. "But if it comes, I don't want to be around. You're down here and you can't get out. You have to hope the wind doesn't blow too hard and the water doesn't rise and there's not too much junk floating around to beat you to death. That's what you're up against. You're helpless. People just don't realize that anymore." Albury was a man who knew about hurricanes, but nobody seemed to listen.

★ St. Augustine

The Fantasy Fixation

From the crest of St. Augustine's Bridge of Lions, you can see the most history-loaded view in Florida: Not only the old city itself, the birthplace of Western civilization in North America, but also the state's two most historically significant buildings still standing in original appearance and being freely used.

The Castillo de San Marcos, the great stone fort that the Spanish built, symbolizes the European colonization of the state.

The other building, the former Ponce de Leon Hotel (built in 1887), with its twin 165-foot towers rising into St. Augustine's skyline, symbolizes the loosing of fantasy tourism upon Florida — an infectious malady for which no cure yet has been found.

All manner of wisdom may be gleaned from a study of the human experience represented by either, but the old hotel — now Flagler College — more directly links up with a dilemma that survives in today's Florida.

Pioneer Henry M. Flagler, a man who made his millions in an oil partnership with John D. Rockefeller, conceived the notion that Florida was a patch of sand that had to be tricked up into something else if it ever was to be anything of value.

The growth of that notion exploded a thousand seeds, some of them producing mutations, which resulted in a peculiar fantasy fixation.

In reasoning, it was the equivalent of hanging apples upon orange trees on the premise that this would please tourists because they had been accustomed to seeing apples on the trees back home. Amazingly, while horse-drawn carriages and other popular things of Flagler's day have passed into curiosities, the fantasy fixation survives.

Out of it sprang the tacky roadside zoos, the rubber alligators and the plastic flamingoes and wire-limbed palms and all the other make-believe. The coming of high costs and interstate highways hurt the small-time tackiness but it only subsided; it did not go away. Instead the ultimate in sophisticated fantasy (we hope), Disney World, emerged in a grand style somewhat akin to that of the old oil baron.

Flagler began it all in highly genteel form but at base it still was a distortion of the fact that natural Florida was a powerful attraction that, if preserved, was a better and more lasting investment than any fantasy ever invented.

In Flagler's day, at least, there was more excuse for the distortion than at any time since. His railroads and hotels transformed Florida for all time, but the spectacular beginning was with the Ponce de Leon Hotel in St. Augustine.

Tom Graham, a professor of history and a native Floridian whose forebears arrived in St. Augustine from Spain in 1602, has a unique perspective from which to study Flagler and the beginnings of tourism. Occasionally, he lectures on the subject. Among his published works are a small book on the hotel, and a study of Flagler that is included in another book titled, *The Awakening of St. Augustine.* He teaches Florida history in Flagler College (enrollment: 900), housed in the old hotel so much a part of his studies.

"One pitch I make is that it's the most historically significant building in the state — because of who built it, its role in history and its architecture," Graham said. "Maybe you could say that the Castillo is more significant, but those are the two."

When Flagler built the Ponce de Leon, with an extravagant Spanish Renaissance architectural style ("Babylonish luxury," one observer called it), Florida was wilderness. Until then, the state had been promoted mostly as a health spa, a place for consumptives and invalids, where the water and the climate helped rheumatics and bronchitis sufferers.

That did not produce images that would bring the tourists — sometimes known as "strangers," then — galloping. Another handicap was that hotels had the reputation of being noisy places with bad food.

His luxurious hotel, boasting 400 rooms, each with a fireplace, plus inlaid marble, a great rotunda and gargoyles and caryatids, changed that. It was a palace where the Swells could come seeking pleasure, where they could tell themselves — adopting Flagler's promotional blurbs — that they were experiencing "the American Riviera" or "the winter Newport," not just plain old Florida. One fulltime employee had a single job: replacing any of the 5,000 light bulbs burned out by the hotel's early electrical system.

The hotel was such a departure from form for Flagler, a serious businessman, that a friend once questioned his judgment in building it. Flagler replied with a story about the exemplary life of a loyal church member who, in his later years, went on a drunken spree. In response to criticism, the man explained that up to this time he had given all his days to the Lord, and now he felt entitled to take one for himself. "I was pleasing myself," Flagler said.

Within a few years, when St. Augustine was not transformed into either the Riviera or Newport, Flagler felt a frustration that also would become historic in Florida. His hotel magazine, The Tatler, usually devoted to enraptured accounts of glittering society, reflected his impatience. "Shall this be the Newport of the South, or a Coney Island?" it grumbled.

Flagler was ahead of us on that one, too. Fantasy tourism is built on magic, and eventually the tricks get old. We still worry about Coney Island South.

Shell Games at The Carnival

Nothing stimulates the mind in a more worthwhile way than a mild provocation of the body. The January cold in Florida does it nicely. It has a warming nip, but not a demoralizing threat.

The chill reminds me how the years are ripples, not monuments, how the vibrations from my short walk through this world are felt mostly by me, how the view through my eyes can be so strikingly lean and Olympian while I remain remarkably small and plump.

In this mood, I like to get up at sunrise and walk on the beach at Sanibel Island. In the surreal light, stooped figures hurry about, splashing in the sloughs, making wet tracks in the sand. These are not my favorite people. They are collectors.

There is satisfaction in sharing this perspective, this pouting humility, with them. It makes clear the obsessive peculiarity of grabbing little shell creatures from their worlds to slake a greedy urge.

The collectors boil the skeletons in a cleansing chlorine solution, oil the bones to accent their intricate swirls and blends of colors, and then without embarrassment display them in conspicuous places.

Rather than these stony but fragile blossoms continuing to unfurl, they will sit in the cavities of knickknack shelves and strategic corners, catching dust with the efficiency of a Joe DiMaggio who anticipates so well that he misses nothing but never seems to move, acting as a miniature vault into which little insects can crawl and expire after the exterminator has visited.

The collectors try to capture something, but they fail. They consume it, spend it extravagantly in exchange for a brief glow, and then dispose of the waste by placing it in a handy pantheon of irrelevance where it may be worshiped in time of boredom.

The collectors inspire uneasiness in me. Perhaps fear would be a better word. They symbolize shadow, not light. I read somewhere that an explorer named Knud Rasmussen, speaking of such apprehensions, explained it this way: "We fear the cold and things we do not understand. But most of all we fear the doings of the heedless ones among us."

That touches it. The collectors have this whimsically vulturine appetite, but without any true hunger to mitigate the implications of it. They are heedless ones.

Florida attracts collectors. They collect shells in their buckets and bags, sunshine on their skins, take orange trees home in plastic pots, carry little alligators to an environment that substitutes sewers for streams, catch fish and mount them on boards, kill animals and stuff them into illusions of reality.

Their collections cause vacancies, and into them come manufactured creations as substitutes: artificial "worlds" of varying sorts that in themselves are collections, places where the collectors can congregate in cheer because a theater has been crafted. That synthesizes the goals of their mania. The singular thrill that comes from a discovery experience — of finding a shell or feeling warmth in January or being able to touch something that was wild — is contrived mechanically so that for a fee the collector can savor that thrill over and over until the lust for it has been sated.

To satisfy the need to capture a symbol of that experience, these places offer souvenirs that will insure not even a small tingle of delight escapes being wrung out and devalued: bottles that tan without burning, trinkets that evoke nostalgia without mess or maintenance.

Many may not sympathize with this flatulent leak of personal conviction which appears to assail innocent tourists who come to our dunes bringing money that sustains us, and who in return expect only indulgence for minor quirks. I court this displeasure only because they are so clearly wrong, at least to me. The mind-set of the collectors no longer should be considered innocent, nor their quirks minor.

A Florida that continues to cater to the collectors after it has 15 million residents and 40 million annual tourists, a probability that lies not far ahead, will find itself plucked bare of natural mystery and converted into a soul-withering carnival. It need not be.

The collectors are not dedicated irrevocably to their folly. Most of their whims are fueled by ignorance, and encouraged by promoters willing to waste Florida for a short-haul gain. They can be influenced. Anyone who has lived here five years or longer has the responsibility to know better, and to speak when issues teeter on an expression of public will. We can do a kindness and a service to unaware tourists and strangers by showing them how nature in Florida breaks rather than bends, and by sharing with them our fearful vision of the heedless ones.

As I stare at the tiger conch squatting like a tiny tombstone on my file cabinet, turn off the shell lamp in the corner and quit work for this night, as Gloria puts away her shell earrings and pendant and I fret about these evidences around me for a sleepless hour, just remember two things before you ignore me: Only a believer can blaspheme, and anyone can reform.

Pensacola

Shape-Note Singing: Genuine, Defiant

The singers formed a square, and Deacon Willie J. Milton stepped into the middle. He was tall, bald, powerful, intense. He tapped his feet and clapped his hands and began a kind of chant that animated the singers. They jumped into a fast, rhythmic, emotional song.

Milton stepped, virtually danced a beat, and the singers kept pace, full and loud. On the second round, the familiar words of a hymn replaced the chant, but it was more than the usual hymn. It had the soulful qualities of gospel music and faint hints of Dixieland jazz, and the lively presentation created the spirit of the old-time religious camp meeting. It was as beautiful and startling as a primitive painting.

This was shape-note singing, a rural folk expression popularized in 18th Century New England, and kept alive in Florida by a trickle of religiously bent individualists whose forebears found it personally meaningful and passed it on as part of the family heritage.

Deacon Milton led the singers at a folk festival in Pensacola, and in that carnival air their audience loved it without fully understanding that this music had a special beauty because it represented in American history the persistence of common folk in pursuing the significant freedoms that enlarge ordinary lives.

"We sing it because we like it," Milton said. "It's a little different from regular singing. You don't just sing along. Most people that sing this type music sing it because it means something to them. Some folks call it bogey music, and they don't like it, but we do."

Shape-note signing was born out of the democratic feeling turned

39

loose in post-Revolution America. It was native, unconventional, exuberant, in some ways defiant. The songs needed no accompaniment and tolerated no soloists, relying on strong voices and harmony. They could be sung impromptu, wherever a few of the faithful gathered.

In earlier years, the Puritans — the establishment of that time — disdained most church music but many colonists in the backwoods communities sang anyway. They followed a rural folk tradition brought over from England, one that had existed before Christianity, which taught songs without benefit of written music. Unschooled singers learned tunes by ear, associating the rise and fall of a melody with a sequence of syllables, *fa-sol-la,* that represented the musical scale.

The name evolved when a system was invented to put the syllable-notes on paper in a way that could be sight-read by someone without musical training. Each note was given a different shape on the musical clef. First, there were four shapes — a triangle for *fa,* a circle for *sol,* a square for *la,* a diamond for *mi* — and later these were expanded to the full range of seven. Shape-note singing books then could be published, and still are.

Shape-note singing, and its reflections of rural or unconventional folk rejecting dominance by the privileged, spread into the frontier of the South and took hold in religious revivals. At camp meetings, those intense religious gatherings where participants dramatized in song and personal testimony the trials of struggling against sin, shape-note singing flourished and established a tradition whose appeal had no racial connotation. Later, different styles developed out of preference.

At the Pensacola folk festival, Deacon Milton, representing the St. Mark Missionary Baptist Church in the Flowersview Community, which is 20 miles northwest of DeFuniak Springs in Walton County, demonstrated how it is done. Each side of the singers' square represents one of the harmony parts (soprano, tenor, alto, bass). A leader stands in the middle, taps out the beat with hands and feet and leads the group through the melody singing the syllable-notes in a style whose marked, arbitrary rhythm and sliding half-notes might sound to the uninitiated a bit like a musical chant.

Then, with the tune firmly in mind, the group harmonizes using the words.

"It is a tradition that is dying out," said Dr. Ronald Foreman, director of Afro-American Studies at the University of Florida. "Where it exists, it has survived in pockets as an almost defiant resistance to complete change. There is a pronounced, fascinating rhythm. I love it."

What survives of that tradition in Florida, according to Doris Dyen, historian and ethno-musicologist on the staff of the Florida Folklife Program, based at White Springs, centers in the central Panhandle and Pensacola. Her studies turned up this lively vein of shape-noters and she has begun to bring them into the folklife festivals.

During a visit to Flowersview with Deacon Milton, retired Civil Service worker, he made the whole thing sound quite simple. "I learned it from my folks back in Alabama," he said. "My parents and grandparents, as far back as any of them could remember, sang shape-notes. It's all gospel music. It has its own sound, and we try to keep that alive."

The Milton family had been tenant farmers in Alabama, where the deacon was born, and moved to Florida looking for better jobs and a chance to own the land they worked. Shape-note singing came with them and others like them. The Miltons joined the Florida-Alabama Progressive Seven-Shape-Note Singing Convention, founded in 1929.

"In 1979, the 50th anniversary of the convention, we purchased a little patch of ground in Crestview and built our home convention hall," Milton said. "We hold conventions (or sings) there four times a year, and sometimes groups of us will sing around at other places, like we did in Pensacola."

The shape-note singers do it because it has personal meaning, not for any other reason. Although audiences respond enthusiastically, the music's roots and fundamental purpose primarily lie in the benefit to participants.

Shape-note singing is a genuine expression of religious democracy with overtones that defy the dilutions of social pretense. For Florida, it puts a heartbeat into a particular lifestyle, and keeps alive one of this country's most remarkable musical traditions.

Florida's Sunrise Side

The Sunrise Side of Florida begins in Georgia Heaven and steadily improves, curling down a thousand inlets and bays past the Senior City, the Broad Beach, the enchanting Indian River's Slough-Cities, the Certified Sandbox, the Sold Coast and Babylon, and finally stutters to a stop on those bleached, bony Keys that skip toward the sunset.

The sun gives all of it a Gilt Complex, a preoccupation with being out of doors and as near naked as current bounds of decency or, in the absence of any, courage permits. Nice people say Florida looks like the U.S. finger making a happy point, but raunchy frolickers envision it a phallic symbol setting a bacchanalian mood. The more classic-minded, equally imaginative, call it "the American Italy." Whatever, the east side caught the sun first and its 450-mile side of the peninsula (if you count Key West) lured the pioneers.

Ponce de Leon, looking for gold in 1513, found flowers. Poet Sidney Lanier, waxing enthusiastic on railroad promotional money three and one-half centuries later, found that here "it is one's duty to repose broadfaced upward, like fields in the fall, and to lie fallow under suns and airs...."

One winter on the Sunrise Side bewitched oil tycoon Henry Flagler. Just before the 20th century arrived, he began building a railroad down it, posting a luxury hotel first at St. Augustine and at each major stop thereafter. A friend told him, "You have been looking for a place to make a fool of yourself, and you've finally found (it)...."

If he did, his railroad made it possible for millions to follow his example by making similarly serious if not so historical individual decisions. Flagler opened up the Sunrise Side like a can of peas.

People and buildings began to line it, and never have stopped, despite periodic Boom-Bust cycles that have made the growth seem erratic and uncertain.

All of these fellows, Ponce and Sidney and Henry, ought to take a look at it now. To begin at Fernandina Beach and take the ferry across St. Johns River and brave the traffic and tortuous speed limits and narrow bridges and bareskinned jaywalkers all the way down to Key West requires a man with pioneer blood and an unhurried head, but the picture you get of a changing Florida rewards the taxing of your character. It took us three days but, as the poets say, we like to stop and smell the sea oats.

You have to begin in Georgia Heaven, Fernandina Beach, the closest piece of Florida Seashore to Georgia. Maybe it looks a little like Jekyll Island, but it has the magic of the Florida vacation and Georgia summer tourists fill it up during the hot months.

Going south, the Jacksonville beaches reflect the same riptide of past and future. Modern motels rise among weatherbeaten shingled houses and the old Boardwalk is a honky-tonk candidate for urban renewal.

St. Augustine, the Senior City, has no identity problem. It has committed itself to the truths of a 400-year-old history and it offers nostalgia and comfort in discovery.

Daytona Beach long ago opted to be the Miami Beach of the North and it has succeeded. The Broad Beach, which collegiate vacationers interpret less as a matter of width than as a place of companionship, still is the widest and the motels still range from the Sid-and-Sybil places to Miami Beach in the 1950s and ahead somewhere looms the specter of Atlantic City.

Around Titusville, the Slough-Cities begin along the giant lagoon that is the Indian River and go south to Stuart. The climate gradually changes to semi-tropical and the foliage to heavier greens and brighter colors and Cracker accents become rare and the prices go up for tourists more likely to arrive in winter than summer.

Elegant old Palm Beach still reigns as the Certified Sandbox where the rich play behind hedges and walls and follow tunnels to the beach so that tourists never see them wet. Palm Beach begins the Sold Coast, the stretch to Miami Beach's Babylon astonishingly choked with mansions and hotels and condominiums. Babylon itself, so named by author Pat Frank, suffers an identity crisis trying to decide whether it can be again the prestige winter vacation place or whether it should relax as a resident resort, whether it should roll the dice in desperation or stick to a tested commodity and emphasize climate with renewed class.

Key West retains the fascination of being an island and semi-outlaw where there is constant ferment among conservative Conchs, vagabonds and Babbits, or those aspiring to be one of the three.

The Sunrise Side has surprises. On even a cloudy day you can see from the past to the present to the future. While parts of the north risk development mistakes of the past, the Slough-Cities area has benefited from bad example and the Sold Coast has come under siege by an urban solidity that would have seemed impossible in the more glittering and frivolous times of 20 years ago. Slow, painful correction has set in and, unless jarred awry again by snake-oil spiel, a new kind of respectability and affluence threatens the future.

Florida Heaven has not yet arrived, though, however well Georgia may be accommodated. Some still scratch away the grass and put in pebble or concrete lawns and tear away the trees to make room for concrete hutches, developers still garble history trying to elevate the sound if not the geography of low ground and if honky-tonks have reached a threatened stage they are not yet rare enough to be called endangered.

That is the Sunrise Side of Florida, shadowing and fore-shadowing history: still a place of flowers that tempts you to lie fallow and dream, still a grand place to make a fool of yourself, but rounding into urban middle-age with a promise (if it does not break out with that old impatient itch) of elderly grace to come.

Only Vegetarians Should Argue With Cockfighters

Most people perceive cockfighting to be a barbaric amusement, and Gerald Cruikshank thought that was a shame. "Oh yes," he said. "Some people still frown on it. It's usually the ones that are raised in the city and don't know anything about nature that are against it."

He explained further. "It's like square dancing. Years ago, people frowned on square dancing, but there's not a thing in the world wrong with square dancing. Used to be that a bunch of people would come to square dances and they'd drink too much and they'd get to fighting and they gave square dancing a bad name. Maybe the same thing's happened to cockfighting."

Cruikshank lived in the Picketville community on the north side of Jacksonville. He had 20 acres between a cemetery and a landfill that stretched from a paved road to Six-Mile Creek. A grove of water oaks and pines shaded gamecocks strutting about on 10-foot ropes staked to the ground. He had to keep them apart. "They love to fight," he said.

Cruikshank, a longshoreman, had been a cockfighting aficionado since he was a boy in West Virginia. "Never been without 'em since I was 12," he said in 1979. "Got my first one then and got maybe 120 now."

Cruikshank, stocky and affable, made an ideal spokesman for an enterprise that has been praised and cursed and persistently practiced since the sixth century, B.C. He was president of the Florida chapter of the United Gamefowl Breeders Association and on the national board of directors.

"I don't raise 'em for profit or anything like that," he said. "Just do it because I admire 'em for being so beautiful and for their courage. I do it as a hobby. I don't sell 'em. And I don't bet much on 'em. I lose money on 'em. No way I could break even." The feed bill for his "hobby" runs at least $100 a month.

Cruikshank deplores the association of cockfighting with images of bloodied arenas, frenzied intoxication, violence and illegality. "It's the fairest, most honest sport there is. And popular too," he defended. Between Thanksgiving and July 1, the fighting season, he said he could attend a cockfight somewhere in Florida every Sunday if he wished.

No state law forbids it (although federal law prohibits transporting animals across state lines for the purpose of fighting), but most cockfights are held clandestinely because of the gambling and because the Humane Society sometimes brings charges of cruelty to animals. Although practices vary, the gamecocks usually wear 2.5-inch bayonet gaffs — curved steel talons tapered to needle sharpness, strapped to the nub where their natural spur has been cut off. The secrecy generates a suspicious climate that grows as incidents periodically surface in police action.

There are many examples. Two men were shot to death at a Dade County farm used to train fighting cocks. Lake County lawmen raided an elaborate two-story arena in Central Florida that offered a snack bar, printed cards and seven tiers of theater seats. In 1976 a federal grand jury accused dogfight promoters of bribing deputy sheriffs in North Florida to permit cockfighting.

That sort of notice greatly distressed Cruikshank, and he responded by naming a string of famous men who approved, including George Washington, Thomas Jefferson, Abraham Lincoln, Andrew Jackson, Teddy Roosevelt and Lyndon Baines Johnson.

When the Oklahoma legislature considered a bill to prohibit cockfighting, a lawmaker there defended it as the "sport of all free countries" and implied that it was politically purifying. "In every country where the Communists have taken over," he alleged, "the first thing they do is outlaw cockfighting."

Harry Crews, the novelist and modern chronicler of blood and grits, appraised cockfighting as a blood sport no worse than prize-fighting, football or automobile racing. He offered no apology for liking them all. "Where I come from," he has written, "we don't confuse animals with people. We don't sleep with poodles or whisper baby talk to horses."

An arena is usually a circular pit about 20 feet in diameter, surrounded by a two-foot high fence. The two handlers and a referee are in the ring. The fight frequently lasts but minutes, and one rooster often dies, but not always; he may quit, turn away. Once during a match in the Philippines, a roster attacked his owner, so badly slashing him with the bayonet spurs that the man bled to death.

"The rooster makes up his own mind," Cruikshank emphasized. "If he don't want to fight, he can quit. But he loves it. Fighting's good for them. Some say the gaffs are cruel but I say that's foolish. The rooster's natural spur is about as thick as a pencil and it causes infections. The gaff wound heals faster. Which had you rather be jabbed with?

"The game rooster has every advantage in the world over the barnyard rooster," he continued. His roosters begin fighting at about age 2, and if successful may continue until age 10 or longer; a poultry broiler gets hung up by its heels, its throat slit and feathers boiled off about 60 days after it cracks out of the egg.

"Go over to a poultry place and look at the conditions there, how they live and die, and then look at how my roosters live and die," Cruikshank said. "If you had a choice, the odds would be a million to nothing you'd rather be a game rooster."

A fight is neither pretty to see nor to contemplate. Revulsion is reflexive, yet, as Gerald Cruikshank and Harry Crews said, there is inconsistency in that perception. When the blood flows, we do not make charges of cruelty and send police after promoters of prize-fighting, football and automobile racing.

If we were to make a judgment from the chicken's viewpoint, purely on blood and pain and style of life, would we outlaw cockfighting or fried chicken? Only vegetarians have a neat answer.

★ St. Augustine

For The Elderly, A Graceful Alamo

A great stone gate gives the Fountain of Youth just the right historic look. Beneath an umbrella of trees, with water drawn from a shallow well inside a rocky grotto, the place perpetuates our fondest delusion.

Anywhere but Florida such a straight-faced depiction of the absurd would deserve a medal for courage. But here, in the land of the youthful ancients, it might be the most apt sideshow attraction of all.

About it there are so many poetic touches. Not only is it located in the grayest state in the nation, but also in the oldest city, just a short walk outside the historic district in St. Augustine.

Old age has been called the greatest surprise in life, and that sheds light. We choose to believe in spite of the facts. The surprise becomes great because it is exactly the conclusion we refuse to accept.

The Fountain of Youth touches that same willing gull in us, like a wry jester. We pay $3 each to sip water from a paper cup, drawn from a 28-foot well, in a stone room where mechanical, Disney-esque Indians robotically perform chores.

Many visitors joke cynically as they drink, but nearly all drink. The mind keeps handy, on ready reserve, a place for speculations about what-might-be, no matter the strain on imagination and credulity.

Much has been written about the miseries of old age but in Florida — the Alamo of the elderly, where the last historic stand may be made with some grace and style — there is a happier phase that gets not enough attention.

Not every person can handle it, but many do. They are the cham-

48

pions who acknowledge their mileage and treat their infirmities like honorable war wounds. The knotty arthritic joints, the clouds in the eyes, the distant thunder that persists in the ears, the majestically wrinkled faces, the soft wisps of hair where once grew dark bushes — all of these — become credentials of past campaigns.

They have been told that age makes a winter of the heart, and so they have come where the winter is warm. If this be the fabled evening of life, the sunset, if the clock is striking an actuarial midnight — whatever euphemism you prefer — a remarkable number of them treat it as a going-away party. In age, as the poet said, they bud again.

Across Florida, in these prime winter days, there may be more calculated jocularity per capita on display among the grayheads than any other group. They dwell in their own dimension, where experience is as high as the humidity, where reality distills high-proof pleasure from limited fare.

Their numbers testify that Florida is as good for them as prunes. Already this is the nation's eldest state in terms of residents' age, and the percentages grow. Each year, it adds at least the equivalent of a new retirement city: 50,000. By the year 2000, the state will have nearly 3 million over-65s and Dade, Broward and Palm Beach counties will be home to a million of them.

While Southeast Florida holds the greatest numbers of the elderly, the greatest rates of gain in aged population (according to University of Florida population studies) go to two hot spots: a cluster of Southwest Gulf Coast counties including Sarasota, Charlotte, Lee and Collier; an area farther north that lumps interior Marion with coastal Levy, Citrus and Hernando counties.

Ponce de Leon supposedly set the pattern for this cane-and-crutch migration 4½ centuries ago. After age 50, Ponce ventured from his governor's post in Puerto Rico seeking — legend says — a storied fountain of youth that would restore his vigor, and instead found Florida during the Easter season of 1513. Historians puncture the romance of that story by telling us he was looking for land and gold.

"If he had heard the Indian legend of the Fountain of Youth, he gave no indication of it. What he wanted was land of his own," wrote Miami's Marjory Stoneman Douglas in her book, *Florida: The Long Frontier.*

"Ponce undoubtedly knew of the fountain fables so common in that day, and the near legendary search for the Fountain of Youth was neither unique nor vitally important in his thinking," wrote the University of Miami's Charlton W. Tebeau in *A History of Florida,* the premier study of this state's past.

The Fountain of Youth attraction suggests that Ponce de Leon came to that very spot, laid a stone cross in the ground that is on display, and states that the attraction was created as a memorial to his journey. But historians such as Douglas, Tebeau and others have dug up no such detail. They say only that Ponce probably landed somewhere between St. Augustine and the St. Johns River.

Whether founded on myth, history or hype, the fountain nevertheless symbolizes a legend that harmonizes with a popular aspect of tourist Florida. In a land of plastic alligators, cement flamingos and inflatable porpoises and mice that talk, the Fountain of Youth almost comes as a relief.

Maybe Ponce de Leon did not come here looking for eternal youth. Maybe he only wanted a little real estate. But millions since then have come for those reasons of legend and many, for a few splendid years, have found an illusion that comes close enough.

With that in mind, it seems not so bizarre to hoist a paper cup filled with well water, and drink deeply of faint hope.

Horseshoe Beach

In Dixie, Oldtime Hogs Are Not Forgotten

In Cracker Florida, hog claims were a matter of honor, not paper. Nobody wrote down the boundaries. They were defined by word and memory. When a dispute came up, it meant that somebody's honor was being questioned. That was trouble. Men sometimes fought over who owned a hog trotting free in the woods. Some died. Others went to prison.

In most of Florida, that ancient custom passed into history, but not in Dixie County. Dixie, a patch of the Gulf Coast between the Suwannee and Steinhatchee Rivers, 80 per cent covered by swamps and timber lands, has not forgotten. The law says old-style hog claims no longer exist, but in Dixie they do.

Strangers have gotten into the thing now, meddling with customs they do not understand and causing trouble and then hollering to the outside law for help. Things are different. Honor prevails against paper only when Dixie contrives to handle the matter informally.

"The hog claim," explained John Osteen of Horseshoe Beach, a longtime Dixie County commissioner, "began as a gentleman's agreement. In the old days, people raised hogs around the house, you know what I mean? They ran loose.

"The settlers around here would say, well now, this is my claim. My hogs range up here to Road 42, or over to the old Cannon place road, or some other road. Another fellow would say, well then, his hogs would range from there on over to his place. They just made it up, without signing any paper or paying anything. The land usually belonged to one of the timber companies, but they didn't care. That's how it got started."

In 1921, the county set up a marking system so that ranging hogs could be identified. A farmer would take his pocketknife and notch the ears of his hogs a certain way, and then he would go down to the courthouse and register the mark. Hogs with that mark were recognized as his. If they strayed to another claim, the issue was compromised.

In 1937, the state in effect reinforced the custom with a law stating that in Florida there was no such thing as a wild hog; all of them belonged to somebody. No longer could a man plead, as was common in hog theft cases, that the animal was wild.

For a long time, hog claims were a way of life that worked, but the old codes wore thin. With new residents, and increased penetration by visitors, change inevitably strained what was a delicately balanced working order. Troubles that once had a chance of being worked out amiably among lifetime acquaintances more and more often became angry disputes among strangers.

Hog claims passed from one generation to another as real property. John Osteen, for example, inherited one from his father. But he saw trouble coming, and converted his claim to a lease. He operated part of it as a hunting club for South Floridians.

But not everyone grasped the change as well as Osteen. As unwritten claims changed hands, through inheritance or sale or lease, their boundaries blurred. In some cases, claims were sold that did not exist at all. Strangers bought, or sold, the Brooklyn Bridge in Dixie County. The sensitivity remained, but the bases for friendly settlement of disputes frequently did not.

In 1979, state law seeped in and declared no hog claim existed without paper to prove it. The law declared it, but Dixie was still deciding how it should be worked out.

That was a bit of a tangle. Sometime in years past, the state gave each county the option of designating the hog as legal game. Because the hogs ran loose, they were wild in manner if not in definition, and hunting them was considered good sport. When so designated, hogs came under the jurisdiction of the Florida Game and Fresh Water Fish Commission. That meant rules, regulations and a legal hunting season that corresponds to deer season. Dixie declined the option, preferring to hunt as it pleased with the home-grown hog claims system.

Joe Hubert Allen, clerk of the Dixie County Court, made the surprising discovery. He was accepting the registration of hog marks as usual, just as clerks before him had, and his authority to do so was challenged. He queried the Florida attorney general and was informed that the law had changed. "Nobody ever had told us that before," Allen said. Anyway, hog marks no longer could be registered in Tallahassee with the Department of Agriculture and Consumer services.

That discovery, and the impact of a hog claims case that reached Circuit Court, eliminated Dixie's legal authority to enforce hog claims. The judge ruled no claim existed unless there was paper to prove it. That stripped away all except tradition. But, in some ways, tradition in Dixie County is as powerful as the law.

There followed a series of meetings among holders of hog claims, hunters, timber companies, legislators and the county commission. The honor in hog claims was endorsed, the legal complications explained and it was recommended that hog claims be converted to paper. But that illusory process, of defining claims recorded only in memory, merely shifted the battle to other grounds.

"Those old hog claims depend on people trusting one another," Commissioner Osteen said. "We were always proud that we could do that around here. If problems come up again, we will find a way to make them right. Yes, sir. I think Dixie County can handle this thing itself."

Sheriff Glen Dyals agreed. "The state says there's no such thing as a claim now, but the oldtimers still believe in claims and I'm for 'em. Hog claims been here since before I was born in this world. If something happens, it don't necessarily have to go to court. We'll just get everybody concerned to set down together and work it out."

Dixie County forget? Hell, no.

Okeechobee

The Return of The Song-Dog

On the top shelf of a dry-goods section at Guynn's Grocery, its feet planted among pictures of Lenore Guynn's grandchildren, stood a yellowish doglike creature with lips peeled back by a taxidermist into a snarl.

"It's a coyote," Mrs. Guynn said as strangers stared at the fierce-looking animal. "They've been killing calves and goats around here. They're all over the place in these woods."

Mrs. Guynn's grocery served a farm and ranch section north of High Springs near where the Santa Fe River separates Gilchrist and Alachua counties. Foxhunters ran over the coyote in a pickup truck in 1978.

Her estimate of numbers may be unscientific, but in fact the sun-down yip-yip and mournful howl of the coyote — the prairie wolf that Indian legend says will be the last animal alive on earth — has sounded in at least 16 Florida counties in a broken path from the Panhandle down through the central ridge into the Everglades. The nature of the animal and Florida terrain adjoining the 16 suggest probable presence of coyotes in other counties.

Their future in Florida cannot be charted with any certainty, but the coyote could have noticeable impact. Mexican peasant farmers have described it as the most astute being on earth, second only to God. Biologists call it the most compelling wildlife success story. Officials out West warn that even a few of the little animals (about two feet high, four feet long and 40 pounds) can be a serious problem. Naturalists admire it as the song-dog, extol its intelligence and even praise its sense of humor.

Defining Florida's situation even as it existed in 1978 was almost impossible. Coyotes are famed for their cunning, their adaptability to any environment (even urban) and their capacity to create problems. In the forests and wild areas of Florida they can exist unknown. Only when they venture out to farms or ranches for food, or when they are encountered by hunters, does confirmed identification occur.

Because a wild dog can be mistaken for a coyote, and because an ancient enmity that exists between man and coyote quickly stirs man to kill, wildlife officials treated the subject cautiously. A coyote scare puts them in the middle of warring foxhunters, who favor the coyote as bait for running their hounds, naturalists who want to encourage the species and the farmers-ranchers who want to protect their small livestock.

Coyotes flourised in Florida before Columbus arrived, but were driven West by settlers. In the West, literally millions of them were killed through the offering of bounties, through federal predatory control projects and by sheepmen trying to protect their individual herds. With that threat, coyotes migrated from the Western prairies south to Central America, north to Alaska and east to the Atlantic seaboard.

The coyote's return to Florida was noted at least as early as 1925, when four of the animals were released or escaped in Palm Beach County. Within the next few years, 16 were killed in Collier County, one was killed in Monroe County near Key largo and one was killed in Marion County.

Coyotes reappeared in Polk and Osceola counties in the 1950s and established population. Since 1976 they have been sighted or killed in Alachua, Columbia, Hendry, Hernando, Jackson, Lake, Okaloosa, Osceola, Polk, Suwannee and Washington counties. In four south Georgia counties, farmers and ranchers have been harassed by coyotes.

The coyote is not protected by Florida law, but use of steel traps and poison are illegal. Ranchers have put out butchered cattle as bait, and shot coyotes that gathered. They have penned up dogs in heat (the highly democratic coyote will breed with a dog, producing a "coydog," further complicating identification) to lure coyotes within shooting distance.

The most notable coyote scare so far occurred in Polk County in

1969. A sheepman-rancher complained of heavy losses and organized a hunt. They got four, but six years later he quit the sheep business, saying the coyote had beaten him. The animal was too elusive.

Coyote reports accumulated in the High Springs area served by Guynn Grocery. L.W. Allen, a rancher, in 1978 estimated a pack of 25 near his place. "We sit on the porch at night and hear 'em hollering. They hit all my calves last winter except the seven big ones. Pretty near wiped me out. No way in the world we'll ever get rid of them."

Dewey Lee, a rancher neighbor of Allen's, said coyotes attacked his calves. "First thing the coyote's do is eat the calves' liver," he said. "I'm afraid we'll be fighting those things a long time."

In Florida, the coyote may have found a natural home. There is abundant precedent here for the survival of a creature who lives by his wits, eats anything, breeds with anything, howls at a full moon and moves fast. It is just too early to tell whether he is nimble enough to compete with tourists.

The Festivals: Florida's Glue

In Florida, a patch-quilt of a state, almost everybody loves a festival. The celebration of life never stops, rarely pauses. From the villages to the cities, more than 600 annual public parties spread across the peninsula like so many happy-time town meetings.

The object is pleasure, not civics, but among them there is an old-fashioned sense of community that, in the absence of much other statewide cement, does more to encourage Florida's varied pieces to cling together than any other non-governmental thing.

They make a trail that covers almost every weekend on the calendar, though the string gets thin in August, and sets up great open-air huzzahs for things that Floridians find worthy for any reason, whimsical or serious.

At least 5 million persons a year (my estimate) attend festivals celebrating food, music, art, folklife, history and whatever. The festivals identify and reveal Florida's splendid variety, its fancies and even its problems.

Florida defines its festivals loosely. They range from a belly-flop diving contest each July at a place called Otter Springs in north Florida, which draws 5,000, to the street party Calle Ocho in Miami each March where Latin rhythms and food attract 600,000.

The Keys and coastal cities pay homage to seafood, LaBelle honors swamp cabbage and at Belle Glade winter vegetables get the glory at a Black Gold Jubilee. In the Panhandle, Niceville memorializes mullet and Wausau, possums. For Macclenny it is moonshine and Okeechobee, speckled perch.

The festivals are an evolution from the barn-raisings, hog-killings, corn-shuckings, cakewalks and church bazaars of earlier times and have the effect of reviving some of what they represented.

They have grown to include almost any single-theme public wing-ding that has been elevated beyond neighborhood dimensions.

In *The Book of Festivals,* Dorothy Gladys Spicer offered a formal definition: "Festivals are the outward expression of man's common heritage of fear and thanksgiving...for harvests...fear of hostile forces, joy in sunshine, rain and renewal of life...."

Florida's festivals combine folk culture and show business. They have developed into a kind of hey-look-at-what-we've-got boast that in an extraordinary way generates warm response.

Their numbers appear to be increasing, but there is no official count. April Athey at the Florida Division of Tourism in Tallahassee produces the closest thing to a catalogue, but it is only a promotional directory of the major or most unusual festivals to assist news media coverage.

"We list about 350, but there probably are twice that many," she said. "There seem to be more in recent years, but they come and go. Some communities drop them, and others start them. A lot of small places feel like it keeps their town on the map."

For some, it has been like tieing themselves to a rocket and lighting the fuse. The crowds lurched upwards so suddenly that they reached unmanageable proportions.

The Cedar Key Art Festival may be the best example. Cedar Key (population 900), a one-square mile island city and gulf coast fishing village, had been drawing some 35,000 a year to the April event. In 1975, with no warning, 100,000 came.

In response to food and water shortages, sewage incapacity and friction between tourists and locals, the Cedar Key Council announced there would be no more art festivals. Later it relented, on condition that sponsoring clubs quit advertising the affair.

The Apalachicola Seafood Festival (begun in 1915 as the Apalachicola Carnival), probably the most renowned of the village festivals statewide, had similar troubles. Apalachicola (population 3,100), on the Panhandle coast, regularly drew 10 times its population for the November event. As Florida oyster supplies dwindled, and Apalachicola could sell all it produced without promotions, some of the townspeople tired of having to clean up after 35,000 guests each year.

When Apalachicola tried to scale down the party, though, it experienced the other side of festival volatility. That year, 1981, only 10,000 attended. The next year, they prepared accordingly, and the numbers swelled back to 35,000.

"We have decided that we can't tell what to expect," said Alice Leavins, festival director for 1983. "There's no way to control the size. We never can tell. It can be a real disaster." Noted Leon Bloodworth, a former director, "Once something like this gets going, it's hard to stop. We may not be able to keep it small without killing it."

Grant, an unincorporated Brevard County community on the Indian River, started a seafood festival in February, 1976. The sponsoring Community Club expected maybe 500 to 1,000; 5,000 came. "Traffic backed up on the highway for 10 miles," said Margaret Senne, 1983 chairman. With planning and better equipment, Grant geared up for greater crowds and now handles about 30,000 each year with relative ease.

In Florida, festivals are a powerful force. They thrive on benign climate and a casual populace. Encouraged by nostalgia, they conjure up an identifiable state spirit. They establish threads of commonality among the disparate.

Festivals give us a whiff of Florida's essence. In offering a respite of comfortably accepted themes, a rare and welcome gift in this fermenting state, they make a special contribution. But, above all, they are fun.

Upstairs Florida

The mountains in winter have a harsh beauty, like truth. Nature goes to the confessional, exposing all the skeletons. Trees and bushes, stripped naked of leaves, hide nothing.

The landscape is as stern as the Old Testament. Where erosion has cracked the scruffy slopes, red earth shows like frozen blood.

From a distance, leafless forests on the peaks and ridges look like the stubble of a beard on a reclining giant.

Ice silvers over the muddy edges of mountain streams and ponds. Cows shatter it with their hooves, and drink. Motorists peer at the road through holes scraped in the sheen on their windshields.

But by April, the mountains begin to soften and dissemble. As spring comes, they pretty up the hard facts like children learning the rewards of pleasant evasiveness.

April in the mountains marks a riptide of the seasons, a chiaroscuro of melancholy and cheer. Among days still christened by snow and sleet, there are bright and warm afternoons that lure the green out of dead-looking limbs.

Before April has gone, blossoms burst into that bleak landscape like tiny, silent explosions of exuberance. While smoke curls out of chimneys, flowering peach and plum trees raise the first cheers to approaching summer.

In the flatlands, across South Georgia and down the peninsula to South Florida — to another land and another people — steady sunshine and summer calm already have come.

But in the mountains of northern Georgia and North Carolina the seasons still struggle with each other. It is a fierce battle for clemency, and always successful.

Spring, marking the victory, begins at the bottom of the moun-

60

tains and gradually greens its way upward. The mountain people can read that rising level of green as though it were a blackboard chart.

Not until May or maybe even June does spring crawl all the way to the top and give the mountains their seasonal identity as Upstairs Florida. When that happens, the gates fly open.

Up those stairs from the south the summer people begin flooding in with another load of money and another wave of city ways to plant among a people not fully decided whether they are victims or con artists.

"Picking flatlanders beats picking beans," they always say, but the flatlanders do some picking of their own. It is difficult to tell the pigeons from the hawks. The isolated mountain villages pop out with commercial zits: the real estate frenzy, billboards, pizza parlors, discount houses, curiosity shops.

This summer tide of Floridians began on practicality, decades ago, before air conditioning developed as routine relief for the rigors of tropical Julys and Augusts.

Then, rather than snapping on a cooling machine, Floridians piled into their cars and headed north toward the cool mountains. South Florida, especially, would empty out. Families who could afford it had high summer places. Workers and husbands stayed behind, except for brief vacations, to keep the essential functions going.

What had been a near necessity in time became a custom and eventually a tradition. Though South Florida no longer collapses in summertime, each year the heat migrants reaffirm Florida's seasonal territorial claim.

Once, that summer flight followed U.S. 441 north as it wound through quaint Georgia villages, up through the foothills and finally to the first real mountains surrounding the Little Tennessee Valley along the Georgia-North Carolina line.

There, where the floor of the valley has a 2,400-foot altitude, was the gateway and staging area to Upstairs Florida.

From the valley, which contained the villages of Dillard, Clayton, Mountain City and Rabun Gap, the summer people could go east up the mountains and 13 miles to Highlands, N.C., and on to Cashiers and Hendersonville and all the way up to Blowing Rock and Boone.

Or, they could go north 12 miles to Franklin, N.C., and fan out through the Smokies to Cherokee and Gatlinburg and any number of other mountain towns and resorts.

Now, with Interstates 75 and 95 and their east-west connections, there are other routes from South Florida to the mountains but the old one through the valley probably remains the favorite.

But however the flatlanders get there, the seasonal colony of Upstairs Florida awaits. It has been established on firm mutuality and nothing is likely to change it. There are too many second homes and condos and friendships and other appetites for the beguiling mountain ways.

April is the month when Upstairs Florida spruces up and gets ready, for it is spring in the mountains and the heat migrants are coming. It is one of those facts of life anchored implausibly by threads of delight attached to changing lights and temperatures.

The migratory phenomenon, covering nearly 1,000 miles, begins with the spring riptide and closes with its opposite number in October — when the leaves take on flaming colors, summer loses the battle for clemency and the chigger-bitten flatlanders then follow the warm air back downstairs.

As some of the mountain people say when the invasion ends, the winter truths shall set you free, especially if accompanied by sleet.

Lake Placid

Scavengers: Wildlife Heirs of Florida

Dr. James Layne has a democratic love of life, all of it. He speaks as lovingly of a sand skink as a panther, as respectfully of a scrub jay as a bald eagle, as proudly of the Florida mouse as a black bear.

It is not animal snobbery that makes him look with dismay upon what he foresees to be the wildlife heirs of Florida — such creatures as the raccoon, the gray squirrel and the cattle egret.

Zoological aristocracy does not make him biased toward a coming reign of wildlife types that adapt to whatever bastardized tastes and mongrelized instincts that survival demands.

Dr. Layne respects the survival capacity of the possum, the armadillo, the cottontail rabbit, the common rat. Unnatural disasters that rip away natural habitat isolate some animals from the only life processes they know, but not these. They scramble and survive. They are streetfighters and scavengers, and they loom as eventual inheritors.

They sleep almost anywhere, eat almost anything, search out patches of trees and bushes in parks and yards and seem undisturbed by the screeching and grinding of the cities. Or they can romp contentedly through the biological deserts of groves and fields, through the great forests lacerated by multiple abuses, and find make-do havens.

Layne perceives the inevitability of the future, gauged by the tumbling of natural cathedrals, but feels Florida diminished by it.

"We are losing the diversity, the uniqueness of wildlife in Florida," he said. "Everybody knows about the panther and the bald eagle but who ever heard of a skink or the Florida mouse or the gopher frog? They live only in the sand pine scrub habitat that is rapidly being lost.

"To the average person these mean nothing. These small, inconspicuous creatures are a matter of complete apathy, yet they probably are just as important as the eagle and panther. It gets even worse when you talk about the species of insects we are losing. People start rolling their eyes."

Layne spoke from a fenced-in, 3,800-acre scrub empire in South Central Florida where the skink (a kind of lizard) and the Florida mouse and the scrub jay have equal rights. Man does not tamper with nature there. He only observes. Not even lightning may start a fire and burn the scrub. Sometimes Dr. Layne worries that overprotection itself may become an unnatural influence. Does an occasional, naturally caused fire benefit the scrub? It has become a matter of research.

He works from a second-story office at the end of a long, depotlike building put together with elegant strength nearly a half-century ago by John A. Roebling, grandson of the man who designed the Brooklyn Bridge and son of the man who finished it.

This is the Archbold Biological Research Station of the American Museum of Natural History, located near the south end of a 100-mile ridge that runs down the middle of Florida into Highlands County. As the ridge tapers away, on the station grounds eight miles south of Lake Placid, elevation varies from 222 feet down to 125. The Gulf and Atlantic coasts are equidistant.

The station looks, and operates, something like a foreign service colony. The facilities, a 4,000-volume library, laboratories, catalogued recordings and films and surrounding natural habitat attract scientists from the Caribbean to California and Canada to come here for study. State and federal agencies call on the station for counsel.

The Roebling family had intended this to be a private estate but finished only the warehouse and sub-buildings before giving the property in 1941 to a family friend, Richard Archbold, to be used for biological research. Archbold, whose grandfather had been president of the original Standard Oil Company, lived at the station and steadily expanded its holdings until his death in 1976.

The station continued under the guidance of Archbold Expeditions with Dr. Layne as its executive director. Layne, whose credentials and stature within the scientific community are giant-sized, served 13 years on the faculties of the universities of Florida and Cornell before coming here in 1967. He directs specialized research in habitat, evolution of adaptations and population survival in Florida.

His personal opinions are close to prophecy.

For Florida, most of the unique wildlife and most of the larger and more romanticized animals will disappear. Whitetailed deer will continue to thrive, an example of one exception at least in size, because they are managed, almost like freeranging cattle. The state permits hunters to keep herds healthily culled to numbers that available forest habitat will support.

But the general promise of wildlife appears lukewarm, or worse. Survivors will be more maverick than wild, less afraid of man, more familiar than mysterious, not physical dangers but physical nuisances, probably less a contribution to healthy balance than to health hazard. There will be a prevalence of small, hardy, fast-reproducing pests.

"The critical thing," said Dr. Layne, preferring to take a broader view, "is that the loss of sensitive wildlife forms is a signal that we're disrupting the natural systems of Florida. We ourselves depend on those, what they mean to the water and the air and the soil, and ultimately we will pay for it."

No hurry, right now. Watch for the coming of the pests. They will tell us when it is time to panic.

Umatilla

Keeping The Oranges Warm

A cold wave brings a look of doomsday to Umatilla and the orange country. Dark clouds hang over the groves and dusk comes early on a December afternoon. Shivering pickers move through the groves plucking the legendary golden apples, and many an owner warms his hands before a stack heater and prays it will not freeze.

Freezes are fearsome things in Lake County, an hour's drive north of Orlando. Fortunately, they do not come often, but when they do it can be disaster for a grove man.

In December of 1895, one hard freeze followed after another and the bark on the trees split and popped with the sound of gunshots. When some owners heard, they got directly up from their dinner tables and fled the state. Others replanted, others moved a little farther south. Other historic freezes came in 1962 and 1977.

Grove owners in December, when the fruit is maturing, recall the bad years and worry. They listen closely to the weathermen and restlessly wait for warnings.

"An old rattlesnake now, he'll get him a rabbit and crawl into a gopher hole and he'll be set for the winter. Won't come out until it gets warm again," Lawrence Atkinson, a grove man, said as the winter of 1977 approached.

Atkinson always kept a jar of rattlesnake tails — the rattlers — on his desk. Summers, disk plows behind tractors chop up rattlesnakes that come hunting for rats and rabbits in the groves. "Buzzards eat the meat, and I save the rattles," he said.

But as a grove owner and caretaker since he and his Dad came down from Georgia in 1926, Atkinson has found no such easy answer. In the early years, he and his Dad burned sticks of fat pine

66

wood among the trees to keep down the cold. They would cross-stack three pieces at intervals, and keep an extra wood supply under the trees. But the wood supply became scarce.

Later, they learned to splash old tires with a little gas and oil and burn them in the groves. It did not smell so good, but provided a little heat and a lot of smoke that hung over the trees. "We thought the smoke kept off the frost," Atkinson said.

From that, they turned to open or smudge pots. Sometimes these would be just five gallon cans with fuel oil in them and a lid on top to act as damper. They too produced some heat and a lot of smoke.

But the Environmental Protection Agency discouraged wood, tires and smudge pots for reasons of pollution and now most grove men use portable stack heaters, four-foot high fuel oil burners with a tub at the bottom, a cap on the top to keep out rain and vents on the side to let out heat. They smoke a little but not enough to make the EPA cough. However, they are hard work, too. They have to be put out each winter, fired by hand and refuelled.

Some owners went to the considerably larger investment — but more convenient method — of a permanent installation of pipes that wind through the groves and are fed by a central oil supply. They have a system of small, jet burners. But even for them, a cold wave remains a thing to fear.

"Nobody was equipped for it when that '62 freeze came. The wind blew so hard even those who had wood or tires ready couldn't fire. Just too much wind," Atkinson said. "Now most of us have these stack heaters. I don't fire to save the fruit any more, just the trees. With costs what they are today, I don't think it's worth it. Even if the fruit freezes, some of it can be used by the juice plants.

"I won't fire until midnight, not even if it gets down as low as 24. The coldest time is just before day and a little after sunrise. If you fire too early, the fuel runs out just when you need it most."

"Some of these fellows get excited and go out and fire a little bit every year, but I don't. I just stand by until a big one comes."

Atkinson put out his stack heaters early in December, before the hard winter of 1977, and fuelled then. "I expected a bad one," he said, "Another '62." He was right, and the preparations eased the damage. At times like that, he would have his workers stand by. If he had to call on a cold night, they would gather at his little two-room frame office across from the schoolyard, collect gloves and flashlights and starter fuel (oil spiked with gas) and make a midnight firing run through the groves.

On gloomy December afternoons, Atkinson always would light the little oil heater in his office, warm his hands, and walk to the window often to check the sky. He would sit by the telephone at a littered desk, where the two most prominent objects were a jar of rattlers and a picture of his three pretty daughters, and pray that he would not need to call the workers.

Not many things scare a grove man more than a hard freeze.

Places

Evelyn Shealy at Ochopee Post Office

Walt Disney World

Disney World: Nicey Nice, Cold Turkey

Inside one hall, a $40,000 fabrication of Honest Abe Lincoln rises from a chair and speaks to a gathering of U.S. Presidents. Teddy Roosevelt cocks a hand impatiently on one hip. One President whispers; another fidgets. But they do not interrupt. The late model Lincoln has computers. He can make 47 body movements and 17 different facial expressions. The others can only nod or twitch. They listen respectfully.

Around the corner there is a 65-foot treehouse. The tree has vinyl leaves and hand painted blossoms and the view looks over a crafted world, Walt Disney World, where no paint peels and no soot billows and no horn honks, a sugared world which celebrates human imperfections by transferring them to animals and laughing at them.

Nobody cries because Mickey Mouse is a 50-year-old rat with monstrous ears and a woeful body, because Donald Duck has a lousy voice and a bad temper, because grotesque Goofy has subnormal intelligence, and nobody cares that all the animals are cool, bloodless machines moving on wheels and bearings. They have been burdened so we may be relieved, designed for stupidity and bumbling, created to make human frailty an immense joke.

The fake animals are Orwellian creatures manufactured to be buffoons — emotional targets. Upon them we can shed prejudicial humor without guilt. We can love them for their delight in accepting comic servitude. They never organize or protest or sue. Let your Archie Bunker out. No one will notice.

At Small World dolls sing a chorus in all languages, over and

71

over. The little anchored mechanisms gather dust but never cry or tire of issuing childish joy as though on a Detroit production line. Peter Pan flies over moonlit London, Dumbo the distorted elephant makes wings of his ears and soars. You can ride a toad, laugh at seven dwarfs, visit a haunted mansion where 999 testify mischievously about happy ghosting after death, attend a mad tea party, peer into the future.

Neither death, ignorance, insanity, deformity nor doubt daunt Walt Disney World. Like a puff of cotton candy, imaginative genius briefly overpowers reality. Here there is the ultimate pacifier, and the old accept it as eagerly and unashamedly as the young. It is a walk-around dream. Love the past, revel in the future, forget the present. But after awhile, your feet begin to hurt.

Visitors cannot cast off their private imperfections. It is hot. Who expects to sweat in heaven? There are not enough places to sit. The beautiful old steamboat keeps pushing around in circles, blowing its whistle, demanding a spirit of fun as it offers an example of futility.

Cinderella's Castle rises above all. Imagine glass slippers on these bricks. Still farther, there is a speedway where no one ever crashes and burns, and down the middle there is the kind of Main Street that thrived during a period of easy optimism about the American dream. Sinclair Lewis wrote about it in a cynical novel that deplored the stunting influences of complacency and narrowness when mental boundaries are too closely defined.

In this Magic Kingdom, you begin to get that hemmed-in feeling of a sinner too long in the pews. You hunger for a big piece of cheese and a musical mousetrap. You notice that while homage is paid Mark Twain his favorite animal, the cat, gets no billing at all. "If man could be crossed with the cat, it would improve man, but it would deteriorate the cat," Twain wrote. Take that, Mickey. Emerson said, correctly but callously, that God put a crack in everything he made. Walt Disney too?

The people herd through a candy environment like cows searching for a barn at sundown, with Disney attendants lighting up the way with smiles and courtesy, mimicking the faultless Mickey. There is a dictatorship of the proper and the cordial, a regimenta-

tion of good taste and good humor. A kind of mechanical perfection reigns, a coin-operated warmth, inhumanly humane.
Something is missing.

Coming from a world of porno parlors and anything-goes television and a daily routine of assorted public horrors, the sudden
dead morality creates uneasiness, like the eye of a storm. A casual
wink at Cinderella would seem gross, a leer at Snow White capitally
offensive, an off-color joke probably worth a felony. When you
click through the turnstile, the Magic Kingdom lays nicey-nicey on,
cold turkey.

You find yourself standing in a long line at the Diamond Horseshoe Revue. A sign says there are can-can girls inside. In this
can't-can't atmosphere, a snort of reality. At 5:30 p.m., two of the
four evening shows are filled up. During a 45-minute wait in line for
reservations, the 9:30 show fills up. The little lady behind the
counter flashes you a Mickey Mouse smile and speaks in a Snow
White voice and hands you a pair for the 10:45.

"Better be here at 10:15," she advises. All told, it will only be a
five hour and 15 minute wait for a half-hour of looking at real people.
But the seats run out before the line does, and it is like that almost
every day and every night. The show is free, but the attraction is
relief. A performer may stutter, stumble or otherwise make a
mistake. And there is the can-can. This cannot be pure Cinderella.
Some real skin will have to show.

During the hypnotic Main Street Electrical Parade, a spectacular
consumption of battery power, rain begins to sprinkle down. People
do not seem to mind. The parade has a special peculiarity: so many
lights, and not trying to sell anything. Outside the Diamond
Horseshoe at 9:45 the line already has formed on the wet brick
walks. Reservations in hand, the people crowd and wait. At 10:15
they stampede through the doors to the little wooden tables and belly
up to the bar for a cola and some chips. They stare at the stage. Not
a fake animal anywhere. Ah!

Real girls dance out doing the Charleston and what-not, kicking
high and flashing a daring glimpse of panties. Guys make a lot of
noise playing the banjo and brass and a washboard. They stumble
around and tell suggestive jokes Milton Berle gave up 20 years ago,

and the crowd is on its feet cheering and whistling and stomping feet. None of that wide-eyed blinking and blank smiling that Mickey Mouse gets.

We walk out soothed, and decide that even if it is late maybe we ought to catch that Peter Pan flight. Balance has been restored. The blood has been stirred. We notice two prim girls we had seen earlier, walking around eating popcorn like two little Shirley Temples, talking earnestly.

"My Mama likes my Daddy for his personality, not for his sex," said one. Replied the other: "My Mama likes my Daddy for his money." Not Shirley Temples after all.

We have located the fault here for Emerson. The Magic Kingdom, so perfect and impossible, lacks the full dimension of human flaw. Poor old Mickey and Goofy and Dumbo have been fixed in the head as well as elsewhere. They are doomed to be clowns of minor merit because they never had the chance to be knaves. They will never know the joy in repenting even minor sins, or the pride of growth in resisting the major ones.

Unlike Eve, Snow White may see the apple but will never be offered a bite. When you study the anxious faces and the long lines at the Diamond Horseshoe, you understand. They seek relief from the burdens of impossible standards. Life cannot exist without the spirit of can-can.

Ochopee

From Ochopee, With Love

Next time you have a chance, drive over to Ochopee and visit Florida's most famous and best loved post office. It has the best stamps in the state. You cannot beat the prices.

There are many things distinctive about the Ochopee Post Office, other than the central fact that it is the smallest post office in the United States. In this age of luxury high-rises, it has the look of an elegant old outhouse, and offers poetic perspective on the lightning pace of history in South Florida.

Only technically does it have a postmaster. In reality it has a postal-Mama — Evelyn Shealy — a nice lady who hand cancels every letter with love and Zip Code 33943. She tends the place as though it were her living room and company were coming.

Mrs. Shealy, budget conscious, does everything: She keeps the mails flowing through Ochopee, sells picture postcards, chats with tourists and poses for their pictures, mothers the patrons. She even has considered (and decided against) serving refreshments to visitors during the busier winter months.

She acts as maid and janitor and personally finances all the maintenance. She paid for the blue roof when it was replaced, for the fresh white paint job, for the new linoleum on the floor. Her husband Jack, a machinist, built and donated the flagpole.

"I like my job," Mrs. Shealy explained. "This way I feel like I'm sharing. And it's not that much, really, to bother anybody about." She laughed, "I don't always get rid of every cobweb, maybe, but they kind of help to hold the building together."

The postal-Mama keeps a post office that Ochopee can be proud of, one that merits a presidential parable about the miracles of Reaganomics. When the bosses ask for reports now and then on how money can be saved, Mrs. Shealy has nothing to say. The budget is down to bone.

Her post office measures 8 feet, 4 inches by 7 feet, 3 inches and has been certified by Washington as the nation's smallest. It has no air-conditioning, no water fountain, no restroom.

Like a small white monument, it sits back on the edge of the Big Cypress swamp fronting a rocky drive off the Tamiami Trail (U.S. 41) in Collier County about 35 miles east of Naples or 70 miles west of Miami. It would be wonderfully poetic to be able to say that Ochopee was named for an Irish butcher, but the name in fact is Indian, meaning big field.

Forty families call at the post office for their mail, which Mrs. Shealy personally plucks from a pigeonhole and hands over to them because there are no rental boxes. It allows for customized service, sometimes even a phone alert when long-awaited special mail arrives.

A part-time clerk assists in keeping the post office open 5½ days per week. The only other postal employee at Ochopee is an independent contractor who services 160 roadside mailboxes on a 123-mile rural route.

For Ochopee, a disappearing village, the post office since 1974 has become unusually important. That was the year a federal law declared the surrounding Big Cypress a national preserve, to protect the South Florida watershed. The government then began buying (condemning, if necessary) the property, and the population dwindled quickly. Even the Trailways bus no longer stops there. A few residents, like the Shealys, have been allowed to remain because of grandfather clauses in the law.

The process left the post office (which serves about half the number it did in 1974) as the last common link among the citizens of Ochopee. They, the park service rangers and the tourists who stop to marvel at the world's smallest post office (the claims get grander all the time), keep Ochopee on the map.

The village was created in 1929, a year after the Tamiami Trail opened, when a large tomato farm was located there. Other farms followed, a scattering of businesses opened, and by 1940 Ochopee had reached its zenith with a population of 1,200.

Included in that boom was the opening of its first post office in

1932. Capt. J. F. Jaudon put it in one corner of his general store. A year later, Sidney H. Brown took over both the store and the post office.

In 1953, after the general store burned, Brown moved the post office into a toolshed on the property, and it has remained there ever since. The toolshed became the smallest post office. By 1955, the last tomato crop was harvested. The farms moved away to better ground.

Mrs. Shealy became Ochopee's third postmaster in the early 1970s, at a time when Ochopee had begun to muster another boom. A few individualists from the Miami area had begun to move west and one developer had laid out plans for a small city there on property made waterfront by canals connecting to the gulf. There was discussion of building a new, larger post office.

Then came the Big Cypress purchase plan, which helped to preserve a water supply for the exploding South Florida population, but crippled Ochopee permanently and threatened to make even the world's smallest post office too large.

So now Mrs. Shealy, the postal-Mama, lovingly operates a tidy, unique bit of Florida history. It is a place to nurture and honor. She does the extra things with that in mind.

Go visit. Buy stamps. The smallest post office has room to grow. Boost Ochopee.

Jacksonville

Jacksonville: Big Jim's Town

Among the Florida cities, whose tourist and playtime economies give them the images of dilettantes, Jacksonville is the hardworking, self-made man. The St. Johns River curls through downtown like a blue collar. The smell and haze of industry are in its air.

The river winds under the bridges and along a waterfront that gives it both an accomplished look and hints at better things dreamed of and not yet given up.

A mirrored skyscraper anchors the river city, occasionally blinding it with great solar winks, and municipal buildings squat along the river like American pyramids with distant Egyptian genes.

Jacksonville, so scrappingly ambitious, comes on steady and solid. It is Florida by location, Georgia by migration, southern by inclination, cosmopolitan by anticipation.

While I was growing up there during the 1930s and 1940s, it seemed an earthy, quarrelsome, cohesive, wonderful place. I remember it as a brash, old-fashioned, fried chicken kind of a town. (Fried chicken was noble fare then, the food of my soul.)

Jacksonville had a proper Main Street that, as Sinclair Lewis characterized the one in his book, was "the continuation of Main Streets everywhere." In the ignorance of those days we thought it high-minded to have a Confederate Park and a statue to a Confederate soldier in downtown Hemming Park. That excuse vanished in the 1950s, but not the park or the statue.

In memory what symbolized the Jacksonville of that time was Big Jim. Everybody who grew up in Jacksonville knew Big Jim. He was the town crier, the community clock, the thing that tied everything together with a toot.

Big Jim was a giant, hand-operated copper steam-whistle, the invention of a man from Titusville named John Einig. The name honors his brother-in-law, James Patterson, who hammered out the copper. In 1890 when Jacksonville bought the biggest boilers in the state for its Main Street waterworks, Einig and Patterson installed it there.

Back yonder many years ago, Big Jim whistled frantically to alert us that oil tanks along the river had exploded. Oldtimers recalled that it whistled to warn of the great 1901 fire that devastated downtown Jacksonville and to celebrate the ends of World Wars I and II.

But those were the special celebrations and warnings. Big Jim routinely served as the community clock. Jacksonville operated on his schedule. He blew at 7 to start the day, at noon to signal lunch, at 1 to stop it and at 5 to call you home from work.

Sitting out on the brick wall in front of our house, made impatient by the smells of supper cooking, almost every day I waited for the sound of Big Jim. As soon as he whistled, I could look for Dad's old Model A Ford to come shuddering down the street. Then it was time to eat.

You never had to worry when old Big Jim was around. Good, bad or routine, he would give a whistle to let you know the state of the community. But Jacksonville was a smaller and less busy place then.

In 1968, Big Jim was moved crosstown and automated. It cost too much to have an attendant stand by, watch the clock and pull the cord. Big Jim still routinely delivers the time-of-day signals but no longer tries to be a town crier. Nobody seems to hear it anymore.

Jacksonville now is spread out over almost all Duval County. Air conditioning and air pollution mute sounds. Even if Big Jim still had his full vigor, it would be too much for him.

Still, Jacksonville clings to individuality. Among Florida cities with rocketing population numbers even during recessionary times, cities happy to bend themselves into whatever shapes will delight the tourists, it grows more in the deliberate, old-fashioned way — through baby production rather than migration.

The population transfusion that shatters the sense of identity in most Florida cities, producing an anxious search for something still being formed, not yet existing, is a mild process here. The future does not race away from the past so quickly, and that makes a difference in stability.

But like most cities and all people, Jacksonville occasionally suffers tasteless public blunders within the family that taint its image disproportionately. For example, in recent years, an avowed redneck disc jocky became a popular public figure; its Chamber of Commerce denigrated Atlanta and New York trying to generate a publicity fight; some of its policemen sold T-shirts crudely boosting the death penalty.

Outsiders gleefully pick on such easy targets, and continue to call Jacksonville the largest city in South Georgia (when a Georgia company recently bought the local newspapers, that at least partially accounted for the public expression of dismay).

Jacksonville is not just the fried chicken town of memory any more, despite those relapses. The civic conscience that always has graced its better side, that produced the extraordinary riverfront revitalization and the persistent pursuit of downtown revival, gives it broad and admirable dimension.

Sometimes it may seem to lurch this way and that, and local politics may seem distractingly raucous at times, but the city appears to keep working its way steadily toward a vision of the future that (like its past) centers around the river. Somehow, purposeful direction emerges.

In Jacksonville today, not many know Big Jim and that instant feeling of community he gave, but it still looks like an earthy, quarrelsome, wonderful place. Yet, unexplainably, most newcomers to Florida — excepting Georgians — still overlook it.

Canal Point

Custard Apples and Sawgrass

The muck lands along the south and east shores of Lake Okeechobee always had a touch of black magic about them. To the farmer who learned their secrets, they promised treasure. But to the unwary ones, they offered deception and danger.

The best were the custard apple lands, a belt some 50 miles long and a half-mile or so wide along the edge of the lake. They submitted richly. Beans and peppers popped out of the ground fast, lush and fruitful. A man could make two, and sometimes three, crops a year.

But that belt was special. On it had grown masses of the twisting, brittle custard apple trees, 15 to 20 feet high and perfect as rookeries for the great clouds of birds that lived around the lake.

By the time the pioneer farmers came, attracted by the Florida Boom that peaked in the early 1920s, the custard apple lands were rich from decaying vegetation and bird droppings applied generously for hundreds of years to warm, wet soil.

The pioneers cleared those lands, planted vegetables and got fabulous results. So they ventured farther out, past the cypress and willow trees and into the broad, flat sawgrass lands.

But there, the muck did not perform its magic. The bean plants would pop out of the soil, grow lush and green, then turn yellow and die before any beans were produced. Standard fertilizer did not help.

While farmers were still puzzling about all this, a 1926 hurricane — the first in 16 years — ravaged Miami and swirled up to Lake Okeechobee. In three of the previous five years there had been flooding rains, and the hurricane on top of that was the worst disaster in lake history — until two years later, when another hurricane hit with even greater devastation. For Florida, it was natural tragedy piled upon Depression.

Just after that 1928 hurricane, a 22-year-old schoolteacher from Georgia, A. R. Harrington, arrived at Canal Point, broke and ambitious. Conditions never had been worse nor opportunities better.

Georgia, broke too, owed him a year and a half's back salary. When it finally paid off, he began trying to farm as his parents had. It was a revelation. As long as he stayed on the custard apple lands, all was well, but when he moved beyond, it was science fiction.

Cleared sawgrass soil was loose, porous. It needed irrigation during winter, drainage during summer and fall. The old iron-wheeled tractors bogged up. The farmers learned to use horses, which had bigger feet than mules, and to equip them with oversized shoes — the muck equivalent of snowshoes — so they could pull the plows.

The ground would crack when dry, opening up gaps two and three feet wide and four or five feet deep. During dry season, the muck would catch fire and smoulder for days. Over the years the muck would oxidize, subsiding about an inch a year, causing houses anchored in it gradually to appear to rise on their pillars as though on stilts.

The sawgrass lands were not even good for cattle. The cows would get sickly, come down with diseases and infections. The natural grass was not nutritious enough. The land was strange in so many ways. A man could jump up and down on the muck, and 10 feet away another man would feel the earth billow under him in a wave effect.

Many farmers went broke, got discouraged and left. Harrington stayed. He married Gladys, a Canal Point teacher, bought a place on the custard apple lands and raised three children.

After researchers finally determined that the key to making the sawgrass soil perform like the custard apple land was adding certain elements, and after the federal government built a dike all the way around the lake to curb floodings, he was in place to ride the vegetable boom that followed.

Harrington was thinking about all that in March, 1983, when the rains kept coming and his fields were flooded and his corn that should have been ready for harvest was still dwarf-sized from too much water. A year ago, there was drought; this year floods.

He was one of the few small, independent farmers left around Canal Point and he planted only 100 acres, not the 500 he once worked. In the past 20 years, sugarcane and conglomerate farmers had taken over. Even with the harnessing of that sawgrass soil, it took either bigness or unusual dedication to tolerate this peculiar and tempermental environment.

"There's not many people that want to spend a lifetime making a living," Harrington explained it. "That's what it takes here. You have to put farming first. This is a different, changing land. You don't master it. You have to keep trying to understand it."

All of life is a little like that. We get just enough custard apple to encourage us to plow into the sawgrass, where we sometimes must be willing to accept that putting snowshoes on a Florida horse might be the right thing to do. Then, just as you digest that, somebody drops a match and the dirt catches fire.

Would Eden Be Beautiful
To Us?

The white-columned old plantation house sits in a clearing atop a 150-foot bluff overlooking the muddy Apalachicola River. From a second-floor veranda, there is an invigorating view.

You can look across the lawn, down that high bluff to a river which flows as deliberately as time, across to a mixed pine and hardwoods forest where once there might have been a perfect garden, where Eve completed the job of making Adam a man and where Noah chopped gopherwood. You can stare a long time at that view and still feel you have not seen it well.

For visual impact, it ranks in the company of Florida's best: the sweep of sky and water in the Keys, the fine Gulf beaches on the south rim of Choctawhatchee Bay, the unique Everglades, the confluence of rivers at Stuart, the dynamically alive mangrove islands off the southwest coast.

About it all there is a special dimension for both the eye and the mind, like an arranged stage. The old Jason Gregory House (1849), two stories high, takes you back to more believing days. It has a pair of chimneys that serve eight fireplaces. On the upland side, a long driveway makes a picturesque approach through tall trees. Everything contributes to a mood.

The remote location adds to it. Even in Liberty County, Florida's most sparsely populated, it is out of the way. Yet with all this, peculiarly, Liberty County is better known for its catfish and scandals than for this place of beauty and myth.

Moreover, this is a public park, the Torreya State Park, where anyone can visit free, or camp and hike and picnic and tour the old house for a pittance.

It is one of the few state treasures not heavily plundered. Over the years, I have made a half-dozen midweek visits and often found no one at home but a ranger. Park attendants say 25,000 a year visit, not one good day's crowd at Disney World.

The mythical dimension probably adds most to its enduring interest. This may be the only place in the world where a persistent claim has been made as the original site of the Garden of Eden.

Once, that was something of a sensational claim. The elements of it were examined and debated. Today, like the park, it creates excitement only among a few, for not many any more believe the Garden ever existed. When a legal test is forced on the question, to decide what the schoolchildren should be told, the courts reply in effect that there never was any such garden.

This generates rage among those who insist upon defining promptly and definitively this unanswerable question. It encourages a bloody fight among the civilized at a time when civilization is threatened. It is as mystifying as the Irish troubles, where religion is misused as a symbol for intolerance.

What intrigues me most about the Torreya State Park is the opportunity it affords to sit on a hard wooden bench in a place of beauty and consider all this as though it were the Biblical Garden of Eden, literal and exact. It is neither church nor court, neither all reality nor all myth. You can just suppose, and wonder, privately. No one will protest.

Suppose, for example, that the gates to this once-perfect place have been opened to the public — an invitation to all Adam and Eve's prodigal descendants to come home — and almost no one has responded, maybe only 25,000 a year. Is it because the place is no longer perfect, or because we no longer recognize perfection? I have a suspicion.

Park attendants do not tell you about the Garden of Eden claims unless you ask. You will have to find a library that has the book, *In The Beginning,* by E. E. Callaway, a lawyer and theologian who spent 50 years developing his theories. Since the death of Callaway, who lived in Bristol, no one else presses the argument. Callaway located the Garden in an area astride the Georgia-Florida boundary where four rivers come together to form one, the Apalachicola.

His arguments included the most popularly known one about the Torreya tree, for which the park is named, a tree also called the gopherwood and the stinking cedar (because of its odor). Callaway argued that the Torreya tree grew naturally in the Garden of Eden, and that the only place in the world where the Torreya grows naturally is right here on the shores of the Apalachicola. His theory therefore suggests that Noah's ark, made of stinking cedar and full of animals, would have been distinctly aromatic.

Ironically, in the 1960s, a blight struck the Torreya trees and threatened to eliminate them entirely as Biblical evidence. Maclay Gardens in Tallahassee rescued some specimens, nurtured them and restocked the park. The blight still occurs, a modern phenomenon, but survival of the evergreen, linear-leaved tree appears assured.

Blight in the garden is not the only irony. The history of the property includes land speculation, slavery, floods, biting insects, a plague of malaria, and the threat of Union gunboats along the river during the Civil War. Finally, during the Depression, the abandoned plantation house was dismantled and moved from its original location across the river at Ocheesee Landing to this commanding bluff.

Uneasiness in the garden along the river continues. Now it is the focus of significant environmental battles. Always, there has been something. As Elizabeth Bowen warned, "Once we have lost [innocence], it is futile to attempt a picnic in Eden."

Innocence may be scarce, but it is not lost. The park has the wonderful capacity to inspire fantasies. One of mine is to think of the old house as the homeplace for the family of man. On the mantles of those eight fireplaces, I see pictures of old Adam and Eve and on a little table by the fire there is a box of apple recipes.

Why not? It is a warming fantasy. Not everything can be reduced to scientific text and turned into computable proof. Full truth requires more than that. For it to reach full force, it must have the dimension that is in poetry; it must be able to tolerate fact that does not fit the chosen meter; it must accept foolishness and innocence as spice in the recipe. Even a man descended from an ape should know that.

★ *Monroe County*

The Keys: Awakenings

The longest, lowest, wettest, narrowest, rockiest, most broken county in the United States appears on the map like a Morse Code message that no one ever deciphered.

The Florida Keys (in Monroe County) are 130 miles long, on the average about five feet high, and for most of their length just wide enough to sheathe a highway.

The bleached, bony Keys have more than Florida's most spectacular view; they nudge the soul awake, and the new awareness can be perilous to the old ways.

If ever a man had cue to feel small and at the mercy of uncontrollable elements, the Keys ought to be the place. Only the things of nature hold true significance.

A stiff breeze sweeps them like a broom. High waves wash their spiny backs. The flat islands leave no place to hide. A newcomer is tempted, the Conchs (natives) say, either to curse more or to pray more.

Out of that comes a special bonus. It delivers relief from the bounds of the daily farce. It permits retreat into a philosophy of splendid toleration. Historically, it meant every person could be his own kind of crazy, and few cared.

The Keys mix the simple reality of a country village with the sophistication of a metropolis compacted into a hothouse. The things that nobody cared about in the Keys were as famous as those they did care about.

After God made Florida, a favorite story goes, he threw the scraps into the sea. They became the Keys, curling off Florida's nose like teardrops in an ocean breeze. Ever since, man has been trying to improve on God's job, courting disaster. For a long while, nobody seemed to notice, or to care if they did notice.

But in the 1970s and 1980s that changed. The numbers of people, and the encrustation of condos and a staggering array of inviting claptrap, eliminated some of that old elbow room. As people intruded on each other, as public services stretched thin and traffic on the one big highway took on a near-permanent snarl, tolerance was not so easy.

One thing piled upon another. The Keys' ambience that once so enchanted newcomers that they tended to be swallowed up, either transformed or spit out, faced overload. The ambience did not change but the newcomers and the development came on so fast and so thickly that they exceeded the Keys' ability to digest and transform them.

The result has been the development of a regular static, an awakening to limits and frailties, a need to care and to be concerned, that is at odds with those old carefree traditions. The Keys, like it or not, were aroused from the wonderful old hypnosis of the past.

The rootless and the firmly rooted, the exploiters and the exploited, the money-changers and the escapists, began crashing into each other. Growth brought the old customs under siege.

The Keys had the reputation of being vulnerable every way except politically. By tradition, politics was dominated by the Conchs or Conch-pretenders who were blooded to the Keys' uniqueness by birth, blood or the political equivalent of a born-again embrace.

Almost nobody liked it, but the numbers began crowding out the old lifestyles, shaking up the old political combinations, challenging the set notions. As the pressures of growth rose, everything left began to matter. A simmer began developing into a boil.

The Keys were reaching the time when they had to sacrifice that old toleration to save the beautiful framework of a natural place. The question was no longer whether this would happen, but how many years it would take before environmental concerns, practical worries about costs and the basic fears about despoliation would reflect in the political decisions of the voters. The same political revolutions that had converted other recalcitrant parts of Florida to the environmental camp were coming to the Keys, little by little.

From Key Largo to Key West, flattened mangroves and crushed coral leave a trail that bleeds white. Real estate signs still stand unblushingly in sloughts that barely resemble land. A half-century ago, a Cracker saw stuff like that for sale and commented that it was too shallow for swimming and too wet for farming. But it sells.

In the upper Keys, they tend to attribute the worst aspects of the Keys to the influence of Key West, regarded by some as not only the seat of county govrnment but also county sin. These are the ones who like to think of the Upper Keys as a family place.

Key West, of course, modestly declines that accolade but intra-county dispute is not new. It dates back to the beginning of this century when the bridges were being built for the old Overseas Railroad.

At that tiem, labor camps in Marathon had a reputation as boisterous places and Key West set the upper Keys' view of its character for all time when it sent liquor boats to fuel the high life and followed them up with "gospel" boats to make the most of the remorse that was certain to come with hangovers.

In fact, however, a significant portion of the Keys' problems originate elsewhere. Their uniqueness brings pressures that no small city or cities can handle alone. U.S. 1 cuts a free channel and both the bad and the beautiful come swinging down it.

The Keys are national treasures and their problems have national dimensions. They deserve national responsibilities.

Fortunately, despite all of man's careless rooting about, their peculiar beauty remains, however frail its health. Neither the condos nore the honky-tonks nor the trailer parks nor the bizarre roadside traps can yet obscure the charms of such an incredible mix of rock, sand and sea — the bright glare, the thick smell of the salt air, the flat islands and the dazzling blue waters that glitter around them.

But change was coming, in that wonderfully intoxicating land and seascape, and in that charming old notion that in the Keys nobody cares, and nobody has to care.

Somebody has to care now, and in a special new way in the 1980s the Keys were beginning to nudge awake not only the sould and the body — as they always did — but the brain, too.

Cedar Key ★

Cedar Key:
Hard Times, High Times

Contrasts make life at Cedar Key seem super real. At breakfast, you sit at a Formica table and eat fried mullet with grits while a neon beer sign blinks good morning. The coffee comes without a saucer, and the salt shaker has four black-eyed peas in it.

A New Jersey tourist at the next table wonders why she cannot get French toast and 10 feet away at a bar two fishermen slug down raw whisky and wince while a little girl spins a squeaking stool.

Cedar Key has the romantic life. Long ago, it submitted to becoming Florida's most fashionably authentic gulf coast fishing village, but old salts never surrendered their lifestyle. They make a riptide of hard times and high times.

There is a certain quality here that establishes almost instant kinship with a visitor. It is like someone else's toothache. You can see the pain that history stamped on this place, and the uncertainty that survives, without having to feel it. You can chase it away eating stone crabs and oysters that come out of these shallow waters, or sample it comfortably with the mullet, an inexpensive and peculiar fish beloved by Crackers.

Main Street looks as though it has not made up its mind whether to be New England or the Old West. A few empty storefronts testify that nothing is certain except the seafood industry and tourism, and they vary with the weather.

Most tourists head for the docks where a road makes a short crescent into the gulf, the fanciest restaurants roost along the water with the pelicans, and sea gulls ride the bucking breezes.

You can see just about all of Cedar Key, a small isolated island at the west end of SR 24 south of the Suwannee River and about halfway between Tampa and Tallahassee, in an hour. Or, you can take a lifetime trying to get to know it.

There have been permanent settlers here since the 1840s. Storms and wars and depressions have given it a history adequate for explaining any aberration you might find.

A maverick set of politicians, professors, a few artists and retirees — an assorted lot of individualists — adopted Cedar Key and with the old salts have helped it cultivate the split image of a place that wants tourists but not change.

Oldtimers admire a tub of pompano as though it were an edible Picasso, yet they turn their backs on magnificent winter sunsets as they sail home from a day's fishing.

Cedar Key hides behind a figurative veil of four bridges. Twenty-two miles of uncluttered road through low hammock land separate it from the nearest major highway (U.S. 19-98).

Once, it loved a stranger carrying cash, as long as he did not decide to stay too long. For years, oldtimers were reluctant to sell property to prospective residents, yet once a family managed to settle it was eligible for such niceties as free space in the old cemetery on the island's highest hill.

Like almost no other coastal town in Florida, Cedar Key for years kept its own ways and slowly retreated before the modern plagues. Isolation, and natives stubbornly appreciative of a peculiar heritage, helped.

But, by 1983, a curious thing had happened to Cedar Key. It was losing its balance, threatening even to lose the struggle altogether. The fishing village could become only a resort facade.

While the rest of Florida was suffering a recession, resort Cedar Key boomed. Realtors and builders clucked happily. Condominiums rose prominently, one mushrooming near the dock. There was a new bank, a new restaurant that did not serve fried foods (a first), an emergency heliport. Cedar Key had been penetrated by prosperity and new discontent.

"A lot of people are coming in and building for profit. They've found the place, and we don't like it," said Frances Hodges, town clerk and wife of State Rep. Gene Hodges.

"Cedar Key just isn't like the rest of the world," said Doris Hellermann at Cedar Key Realty. In 1976, there were no Realtors in Cedar Key. Eight years later, two agencies and a dozen salesmen. "I don't know why, but while other agencies around the state are closing up, the two here are expanding. There are 'For Sale' signs all over town."

"We don't want a 'little Miami,'" said then Mayor Gary Haldeman. "People are coming in here with money, paying for property with cash. I don't know where they're coming from, but they're coming."

Haldeman arrived eight years earlier from Pennsylvania, fresh from a year at Penn State University, married into a family that had been here for five generations.

A big part of his job was tending to police problems. With the influx of new people came a rise in complaints about vandalism, break-ins and police handling of them.

Some of the newer townspeople complained that every time someone from an old family was arrested, either the case was dropped or the police chief was harassed out of town. Some counted 28 policemen (the city has a police force of two) who served and left in six years.

Haldeman said this was an exaggeration. "We haven't had over a dozen chiefs in the last six years," he said, adding, "about half the people you talk to in town are somehow related. That makes it hard for 'em on arrests."

Until the 1980s, nobody paid serious attention to what was happening, but with the mix of the new and old populations, and their different perceptions of Cedar Key, the town boiled.

Much of the division focused on the most obvious change: the new condominiums (including a debate whether there were adequate water and sewage facilities to accommodate them).

Old Cedar Key got worried. It responded with a building moratorium, followed by a new and stricter set of zoning regulations.

Cedar Key expected this to shift growth emphasis from large new condos to smaller and more compatible quadriplexes. However, the moves came late.

Maybe Cedar Key can remain an island of old Florida. If it were any place else, I would doubt it. But here, you cannot tell. Unless you have lived here all your life, the bone-deep sensitivities cannot be charted. Ask one of those former police chiefs.

Destin

The Destin Way

The beach along Destin is full of beauty and contrast and illusion. A breeze stirs powdery white sands into tiny land waves that gather and break. The shoreline fades away in the distance to a ghostly white haze. The clear blue water sparkles and jumps and looks as though it ought to smell like shaving lotion.

These are Florida's most spectacular beaches: a scene of almost immaculate perception. Almost. Startlingly tall condominiums rise out of the faint pollution haze so suddenly they seem to be arriving like ships. A few yards offshore, boaters churn up the lotion and skiers skim across it. The sand keeps blowing, settling into little ridges but not forming the big dunes, because anchoring sea oats have been cleared to make way for tender feet. Not immaculate, but nevertheless beautiful.

The Destins came here to fish. Leonard A. Destin, son of a New England seafaring man one generation removed from England, arrived in the 1830s aboard a sailing ship. On this narrow, then-isolated peninsula between the Gulf and Choctawhatchee Bay, 45 miles east of Pensacola, he founded a village.

The oldest remaining Destin in 1979, then 83-year-old Uncle John, the third of seven Destin generations to live here, sat in his cluttered frame house on the bay side of East Pass, carving miniature fishing smacks out of cedar and painting sea scenes in a strong, unschooled style.

John A. Destin, a bachelor, petted the little dog that kept him company and fretted over his first electric bill to reach $25. He refused a heater or an air conditioner and wanted his monthly bill to reflect appreciation of that thrift.

He complained principally to his nephew, Bill Burleson, who lived next door. He did not call the electric company because he had no telephone. Anyway, he did not hear so well and did not care to talk with strangers, not even if they were sending him bills.

Although his artistry had become prized among those who knew Destin, he never sold a painting or a carving. He gave them to selected friends. That was his way, the Destin way.

Uncle John bought this valuable patch of land on East Pass — where Leonard Destin built his first home — from the government in the 1930s, and paid for it with his World War I bonus. In later years, he gave it to relatives. They lived in finer houses than he, and decorated their living rooms with his artwork.

At a glance, taking in the condominiums and motels and restaurants and advertising celebrations of the 106-boat charter fishing fleet, it was hard for a stranger to regard Destin as still a village. Yet it remained unincorporated and there was a hardcore of permanent residents, many of them oldtimers like the Destins, who persisted in trying to stretch the old village atmosphere — in short, the Destin way — over all the outlanders and their giant human coops.

The task was large. Once the bridge over East Pass was built and the highway (U.S. 98) paved in 1936, making access easy, Destin grew. Commercial fishing gave way to charterboat fishing and tourism. In 1960, the population still was only 900, and the first high-rise condo did not appear until the summer of 1971.

By 1979, there were 3,000 condo units and $80 million worth sold in three years alone. The 6,000 permanent residents swelled to 14,000 during the summer season, and the Chamber of Commerce predicted — almost wide-eyed at the implications of its own figures — that within a decade the total would rise to 50,000.

In 1973, when a charter boat captain died with his boat unpaid for, the villagers held free fish fries and set out a donation bucket. Some $10,000 was raised to save the boat and get the family on its feet. Another charter captain, whose boat burned, was put back into business by competitors who raised money to buy him a new boat.

Destin tried to maintain those old village ways, the communal caring that it grew up with, in a place that was no longer a true village. It was a seaside resort taking on the proportions of a city.

The oldtimers tried to convert the stream of strangers to the Destin way, but the larger the numbers, the more difficult the task.

Already there was division over whether Destin should incorporate so that it could get federal revenue-sharing money and bolster the police force and get better control of zoning and take better care of litter. The arguments revolved around how best to avoid the mistakes that boom growth brought to Panama City.

Destin calls itself The World's Luckiest Fishing Village. A lot of newcomers think that is because the continental shelf runs close to shore, making deep-water fishing possible within yards of the beach and assuring good business for the charter fleet. But that is only part of it.

Uncle John still fretted about a $25 light bill on the same finger of sand where pleasure-seeking strangers shelled out more than 10 times that for a half day's fishing, where a condo no larger than his frame house might sell for more money than he spent in 83 years.

Despite the condos, The Destin Way survived, the old and the new trying to carry it beyond the present, into the future. But that would require more luck than getting a snapper to bite.

★ *Islamorada*

The Storm This Time

The thing that the Florida Keys always taught first was to endure. Hang on, and the storm will pass. The Russell family, which has endured in the Keys for more than 100 years, knows this well.

When the surrounding waters seem a sea of troubles, Bernard Russell tends to dig in. Nothing could be as bad as 1935. That memory freshens his belief in survival.

He was 17 then, a Depression veteran already. The land boom had collapsed, a bank had failed and the family had suffered major losses. On the first day of September 1935, the greatest hurricane in U.S. history destroyed everything else. Of the 408 persons killed, 50 were members of the Russell family, leaving only 11.

After the hurricane, all they had left was the bare land, everything on it blown flat and washed clean. Young Bernard himself saved nothing personal except the wind-torn clothes he wore. He remembers looking around, wondering what would come next.

"Everything was gone," he remembered one summer day in 1982. "I could stand in the middle of Islamorada, and look one way and see the ocean, look the other way and see the bay. I could look from one end of the island to another, and there was nothing."

The Russells were the first white settlers on Upper Matecumbe, which includes Islamorada. They migrated from the Bahama Islands first to Key West and then up the Keys. They and their close friends, the Pinders, who also came over from the Bahamas, pioneered.

The two families established the first church in Islamorada. Preston Pinder became the first bonefish guide. Bernard's father was the first postmaster after the railroad came through, opened the first restaurant and the first service station, had the first chicken

97

farm and the first marine dock. Overnight, all that was gone.

"You've heard the women say they will make a cake from scratch? Well, that's the way we started life again. From scratch. We had nothing," Russell said. The families sent their women and children to Miami to stay with relatives. The men stayed, set up tents and began rebuilding.

By themselves, the Russells and the Pinders make a chapter in Keys history. Bernard further united the two families by marrying one of the Pinder daughters. He became a yacht captain for the wealthy, a master boatbuilder and a cabinetmaker. He organized the volunteer fire department and was its chief for 18 years, helped start the ambulance service, served with Red Cross in hurricane relief.

The Russells are imbedded deeply in the Keys. A measure of their stoic attachment was indicated in 1960, a quarter century after the family horror of the 1935 hurricane, when they chose to ride out another bad one, Hurricane Donna, in their home. At one point, the Russells saw the ocean in their front yard, a foot deep. But they endured.

But in the 1980s, Bernard had some doubts. A lot of his friends had left. There had been so many changes in the Keys; so much had been wiped out. He considered it, and decided he simply could not go. The family stake was too great. "I'm going to stay and fight as long as I can," he said.

But what hurricanes and hardship could not do, a tidal wave of homogenizing growth and convenience threatened. They had shaken beliefs he never questioned before.

"I'm not against progress," he said. "Building is my trade. To say don't build is crazy. But they're changing us into a melting pot, making us like everybody else. We had something unique and they're making it common. They're changing the Keys, and they've changed my view of what progress is."

Russell did not like saying these things. They moved him toward political involvement and he always stayed out of politics, except to support his friend Wilhelmina Harvey, a Monroe County commissioner.

He felt that the traditions of the Conchs, the natives, had been manipulated and distorted, sometimes by other Conchs, sometimes by later comers trading on Conch ways for personal and political gain.

The feeling grew among him and his friends that they could not influence the course of local government. When they went before government boards they were faced with an attitude of, "Take what we do or leave it, like it or get out."

"You get this feeling that you have nowhere to turn, nowhere to go. You can get all the petitions you want, but it doesn't make any difference. They don't listen," he said.

"I've seen them come in office saying, oh man, we're going to change things. In a few months, they're flowing with it. If someone tries to battle it, like Wilhelmina, they're out. They mow them down. These are the kinds of things that get you to the point where you have no trust."

For the first time, Russell hedged his faith in his ability to endure. He bought some property near Ocala, where many Keys refugees go, but hoped never to use it. Meanwhile, he digs in, as he always has.

Nobody loved the islands more, or invested more blood, sweat and years in them. The Russells always have been Keys boosters, believers in progress. They accept change as inevitable.

What troubled them was that traditional progress seemed to hurt rather than to help, and they wanted better answers. The things they treasured were being flattened again, and this storm showed no sign of passing.

★ *Melbourne Village*

The Women Did It All

Three wonderfully hardheaded, idealistic women created Melbourne Village as a refuge for simple living and high thinking. They did it right, but the world seeped in and the village learned to live with the threat of high living and simple thinking.

Melbourne Village became a patch of soft green encircled by concrete and asphalt callouses. It is in the eye of the Brevard County urban boom. Its curbless and quiet streets, trees, parks and comfortable homes testify to a different dimension in time and progress.

How the village came into being is a remarkable tale of unselfconscious, pioneering feminism. During the Big Depression of a half-century ago, three women prominent in the civic life of Dayton, Ohio, got an idea.

They were looking for ways to help the masses of unemployed, dispirited men waiting in lines for bread, soup and relief. The women thought the men needed something more: They needed to regain their sense of dignity as well. The women decided that the best way to help was to put these fellows back on the land as homesteaders. Let them raise their own food, build their own homes and recapture to some degree the pride of being independent.

The idea fit nicely into Roosevelt's New Deal programs, but a few fat cats mangled it. Some Dayton merchants complained that the competition of self-supplied food might hurt their profits. Some industries grumbled that this small draft of independence might encourage workers to strike.

The New Deal backed out. In Dayton, there was no chance. "Never mind," said Dr. Elizabeth Nutting, one of the three women. "Some day we'll do it someplace else." The idea lay dormant until after World War II, a restless time.

In 1946, attracted to Florida by real estate pitches, the women sent a scouting party that found and anointed a ragged-looking piece of ground about four miles west of the Indian River, a place where cows roamed around a beautiful hammock.

By then, times had changed. That sense of dignity they cherished had begun to become elusive for everyone, not just the unemployed. They altered the plan, relying on an eclectic philosophy that probably first borrowed from Thoreau, one that evolved loosely along the lines of a commune that idealized individual worth and self-reliance. But this plan would include the founders themselves.

They chartered the nonprofit but taxable American Homesteading Foundation and with that tool founded Melbourne Village, an "intentional" community, laid out around that hammock. They planned the good and natural family life. There would be large lots, town hall meetings to govern and volunteers to do the work, lots of trees, gardens, livestock, crafts, a barter economy and a simple life of high ideals.

Florida's history is full of such dreams. In its pioneer days, the state inspired many visions of individual utopias. The Czechs tried it at Masaryktown. A religious and philosophical order, Koreshan Unity, tried it at Estero. There have been Greek communities, Polish communities, Italian communities and a selection of others cemented by nationality or inclination. But this one was distinctive as probably the only one conceived, founded, nursed to maturity and beyond principally by women.

"Why did we go to all this trouble? Because we wanted to live a certain kind of good life," explained Mrs. Virginia Wood, a founder. "It wasn't a matter of women's rights. It was just the natural thing for us to do." Mrs. Wood, a fine and feisty great-grandmother, in 1982 at age 94 still served on the village beautification committee.

The foundation bought the land (beginning with 80 acres, later enlarged to 360) and resold it to selected persons if they first joined the foundation at $500 per membership. The first lots sold for $250. Members were screened by a committee that investigated desirability, credit rating and probable harmony with the naturalist approach. Street access to the village was limited.

Deed restrictions protected the concept. This insured greenery, limited structures to a certain percentage of lot space and gave the foundation the right to approve resales or to repurchase the property. This at times inspired charges of snobbery and prejudice, but none stuck.

Fearing annexation by the city of Melbourne, and possible loss of control, the village incorporated in 1957. An unpaid mayor-commission government and the foundation shared authority. As new people and new ideas entered, the arrangement sometimes became fractious but it endured.

The original concept gradually has diluted. The barter economy never really developed. The village evolved into a place regarded by outsiders as casual and exclusive. That reputation reached the founders last, and surprised them. "When we discovered that, it amused us," said Mrs. Wood. "We always thought of ourselves as a simple little village. We like the way it has developed, but it isn't exactly what we set out to do."

Melbourne Village (estimated population 900) survived suspicion (Why so intent on being secluded? Communists? Nudists? Bigots?), plagues of insects, the space-industry boom, the omnipresent transience of Florida and mini-rebellions by a few men who (the women said) chafed over the knowledge that women pioneered the whole thing.

"Some of the men just couldn't tolerate the idea," said Mrs. Wood. "We like to say it was because they were very much annoyed because we did not leave it for them to create."

Melbourne Village is a pretty place, but its uniqueness lies in its history. When the men were dispirited, the women responded with an idea and fought hard times and fat cats to prove its worth. After 50 years, it was clear they overcame.

Some of the men found this a burr in their dignity, but of course the women understood — and smiled.

Mexico Beach

One Rainbow In Florida

In the 1940s Mexico Beach was a nameless rainbow curve of white beaches and blue water and sloping dunes speckled with sea oats the color of weathered gold. There were no piers, no roadhouses, no motels. Only U.S. 98, within sprayshot of the water, laid a track across sand so fine that it was compared to sugar and sometimes was bagged and shipped north to spread across barroom floors, upstaging saloons which used the less elegant sawdust.

Going west across the lower rim of Florida's Panhandle, it was the first of those spectacular beaches that began near Port St. Joe and stretched all the way to Pensacola. Along the highway, then, you came onto them suddenly — from out of the dark browns and grays of old Florida to a great, bright window — and a wider world opened up.

Gordon U. Parker, a land buyer for a lumber company, liked it. He selected about 4 miles of beachfront, a narrow swatch of dunes between the Gulf and some lowland swamps amounting to 1,850 acres, and with two partners bought it on speculation in 1946 for $65,000.

Around Blountstown, his hometown 40 miles to the north, men who judged land by its fertility snickered about old man Parker's pretty desert. But he ignored them, and eventually swallowed up his partners to become sole owner of what would become the town of Mexico Beach.

Parker thought of it as a subdivision and considered calling it Rainbow Beach, because of the way the shoreline curved, but decided instead to name it for the Gulf. He peeled off the first pieces of land in 50-foot oceanfront lots and sold them for $600, but the price crept up fast. Everything in fact worked better than Parker ever had hoped. Those first lots, if sold today, would bring almost as much as the original price of the entire tract.

The Parker success story is only a small pop in the Florida land boom, but its proportions and prospects are typical. Mexico Beach (population 1,100) by the 1940s was a budding resort town, drawing enough visitors to treble or even quadruple in size each summer. It was still a place of cottages and small motels, still had a down-home look, but it was hurrying toward the risks that are the curse of sudden growth: reverse metamorphosis, from a windblown butterfly into a sweating caterpillar. The change is the equivalent of slicing up orchids to make hash.

West along the coast there have been miracles of development in similar villages, in places like Destin, and Mexico Beach had eyes for that kind of miracle. But it was finding that as dreams come true, they create more dreams, and desires turn into urgent needs.

The town incorporated in 1966, with a mayor and a council, and therefore learned the political disputes that exist when zoning and other regulations are introduced into tight quarters with business ambition.

About 2,000 lots were sold and over 700 houses built on them. The blessings of high-rises were yet to come, but already there were two traffic lights, a demand for more police protection, a need for a new fire truck and a new bridge. Further development and perhaps even industry were discussed, and that meant an expansion of the water system and an expensive new sewage system.

Mexico Beach sat far into the southeast corner of Bay County, with the huge Tyndall Air Force Base between it and the county seat Panama City. It was a long distance call to the courthouse, and the cost of a call was an uncertain investment.

So the town in practical fashion leaned toward the Gulf County seat, Port St. Joe, only 9 miles away, where its children went to school, where the doctors were, where the utilities companies had offices and where some commuted to work. Cross-county tugs became so complicated that Mexico Beach felt it ought to have one city officer designated as intergovernment coordinator.

In 1979, Mexico Beach in a referendum expressed a wish to secede from Bay and become part of Gulf. That was the town's preference, but not necessarily its future. For example, there was the question whether if Gulf accepted the town it would have to assume a pro rata share of Bay County's bonded indebtedness. Some suggested that might equal what Gulf already had.

Old man Parker turned over the family business in 1961 to his youngest son, Charles M. Parker, who became the town's first mayor and operated the first real estate office. His help included a third and fourth generation of Parkers. His daughter was a saleswoman and his granddaughter a receptionist.

The town grew beyond the Parkers. The original $65,000 speculation returned several million and the future looks just as profitable if not as comfortable. "There's more money to be made here than has already been made," Parker said in 1981. "I'm not too carried away with the changes but I certainly cannot let sentiment override my better business judgment."

In the Panhandle, people traditionally have been tied to the land, and have measured those ties in decades and acres. That was reduced to feet and now is being reduced again by newcomers who find comfort in communal shares of feet.

Parker, an affable man, compared it to the refugee experiences of South Florida. That transformation of a culture created its own flow of refugees. "It gets to be too much for them down there and they come up here hoping to find 10 or 15 years' reprieve from the rat race," he said. "When I have a choice piece of property, you know where I advertise it? Miami. Half our sales are to people from South Florida."

There was no question whether sentiment or business judgment represented the greater wisdom in this situation, for in practical terms it did not matter. In Florida, a secondary tide flowed northward and made its own changes. Practical men like Charlie Parker found that it was foolish to try to stand fast before such a tide. They recognized and accepted it as manifest, and profitable, destiny.

Tarpon Springs ★

The Greeks and The Sponges

A few hardy Greeks still pursue the old sponge industry dream in Tarpon Springs. They have struggled — and have not always won — against boom-bust cycles, generational blurring of ethnic customs, the appeal of easier work and higher pay, and the temptations of the federal teat.

The Greeks, with 3,000 years experience at it in the Mediterranean, came three-quarters of a century ago and revolutionized the sponging industry on this side of the world with dangerous but effective hardhat diving. They battled Conch spongers from the Keys (free divers or boat hookers) who accused them of ruining the sea bottom with metal-weighted shoes, struggled against an ocean bottom blight in 1947 and destructive pollution in 1970.

By 1978, only five commercial sponge boats worked at it, and even that number represented a revival of the industry. The old men sat in open-air coffee shops off Dodecanese Boulevard, near the docks, close enough to smell both the salt air and the olive oil and cheese and peppers and lamb cooking in the restaurants, and to keep an eye on tourists picking their way along sponge-laden sidewalks and peering into exotic trinket shops. The docks and their satellite shops were a tiny Greek tourist village encircled by a pretty Gulf Coast suburban community 35 miles north of St. Petersburg.

Like sponges, the old divers soaked it all up, and then talked about it. "As long as I'm alive, there's going to be one boat working," said George Billiris, whose grandfather came in 1907 (the year the Sponge Exchange was established) to dive. In 1924 his father, also a diver, opened a tourist shop. Billiris owned three of the operating sponge boats and captained one, The Agatha. He was the 10th generation of his family (his brothers have provided an 11th

106

generation) in the sponge business, the first of them born in this country, and purposefully optimistic.

"We stand a good chance now," Billiris said. "I get a little keyed up about it. The commercial demand for natural sponge is enormous — seven times greater than the supply — and the sponge is coming back in the Gulf. The pollution is gone. Where the sea bottom has not been disturbed by shrimpers, the sponges are healthy."

The sponge industry here probably reached its peak in the late 1930s, when there were nearly 2,500 men employed, some 180 sponge boats plus 25 to 30 warehouses and buyers. Sponges put $3 million a year into the Tarpon Springs economy.

Tarpon Springs boats discovered the blight in 1947, and the industry almost disappeared. Sponges disintegrated at the touch of a hook. Until then, sponging had been a father-son business, as it was in Greece. Afterward, fathers encouraged sons to enter other fields. Not until about 1960 was the blight gone, permitting a revival. But by then many of the experienced divers had abandoned the field, and sponge buyers had become oriented to Mediterranean sponges. More divers were imported from Greece, and Tarpon Springs launched an educational program boosting their best sponge, the rock island wool.

In the late 1960s, spongemen gave up hardhat diving and turned to the use of a lightweight full-face mask and airline rather than the classic portholed metal helmet and cumbersome suit. Desco divers can move more freely but cannot dive as deeply and do not dive in the winter when the waters are cold. A desco diver normally works in waters up to seven fathoms deep, diving for two hours at a time, totalling not more than six hours a day.

By 1970, technique mattered little. All appeared lost again. Pollution replaced the blight as a menace to sponges. "Everything on the bottom started looking bleak again," said Billiris. Once more, the industry slumped and what the tourists saw at the docks was about all there was left of sponging.

Billiris was one of the few who did not give up. The years have confirmed his faith. "I don't know who is doing it, but they're doing it right," he said. "The bottom again is in a healthy state. There's growth and life everywhere. The sponges are back. We're seeing the best I've seen in 25 years. We work from St. Marks down to Everglades, and it looks good."

But the way was not clear yet for that sponge revival. To Billiris at least, there was a new nemesis: shrimpboats. A lot of new ones entered the waters as shrimp harvests dwindled elsewhere, and some of them, he said, care only about today's catch. They drag the bottom with chains and then make a sweep with their nets. They may get shrimp, but Billiris said they left the bottom like a desert.

To preserve and maintain the sponge industry, Billiris believes spongers may have to return to the hardhat and work year-round (instead of scrambling as weather and season permit to make enough trips — each stretching 10 days to a month — to reach a goal of 120 work-days). Not even the hard-hat will help unless the seabottom is protected, and unless new divers can be trained.

To Billiris and the older Greeks who sit in the coffee shops and remember the struggle, to let the Greek ways and sponge industry become items only for history and museums would be to waste a hard-bought heritage that contributes a valuable piece of the Florida mosaic attracting tourists.

"We've got something to be proud of," he said. His arguments had merit and logic and practicality but they may be the answer to the wrong question. No more do you survive by being the fittest; the question is whether you fit.

Lake Wales

A Quiet Place of Beauty

During the Roaring Twenties, when life was a carnival, a wealthy old Dutchman turned a Florida hilltop into a sanctuary of beauty and in effect gave it to the public. The gift would be a trust, one insured place of serenity where harried citizens of the world could "fill their souls with the...influence of the beautiful."

For Edward V. Bok, it was an act of faith. The world needed such a place. The implication was that he had done his part, and the years ahead would determine whether his faith had been justified.

Before rushing to judgment, consider the man Bok. He revered thrift, thoroughness, quality, responsibility and serenity. Putting all these words in one sentence today might hint of a joke, but not then, not to Bok. He wanted the sanctuary to be a place where men and women could rediscover these qualities in themselves.

Bok succeeded with his creation. The Mountain Lake Sanctuary near Lake Wales remains serene, beautiful. The inspiration is there, but the Eighties roared, too. Were Bok alive today, he would find little changed, except that the carnival has grown faster and louder.

Logically, the counter-appeal of his sanctuary ought to be greater than ever. As the number of such places disappear, they should become more valuable. As the world around produces greater contrast, the serenity of his hilltop should become more popular each year. It has not.

The nonprofit sanctuary will survive, as Bok wanted, but it was under greater siege in the 1980s than at any other time since he died half a century ago. Bok's American Foundation, established for the dual purpose of supporting the sanctuary and a civic research program, had to give up the research (most recently concentrating on criminal justice). Costs at the sanctuary were trimmed. Inflation had eaten up income from the endowment.

Though Florida's population and the number of annual tourists it attracts trebled since World War II, attendance at the sanctuary declined from nearly a half million then to about 200,000 in 1981. Token admission fees ($2 per vehicle), held low on Bok's orders, paid no more than one-sixth the operation's expenses.

Serenity and beauty, offered as a tourist attraction and virtually given away free, did not attract crowds. It is as though heaven offered a visitor's day, but almost everyone passed it up to go to a fair.

Bok, a philosophic man, probably understood this puzzle of the human condition that gives most of us appetites for the glitter rather than the gold. He was an extraordinary, staunch man who acknowledged a debt to this country which he feared was losing its true spirit.

Bok came to the United States from the Netherlands at age 7, worked his way into the publishing business as a stenographer, wrote many books, served as editor of The Ladies Home Journal for 30 years, and discovered his dream of the sanctuary late in life at his winter home in the Mountain Lake Colony near Lake Wales.

He liked to walk up the hill called Iron Mountain and watch the sun set across the Central Florida countryside. To preserve that place, he bought the hilltop. To give it further distinction, he brought in landscape architect Frederick Law Olmsted, Jr., to create gardens and a place of quiet repose.

He was a prim man. He disliked seeing men wearing tams, and banned them. Until his death in 1929, he insisted that men wear coats and he kept a supply of them handy for those who came unprepared. He disapproved of negativism, and allowed no signs advising visitors what not to do.

The most singular feature of the sanctuary, the tower, was created because he disliked the sight of two old wooden towers used to store water for nourishing the gardens. Bok hired another well-known architect, Milton Medary, to design a beautiful housing for the water tanks. The result was a pink marble tower — sometimes called Florida's Taj Mahal — that would hide the tanks. It had stone herons at its top and a frieze of Florida wildlife.

A carillon was added to complete the disguise. Fifty-three bronze bells from England, the largest of them weighing 11 tons, were installed. For tourists The Singing Tower, as it was called then, became the most distinctive feature in Mountain Lake Sanctuary. Daily recitals still are given.

The 128-acre sanctuary and the tower, renamed the Bok Tower Gardens to be more descriptive, sit like a serene island among a field of citrus trees contained within an exclusive 3,500-acre colony of about 100 homes. The Bok family no longer owns one of them, but it retains ties. When grandson Dr. Derek Bok, president of Harvard University, spoke at a ceremony here in 1978 he noted the need of accommodating human rights and interests with nature's rights and interests. It was the kind of topic that might have intrigued the old Dutchman.

Ken Morrison, former editor of Audubon Magazine, directed the affairs of the sanctuary from 1956 to the early 1980s. "This was Mr. Bok's gift to the American people," said Morrison. "We still hope and expect that it will be here, pretty much the same, 50 or even 100 years from now."

Survival of the sanctuary is justification of Bok's faith, though it might not fit the full measure of his dream. Morrison believes he neither expected this to be a place for crowds, nor felt that it should be. That was not his aim. He simply wanted a quiet place of beauty available to those who appreciate such things. He always believed opportunity should be gift enough for anyone.

Yankee Town ★

Knotts On The Crackers

The Knotts family created Yankeetown. It was an outpost in the wild gulf hammock, inhabited by proud but hostile Crackers, and the Knotts were missionaries for the future.

For most of his pioneering years here, Eugene Knotts revelled in life along the Withlacoochee River. He predicted big things and sorrowed that the snowbirds were so slow catching on. Most of them went farther south.

But in the late 1970s, he stopped sorrowing. The parade was coming back his way. He was on the fringe of tourist Florida. Clusters of neon-blooming concrete spread in hops and skips up the gulf coast to Crystal River, 14 miles south. Yankeetown was next.

Knotts, a spirited gentleman born in 1894, had waited so long for this that the reality stunned him. He always had combined the role of nature-lover and promoter. He built a showplace glass house (every exterior wall a plate glass door) on a bend of the river. "Because I wanted sales prospects to see that houses here could be as nice as anywhere else," he said. He also wanted to be able to see the river and the hammock from every room.

Which meant more: the old dream of Yankeetown commerce, or preserving Yankeetown's serenity? History caught up with Knotts. He could not for long have both. The missionary stayed too long in the wilds. He had doubts and grandchildren.

Yankeetown (population 400, about 80 per cent of them retirees) had not gone commercial yet, though, not in 1978. Trees dominated the curbless streets that follow the curves of the river which serves as the boundary between Levy and Citrus counties. "I wouldn't let 'em cut down a single tree that wasn't necessary," Knotts said. There were no sidewalks, no drugstores, no department stores.

Town Hall sat on Harmony Lane and volunteers manned the fire department.

A. F. Knotts, Eugene's uncle, came here from Gary, Ind., in 1920 to hunt and fish. Two years later, he bought property and in 1923 Eugene and his wife Norma arrived to help create a town out of a wilderness. The Knotts saw it as a hunting and fishing paradise that would become a booming port city when the cross-Florida barge canal was built.

They built the road, set up their own water and power systems, brought in telephones, built the Izaak Walton fishing lodge and later a new limestone rock school, opened a subdivision and, naturally, wanted to name the place Knotts.

But A. F. Knotts not only was a Yankee, he was a Republican. Native Crackers, with some derision, labelled his creation Yankeetown, and it stuck.

To some Crackers, Yankeetown seemed a touch snooty. In 1927, a counterpoint Crackertown subdivision was laid out on Yankeetown's eastern border. Those beginnings never have been completely overcome, even though Crackertown has been annexed by Inglis.

During the 1930s, A. F. Knotts built a dance pavilion exclusively for Yankeetown and its visitors. Some of the Crackers regarded it as class distinction and demanded admission one Saturday night. "We're just as good as any damned Yankee," they said, according to A. F. Knotts (who died in 1937). The incident is recorded in a Yankeetown history written by Eugene's son, Tom Knotts. While A. F. and Eugene argued with armed Crackers at the door, their fellow Yankees went home, got their own rifles and brandished them. The Crackers left under threat, straining relations further.

Though Inglis and Yankeetown butt up against each other, their differences are apparent and the oldtime feud still simmers and pops sometimes. Alongside Yankeetown's non-commercial scene, Inglis (at the intersection of SR 40 and U.S. 19-98) takes pride in such conveniences as a restaurant, two motels, service stations, fast-food stores, a bank, a bar and lounge. "They still see us as a bunch of Yankees," said Yankeetown Councilman Bob Butler, "and I'm from Arkansas."

A. F. Knotts was mayor of Yankeetown from 1925 until his

death. Eugene then took over and held office until 1970. After that, the Knotts were influential but not decisive in community affairs. Strangers came in and the town changed. Riverfront property in 1978 sold at $200 a front foot and was hard to find. The town budget reached $60,000 and nearly half of it came from revenue-sharing funds. But, biggest of all, the mayor and town council unanimously passed a resolution opposing the cross-Florida barge canal, one of the reasons A. F. Knotts came here in the first place.

Finally, after a long hassle, the town adopted a comprehensive land-use plan which recognized the river and swamps and marshes as its greatest natural resource. The future of Yankeetown would be built around their protection.

The plan cost $12,000 — or about $30 per resident of Yankeetown — and at the final hearing the Town Hall was packed. The crowd parted and emptied a chair when the grand old man, Eugene Knotts, entered. He listened for awhile, and left. He said the meeting made him feel uncomfortable. "That's the same damned bunch that opposed the barge canal," he said. "They don't know what the hell they're doing. I didn't know half the people there. There's nothing wrong with being an environmentalist. We've always tried to save things. But you don't have to go crazy."

From the beginning, Yankeetown was built on opposing dreams — the natural paradise vs. the dream of a bustling city — but for its first half-century it had the luxury of enjoying the one and holding to the other without real conflict. The Knotts never had to make the choice. It was taken out of their hands. Virtual strangers, non-pioneers, made the decision with the land-use plan. Yankeetown opted for serenity.

Eugene Knotts sat in his glass house looking out at the dark river where mullet were jumping and an alligator glided along the bank, and talked like a man who agreed but was conscience-stricken at breaking with the old faith. It made him feel better to grumble about it, he admitted. "They're coming up the road towards us. They'll be here next. No, we're not so crazy about the idea any more. We've got to have some quiet places left."

The Daddy Yankee in Yankeetown sounded almost like a Cracker.

★ *Daytona Beach*

Daytona Beach:
Proud Blue-Collar

Daytona Beach, The World's Most Famous Beach, decided to be realistic. It is a blue-collar tourist town. Nothing will change that. Moderate-income families, racing-car fans, motorcycle enthusiasts, college students and senior citizens pay the bills here, and Daytona Beach is glad to have them. Let the country music and good times roll. Daytona Beach aims to be the best blue-collar tourist town in the country.

A startling thing happened in 1981 to emphasize what was involved in accepting this reality. The Daytona Beach area Chamber of Commerce polled its members to determine the most urgent needs of the community. Historically, such polls reveal a craving for new industry. Not this one. Daytona Beach wanted a new image more than anything else.

But how could it acknowledge its identity as a blue-collar tourist town and get a new image at the same time? On examination, the task seemed to be that of establishing the difference between blue-collar and ring-around-the-collar.

Daytona Beach had built up early as a summertime, small-scale Miami Beach, lining the oceanfront with motels and glitter, spreading north and south along its 23 miles of broad, beautiful beaches. When Disney World came along in 1971 and altered the tourist flow in Florida, the originally developed beach area — where Main Street dead-ended at the oceanfront Broadwalk — had deteriorated. Daytona Beach faced tremendous problems of renewal (no major new motel construction in 10 years) at a time when business was changing course.

115

The energy shortages followed. In 1975, a shark scare roiled up, and the chamber of that time formed a Shark Committee to combat misinformation. The worst problems, though, continued to grow around Main Street, which became known as the Boulevard of the Busted, or the Drink-and-Lust district. Some of the racing-car-and-motorcycle enthusiasts (including gangs) found it a handy wallow. The college students, who came by the thousands during spring vacation, were attracted by easy sin. Dropouts among these visitors and fringe elements that preyed on them turned the area into the focus of crime in Daytona Beach.

When the FBI released figures in 1977 that showed Daytona Beach to be the nation's No. 2 crime city, behind Las Vegas, the city went into shock. The Halifax River divides Daytona into a tourism half and a conventional half. The conventional half, particularly, was outraged.

Daytona Beach, protesting that the figures were distorted because the tourist population (visitor traffic of nearly 6,000,000 per year in a city of 55,000) was not included in computing the proportional incidence of crime, responded with increased police vigilance in the Main Street area. (FBI figures then dropped Daytona Beach to 10th place in crime nationally, behind No. 1 Miami and four other cities in Florida.)

In 1979 a national magazine, which might be regarded as expert in matters of sleaze, had published an article which viewed Daytona Beach as Sleaze Summit, U.S.A. The city, already off balance, went through another spate of attention focused on its problem. It has been trying to recover from the labels of crime and sleaze ever since.

A few raised a question whether the city should alter its tourism appeal. Statistics indicated, for example, that the heaviest incidence of crime occurred from February to April, when racing-car-and-motorcycle events were scheduled, and when the college students got their spring holidays. Some suggested Daytona Beach might be better off without those groups.

But with the decline of both the general economy and tourism in most of Florida, including a tourism dip here, which the chamber estimated at 10 per cent, an emphatic opinion arose that no business should be chased away on a mere gamble for something better.

"We are a blue-collar resort. We have always been a blue-collar resort. We are inexpensive and convenient. We won't ever change the kind of person who comes here," said Jerry Croccow, marketing specialist at the chamber. "We're happy with that."

"Every community should do what it can do best," said Gary Powell, executive vice-president of the chamber. "We have a unique clientele. We're keyed to the blue-collar tourist." Powell stressed, however, that this was not a decision to tolerate crime and sleaze for profit. He said those labels were exaggerated and unfair.

The city decided to pursue a formula whose appeal is varied by the season. February through April, it promotes tourism for racing car fans, motorcycle enthusiasts and college students. Summers are the time for families, many of them from the southern states. Falls, it concentrates on senior citizens.

The polls and marketing surveys and realism spoke. Daytona Beach is a blue-collar resort and it has resolved to be proud of it.

Lakewood

View From The Highlands

You cannot get higher than Lakewood in Florida, at least not with a clear head and both feet on the ground. Neither can you find another spot where you seem closer to God and farther from Miami. What better spot to pause and ponder the fascinating complexities of the Panhandle?

Here on Florida's highest hill, at an elevation of 345 feet (which comes to about a yard of altitude for each local resident), you sit in an old churchyard and look across Walton County hills turning brown and listen to the wind rattle withered corn stalks in the field, and you wonder how North Florida and South Florida got together, or stayed together.

The kinship of the Panhandle with the rest of Florida tapers off as these rolling uplands flatten out in a 500-mile curving slope to the Caribbean. As the climate softens from temperate to tropical, the manners and customs harden from Cracker to cosmopolitan.

Up here, a lot of people would be happy to break off Florida about the level of Tampa. As far as they are concerned, the rest could be another state. . . even another country. They might suggest the entire cast-off piece be called Miami, a name which suggests to them a collection of urban horrors and modern sin (some like to speculate in idle moments on just what the latest sins might be).

The Panhandle itself, that long finger of West Florida upon which Georgia and Alabama sit so heavily, has a range of contrasts that compares to those of the entire state. The line of white beaches and barrier islands that begins just past the Big Bend and stretches all the way to Perdido Bay — the Miracle Strip, dominated by Panama City — creates a tourist attraction and economy that has more kinship to the Gold Coast than most people here would like to

118

admit. One big difference, though, is that the main season is summer, and most visitors drive from neighboring states whose customs and inhibitions are familiar and easily tolerated.

The heart and soul of the Panhandle, however, lie in the high country where the 200 miles between Pensacola and Tallahassee contain no city of size. The scene looks as though it has been plucked from the Carolina foothills. There ought to be blue tips of mountains in the distance.

Here the carnival air winds down to a bucolic quiet and a rugged countryside. The people affect a softened grace in manner and speech that cloaks their human capacity for harshness.

On the radio, mournful country singers set the mood by professing fears of God and jilted women, by reverently celebrating Mom but chuckling at Dad's minor sins, by philosophizing on peculiar forms of tragedy and deprecating money's role in happiness.

Weekly newspapers berate the federal government and the liberals, carry notices of family reunions, promote fish fries and "chitlin" suppers to raise money for churches or Boy Scouts or neighbors who have lost their homes to fire. They list community by community such social activities as the Smiths spending the weekend in Pensacola or the Browns having guests from Atlanta or the Jones boy having the flu.

These reflect a society that thrives on self-inspection, with all the benefits of neighborliness and security that implies, as well as what might to a city-dweller seem a preoccupation with gossip and a nettling loss of anonymity. As some wise fellow once said, there is not much to see in a small town, but what you hear makes up for it.

More squat pickup trucks, rifles bracketed in the rear windows and CB aerials rising off the roofs, buzz through this countryside than foreign compacts. Pastures resemble golf courses, two-rut roads lead off four-lane highways, collapsed farm buildings share hillsides with country gentleman farms, and men cover their heads with hats and tip them to the ladies.

An outsider might look at all this and wonder why the Panhandle should belong to Florida and not Alabama, but it would be best to do so in private. This is a special blend, a different Florida that sees itself as the *real one,* where there is a foundation of red clay and fundamentalism to steady the mix of sandy beaches and frivolous tourists.

Alabama, in fact, has always been sweet on the Panhandle and has tried often to have her. As late as 1963 a state senator from Mobile proposed to the Alabama legislature that steps should be taken to annex the Panhandle, but he was too late with an old idea. From 1818 to 1901 there had been a series of flirtations with that very same notion.

Gen. Andrew Jackson, Florida's first territorial governor, had the original pleasure of rejecting Alabama. "We love her as a sister, but would not be tied," he said. In 1822, U.S. Sen. John Walker of Alabama tried to persuade Congress to give the Panhandle to his state. "Nature has given it to us, and Congress will not always withhold it," he said, unprophetically.

The idea came closest to reality in 1869 when Florida and Alabama reached tentative agreement and a convention was held in Chipley, Fla., to tidy up the bargain. There was a generally favorable vote among the Florida counties involved, but Alabama balked at the cost ($1 million plus a tax break) and as a consequence Florida had to reconsider. To this day, say the solid folk up here, Alabamans are chintzy about Florida's high prices.

In the small towns, men gather early in the mornings to drink coffee and talk politics and football, courteously lowering their voices for four-letter words.

They have been accustomed to seeing one of their own become governor and they would like to keep it that way, though lately they complain that the Good Ol' Boys they send to Tallahassee seem to change and become unduly influenced by eggheads. There is concern because all those people south of Tampa have been carrying the statewide vote and infiltrating the Cabinet, threatening a North Florida (if not Panhandle) tradition of political leadership preserved more by political skill and influence than by population numbers.

Here, beliefs in simplicity and self-sufficiency survive, however threatened they may be by voting patterns and however compromised they may be by national independence, federal subsidy and mandate. In just one day's drive from Miami, the world changes from bright and warm to cold and quaint. Black buzzards circle above cattle gently chewing their cuds in serene pastures, and tall timber forests cover the hills.

Sitting atop Florida's highest hill on a cool Sunday morning in December, one can understand how the Panhandle folk might believe *their* Florida is the only real article left, and that the emphasis on farms and families and fundamentals makes them the backbone and strength of tradition, the last and best of the Florida Crackers. Maybe you will disagree, but you cannot visit and see and hear without being impressed. The difference cannot be measured in miles.

Howey-in-the-Hills:
The City Inevitable

In 1925, despite the Great Depression that threatened, W. J. Howey accelerated his big dream. Even in boomtime Florida, when extravagant promotions and dazzling promises were common, Howey got attention.

Not only did he sell citrus groves and Florida living, all in one exceedingly fancy package, but he guaranteed the groves would bring a profit and advertised that they were nestled in "the Florida Alps."

The highest point in his "Alps" — the central Florida ridge — was Sugarloaf Mountain, for which he claimed a height of 362 feet, and cited an 1870 survey as verification.

Howey did not recognize the then officially accepted top elevation of 324 feet at Iron Mountain near Lake Wales, and the presently acclaimed peak of 345 feet at Lakewood near the Alabama border had not yet been charted.

Howey dreamed for a namesake city whose charm and renown would memorialize his name. He planned to convert 60,000 acres of land here in Lake County, about 40 miles north of Orlando, into the citrus capital of the world.

"Blacksmiths and citrus groves," shouted one of his newspaper advertisement headlines. This explanation followed, "Like the automobile industry, citrus culture is past the blacksmith shop state.... Because it has such an organization...the W. J. Howey Company is able to guarantee you your profits on an investment in a Howey Grove."

The exploits of super-salesman Howey make up a classic tale of

122

developing Florida. All over the state, during the Boom and even later, towns were created by the spur of one man's dream or one group's special hopes. Sometimes these were ethnic, sometimes religious, sometimes snobbish and sometimes merely greedy.

Not all survived when the full force of the Depression hit. Howey himself floundered, but he found an angel and Howey-in-the-Hills survived. He had his memorial.

When debts piled too high, the staggered Howey faced bankruptcy and the death of his dream. In what seemed a dubious gift at the time, Howey turned over the company — and its nearly half million dollars of debts — to a 30-year-old University of Florida graduate and successful fruit packer named C. V. Griffin.

Not only did Griffin supply enough magic to preserve the town, but he made it prosper. Under his guidance, Howey-in-the-Hills paid off all its debts.

It began its fiftieth year free from debt and with a resident population of some 600. Griffin, in 1975 a tall, gray-haired man, remembered both the grandiose Howey schemes, and his own Depression years struggles to overcome their failures.

"Howey was an unusual man. He could sell you anything, and do almost anything," Griffin said.

Howey came to Florida from Chicago in 1912, and planted 200 acres of citrus groves. He closed them during World War I but picked up again late in 1919. The town first was organized as Howey, and changed to Howey-in-the-Hills when incorporated in 1926.

The Howey Company not only owned the 1500 acres that made up the town, but in addition held 60,000 acres. From 1919 until 1932, he converted some 15,000 of these acres into citrus groves.

During the winter season, The Howey Tribune (a company newspaper) entertained, informed and sold such celebrities as writer Opie Read, former President Calvin Coolidge and a variety of other wellknown men of that time, most of whom stayed in the 65-room Hotel Floridian on Palm Avenue overlooking Lake Harris.

In May, 1926, The Tribune headlined the visit of U.S. Secretary of Agriculture William M. Jardine, who took a look around and pronounced in that fateful year, "Florida is agriculturally, horticulturally and economically sound."

Four years later, in the midst of the Depression, The Tribune still was going strong. In January, 1930, it interviewed a Eustis girl who had been judged by a national 4-H competition to be the healthiest young lady in the country. She attributed it to eating a Lake County grapefruit every day.

"I do not smoke cigarets, use rouge or lipstick and while I like to dance I don't because I am a Sunday school teacher in the Christian church," said Florence Smock.

The Tribune bravely quoted Howey, "In my judgment, Florida is entering upon an era of unprecedented substantial prosperity." At the time, real estate values were plummeting.

The Tribune added a wondering quote from the Marion County Sun: "W. J. Howey may be a Republican, but no man in Florida has more faith in the state. . . ."

By 1936, Howey-in-the-Hills and the big dream was going under, and Howey had to admit it. He looked around for someone to save the city, and found Griffin, a young University of Florida graduate from Illinois whom he had helped make a successful fruit shipper.

"When Howey came to me in 1936, the company owed $450,000. All I had to do was assume the debts and he would give it to me. I had to do a lot of talking to creditors," said Griffin.

"I became president of the company in 1937, and there was hardly anybody here then. Maybe 30 people, mostly widows. I didn't want all those debts and burdens, but I didn't want the town to fold up, either.

"So I inherited the town and went into the real estate business. From 1937 to 1956, I both sold acreage and bought back some that Howey had lost. I bought 10,000 acres one time at $7 an acre."

Griffin himself became a promoter in a style that might have made W. J. Howey proud. He arranged package tours out of New York and other cities in the East through a travel agency, and he began holding annual auctions.

The old hotel became a country club and guests who wished could have a private bath (rather than connecting bath) at rates that went up to $134.75 for eight days. The price included transportation, fish fries, cocktail parties, golf, horseback riding, fishing, lake cruises, games, carriage rides — and, of course, a good look at the best groves.

"Anybody who bought a grove got a house," Griffin said. "I figured if I could bring 200 people in here, they'd bring their friends and that'd be enough.

"Our first auction drew 75,000 people, but I spent $75,000 promoting it. We sold 45 houses and gave away a Cadillac. We had that first auction in July and it rained all day, but we sold anyway. After that, we held them in February."

In 1955, Griffin discontinued the auctions, and ran the country club as a hotel. In 1956, he sold most of his groves to a conglomerate, and converted the hotel into a boarding school.

After a somewhat hectic half-century, Howey-in-the-Hills settled into comfortable respectability. It was not the City Inevitable that Howey had imagined, but a piece of the dream lived.

Fernandina Beach: A Palace

In Fernandina Beach, patience is the word. Geography, history and luck have been kicking the quaint island seaport around for 400 years, and each time she struggled back.

Fernandina Beach sits so far north and east in Florida that you can travel south and west and get to Georgia. Eight flags have flown here and all manner of men — from pirates to statesmen — have walked her streets or hooked their heels over a brass rail at the famous old Palace Saloon.

The sea dominates. On the east is the Atlantic Ocean and on all other sides are the Amelia River and a long sweep of salt marshes that flood in high tide and stink at low tide.

The only other strong, permanent force is history. Each boom has been met by a war, an epidemic, a hurricane or a depression. The greatest of them came in the last quarter of the 19th century when the old cross-state railroad to Cedar Key made Fernandina Beach one of Florida's principal links to the world. Most of the town was built then.

Anything that does not depend on the sea or history never had much chance. Once, the area was promoted as "the fig culture center of the South." That did not prove to be the case.

Another time a promoter discovered prolific mulberry trees and pledged to make it "the silk center of the world." He brought in a few silkworms, sold some stock and then vanished.

In the 1920s, the local Chamber of Commerce put out a piece of advertising that typified the boomtime psychology: "The Atlantic to Mississippi Canal will be built just as certain as Nehemiah rebuilt the walls of Jerusalem," the blurb read, "and in the day that is accomplished, Fernandina will be the New York of the South." They could have used Nehemiah here.

In 1971, Fernandina Beach decided to roll with the power of the sea and history. A 30-block section along Centre Street was placed on the National Register of Historic places, and the whole town launched into a fever of restoration, mostly 1890s style, of which the Palace Saloon (1878) and the Courthouse (1891) are the center-pieces.

Since most tourists do not spend time gawking at judges and clerks in solemn judicial surroundings, where fun seems improbable, they venture into the Palace, where all things seem possible.

You enter through swinging doors. A fortress wall seven bricks thick shuts out the heat, or the cold, and red velvet curtains never let the sun pierce the one-and-one-half inch bevelled glass windows.

An ancient, glittering brass lamp hangs over a 40-foot hand-carved mahogany and oak bar in front of a mirror that has survived the arguments of gentlemen and the brawls of sailors. A pair of caryatids — mahogany female forms whose lower halves disappear into the wall — brace the mirror.

Paddle fans hang from a pressed-metal ceiling patterned with square and floral designs, above men and women sitting in captain's chairs or leaning on that magnificent bar watching the swinging pendulum of a grandfather's clock on the wall. They listen to a coin-operated player piano, a jukebox, the sharp ring of a brassy cash register and the chimes that sound when a customer enters the adjacent package store.

The Palace could be a dungeon or a museum, depending upon the bent of your head. It is dark, cool and imaginatively tempting. Only girls work here and fishermen love it, from their breakfast-time snorts to their midnight toddies.

The thirsty and the curious keep the swinging doors swinging, letting in blinding little cracks of sunlight or giving quick peeks at a lamp-lighted street.

The Palace calls itself "Florida's Oldest Saloon," based on the fact that a German immigrant named Louis G. Hirth turned what had been a haberdashery into a saloon here in 1903. He had the help of his friend Augustus Busch, the famed beer man from St. Louis.

It has operated as a bar since, though officially it turned into an ice cream parlor during Prohibition. What was being consumed in the backrooms was another matter.

The Palace's customers have arrived in everything from skiffs to yachts and saddle horses to Rolls Royces. Duponts and Carnegies have bellied up (or their equivalent) to the big bar, as well as Busch and Florida pioneers Barron Collier and Carl Fisher. Even Sam Goldwyn once came. At other times, the clientele has been considerably less affluent and more rowdy.

Once, the Palace imported lake ice from the North to cool its drinks, served beer in crocks, provided 14-pound cuspidors for the convenience of patrons and minted its own coins for in-saloon use.

Now it is a place for tourists to go and sample the raunchiest and the ritziest of old Fernandina, to eat shrimp that her fishermen net from the sea, to wonder at the glories of the 1890s, and the patience that permitted her to survive a poor hand of geography, history and hard luck.

People

Marjory Stoneman Douglas

The Grande Dame of the Everglades

When Marjory Stoneman Douglas enters a room, it tends to quiet down. She has the presence of a rare tropical creature, colorful and commanding. She comes prepared, in the way that untamed things devise their security, either to cast a spell or plant an intimidating sting.

Sometimes, you can tell her mood by her plumage. When expecting to do battle with bureaucrats and developmental bunglers, she wears a red straw hat. Those are her fighting feathers. Other colors indicate she will resort to bewitchery.

One spring evening in 1982, after a 350-mile auto ride from her Coconut Grove cottage, she swept into the living room of Art Marshall's woodsy home (part of a North Central Florida family compound near Interlachen), wearing a yellow hat.

She commandeered an easy chair and a Scotch, nodded to a gathering of naturalists and environmentalists, and then just for fun picked a genteel argument with a man squatting reverently before her on a stool. It was her way of warming the social climate.

In such a gathering there is a tendency to stand back and admire the style of this grand woman who was born in 1890. She is an intellectual Auntie Mame with a cause. She gets the deference due a grandma, but she does not care for it. At heart she is a gladiator.

Her cause is the Everglades but she travels, speaks and writes (she has written eight books) in pursuit of a variety of subjects, including women's rights. One measure of her impact on Florida was indicated last year when the state named its Department of Natural Resources Building for her. Not many nonpoliticians get their

131

names in state stone in Tallahassee.

Neither age nor poor eyesight seem to her handicaps worth dwelling upon. "I see in a bleary sort of way," she said. She tells time by flipping up the crystal on her watch, feeling the raised numbers and the long and the short hands.

She travels alone to such places as England and Argentina.

About a year ago, she went to Patagonia. During a stop in Buenos Aires to change planes, she found she could read neither the taxi meter nor the numbers on the pesos, but successfully bluffed her way along on flair.

"One can always manage somehow. I've caught on to this thing about a wheelchair in airports," she said, chuckling, as if she were a con man revealing secrets. "They put you through ahead of everybody, get you a taxi and you're off to the hotel with no trouble at all."

She was born in Minneapolis, came to Florida in 1915 to get a divorce. Her father, Frank B. Stoneman, owned The Miami Herald. He gave her a job and in time she met a landscape architect named Ernest Coe.

Coe had taken a trip into the Everglades with Harold Bailey, a Coral Gables ornithologist, who remarked that it would make a nice park. For Coe, that was a discovery that became an obsession. In 1928, he committed himself to the idea.

Douglas lists Bailey, Coe, Stoneman and later editor of The Herald, John Pennekamp in her Everglades Hall of Fame. Pennekamp was the principal force in persuading the government to buy the land for the park. For that, he has been called the Father of the Everglades National Park. Douglas, a friend and admirer of Pennekamp, has her own idea. "I would call him the midwife," she said.

Douglas herself belongs in any Everglades Hall of Fame. Her book, *The Everglades, River of Grass,* published the year the park was dedicated (1947), is the classic work on the subject and remains popular today. The Friends of the Everglades, which she organized in 1969, has lobbied and fought effectively for her cause.

The Everglades was the real reason she made this strenuous overnight auto trip. She wanted to deepen her collaboration with Art Marshall in its defense. She regards Marshall, some 30 years her junior but famed for his work in South Florida with natural systems, as its greatest living champion.

Marshall had a plan to save the Everglades, prevent it from completely drying up, and Douglas enthusiastically endorsed it. The Marshall Plan called for the restoration of the Kissimmee River to its meandering channels (the U.S. Corps of Engineers dredged it into a straight ditch leading into Lake Okeechobee), and re-establishing a shallow water flow south of the lake across the Everglades. He sees all of it as one natural system. The state has agreed with him in principle.

Marshall contends that the changes he recommends will give that system a chance to work again, increase rainfall (because evapo-transpiration from the sheet flow is regarded as essential to the rainfall cycle), increase aquifer recharge and boost dwindling marine resources in Florida Bay.

The Douglas book *River of Grass* concluded with this gloomy but accurate forecast: "Overdrainage will go on. The soil will shrink and burn and be wasted and destroyed, in a continuing ruin."

Now Marjory has rewritten the last eight pages and the book will be re-issued with a conclusion that draws hope from the Marshall Plan.

The reunion of these two old Everglades warriors, Douglas and Marshall, formalized a relationship. Marshall has created The Committee for Applied Ecology, which will function independently and statewide but under the tax-free umbrella of Friends of the Everglades.

The two are hatching up a stunt as well. Marshall wants Douglas to don her fighting red hat and go up to the Kissimmee ditch and pitch in the first shovelful of dirt toward the restoration of the river. They are half serious. Laws might be broken. Maybe Douglas would go to jail. There could be a great public uproar.

She came up out of her chair with enthusiasm. "I love it, I love it," she cried. Before she gets old, she would not want to miss a chance to go to jail for the Everglades.

Grand Ridge

The Coon Hunter: Honesty Under A Tree

The Glissons were coon hunters. Edgar learned from his daddy, who had learned from his granddaddy. "I followed my daddy in the woods many a mile," Edgar said. "This rascal here," he said, pointing to his 14-year-old son Dean, "went out when he had to hold my back pocket to keep up."

For the Glissons, hunting raccoons is more than a sport. Pride and reputation are on the line when cold weather arrives and a man and his dogs take to the woods. In rural Florida, particularly the Panhandle, hunting the coon is central to the culture. Success means not just that you catch and kill a coon, but that you do it with style.

It begins with the dogs. At their best, a man and his coon dogs are a matched set. Their personalities mesh. The dog must have a "good mouth," so the hunter can hear him bawl when he strikes a trail. The dog must also tell the hunter how the chase is going and when he has jumped the coon, treed it or cornered it for a fight. He must have enough range, but not more than the hunter. If the dog has a "tight" mouth, he does not bark loudly or expressively. When a good-mouthed dog "trees hard," he barks with a "hard chop" until the hunter arrives to shine a light in the coon's yellow-green eyes and shoot him or shake him out of the tree for the dogs.

Hunters prize a "cold" nose, which means the dog can pick up more than just a fresh trail. But if the nose is too cold, the dog will pick up an old trail and the hunt is spoiled. "If he strikes a trail where a coon walked at first dark, that's no good. He'll hang up too long," Glisson said.

134

The dog must ignore other animals, and stick to tracking raccoons. He and the hunter must not be afraid to tumble into swamps and ponds, where coons usually head when chased. Sometimes, the coon stands and fights, and the dog must be ready to mix it up.

"Hooooooo, man, talk about fighting! Sometimes one coon'll whip a whole pack of dogs. You put a coon in the water where the dog has to swim, he'll drown a dog. Get on his head and duck him under. You get a big boar coon now, and he's a mean joker."

Edgar was born across the street from where he lives, not far from the Providence Baptist Church. His maternal grandparents migrated from Alabama, but his daddy's family goes back generations and generations in the Panhandle. Edgar was a long-distance trucker for 21 years, proud that his wife learned to handle the big rigs and drive with him and proud that his son wants to be a trucker. But in 1978 he quit for an eight-hour-a-day job that would let him stay at home with his family and coon dogs.

Glisson had five coon dogs, three children and a wife, plus five acres and a brick house. He lived near Grand Ridge, a village on U.S. 90 between Marianna and Chattahoochee in Jackson County, which borders both Alabama and Georgia. Except for his youngest daughter, all the family enjoyed coon hunting.

He estimated the value of his dogs — two Blue Ticks, two Walkers and one Black and Tan — at $4,000. He kept them in concrete-floored pens in the yard. Twin dog cages were mounted on the back of his green pickup and a rifle was racked in the rear window.

Getting the right dogs is the secret to coon hunting. "That's the hard number," Glisson said. "You think I got high-priced dogs? They sell registered and trained dogs on up into the thousands. But you better be careful."

Several years ago, Glisson was not. He bought a dog without trying him out, and a dispute developed that landed him in court and made him perhaps the most celebrated coon hunter in Jackson County.

The dog he bought had a decent nose and a pretty good mouth, but he would not tree. Once the coon ran up a tree, the dog lost interest. Glisson sued. He so dazzled the court with his coon dog intelligence that he won the case. Down at the truck stop, notice went on the bulletin board. Edgar was not only a coon hunter, he was a coon dog lawyer.

"That cured me," he said. "The only way I buy a dog now is under the tree. I hunt him first. I wouldn't buy a dog from my brother until I saw him under the tree."

He prefers to train his own, beginning when they are about six months old. The training involves letting a puppy run with older dogs, teaching him to hate coons and coaxing him to trace and tree them exclusively.

"You see that old blue dog there, where the coons have eaten his ears ragged? They just hate coons worse when they get bit like that," he said. "When my puppies start running and treeing, I always try to shake the coon out and let him get ahold of that puppy. Makes him a better coon dog. Once he makes a kill, he gets better and better."

Glisson hunts primarily in winter, because he fears the rattlesnakes that prowl after dark in warm weather. He prefers dark nights. "On bright moonlight nights, coons don't travel as much. And if a dog trees one, it's hard to find him in the tree because he won't look at you. You can't see his eyes. On a dark night, he'll look at that light."

Glisson begins a hunt by parking his pickup, dropping the tailgate and turning two or more dogs loose. "Then I just sit there and listen to them." That is the sweet part. The dogs talk to him across the woods, bawling when they strike a trail and take up the chase, changing voices as the chase changes. "When I hear they got him treed, I go to them on foot. Might be a half mile, might be a mile. Might have to go through briars, wade swamps and creeks, but I go."

The dead raccoon is an anticlimax. The hide can be sold for a few dollars, but Glisson doesn't like hide buyers because their business encourages hunters to overkill. The meat of the raccoon can be eaten, but Glisson is squeamish about it. "Tastes all right," he said. "It's just the idea." He often gives the coon away.

For the coon hunter, the important things are the smell of the woods, the sound of the dog and the final fight. It is a classic adventure in Cracker Florida, settled with cruel honesty under a tree.

Winter Park

May A Butterfly Alight On You, Too

Tall, kinetic Henry Swanson needs all his civic credentials, now that he has taken up with butterflies. He meets them in his backyard, talks to them, courts them, studies them, writes about them. He loves butterflies, and they have changed his life.

To appreciate this, you must understand that Swanson qualifies as a responsible citizen. He is a settled grandfather, a retired agricultural extension agent frequently honored for his dedication to Orange County. He is the kind of man who does not consider church attendance a social activity.

Still, Swanson has developed this passion for butterflies. Furthermore, he suspects that his butterflies think and have feelings. Butterfly experts snort at this but Swanson brandishes his intuition and proceeds.

His wife, Billie, just laughs. Many a supper has grown cold while Henry talked to butterflies. "That's Henry," she said. She is a nice lady. Maybe the situation seems a little peculiar to outsiders, but she thinks on the whole that butterflies have been good for him.

Swanson has the grace and tolerance to laugh with doubters. He invites them to the backyard of his Winter Park home for a command performance. Time after time, the butterflies reward his faith.

One afternoon in 1982, Swanson and two skeptics (my wife Gloria and I) sat in chairs along the edge of the yard waiting for one of those performances. He was nervous. He kept checking his watch. His credibility was at issue.

Out in the middle of the yard, where an opening in the trees permitted a ring of sunshine, he had placed a white lawn chair. This was for the butterfly, the species known as the Red Admiral (or Vanessa Atalanta).

He had estimated the admiral would arrive about 5:15, but now it was 5:20 and he was getting worried. He began to talk fast, filling the time. He reviewed his butterfly experiences.

Swanson is a high-strung, energetic man. As Orange County's agricultural agent for 30 years, he had been a crusading environmentalist. He carried out an exhausting civic campaign and speaking schedule. He warned and warned. He got ulcers.

He began not to sleep well. He would lie in bed, fretting, examining his conscience and his duty. Nobody seemed to see the dangers he saw. "I got where I couldn't relax," he said. He worried about his health.

At this point, the butterfly came into his life. For him, it was like seeing a sunset for the first time. He was enraptured by it. This tiny, beautiful bug became a symbol, a revelation, a religious experience.

He began to regard the butterfly as a messenger telling him to gear his life down, to pace himself more slowly so that he could see not only the butterflies but other small, beautiful, everyday things that enrich life. Anyway, as he looks back at it now, that was his honest feeling about it.

He had his first butterfly experience in 1976 when one lighted on the head of his grandson, age 2. It stayed there while the boy ran across the yard, laughing. Swanson was impressed.

Nine months later, as he stood in his backyard one Friday afternoon, another little brown butterfly landed at his feet. He had not seen one between those times, but he remembered. He held out his finger and the butterfly perched on it. His wife chided him. Reluctantly, he left it to go away for a weekend fishing trip.

Sunday, when he returned, he rushed out to the backyard and the butterfly was there. It returned to his finger. He put some diluted honey on the finger and let it feed. Swanson felt that he and the butterfly communicated.

A routine developed. Every afternoon, he would set out the lawn chair, put a small bowl of diluted honey on it, and almost every day a Red Admiral (predominantly brown but multicolored) came. He began to keep a detailed log of its appearances. If he had to be away, a neighbor, Mrs. Pat Miller, butterfly-sat for him and kept the logbook. In 1981, a butterfly came to his yard 313 of the 365 days. Some years, a butterfly failed to come as many as 47 consecutive days, and then showed up.

After five years, Swanson became convinced that his experience was unique. Who else has pet butterflies? Who else talks with them? He is not sure of the Red Admiral's lifespan (the larger Monarch butterfly, the subject of more study, has an average lifespan of nine months), but he is certain that he has established a generational chain of butterflies coming to his backyard. One butterfly generation passes him on to another, he speculates.

Swanson has written a small book, *Butterfly Revelations,* detailing his experiences and his conclusions from them. All proceeds go to the Presbyterian church. The book is not literature, but it has mystery and wonder, and it is a remarkable record.

At 5:26 p.m. on that June afternoon in 1982, our wait ended. A tiny brown butterfly swooped into the yard. The Red Admiral had arrived. Swanson, elated, danced about the yard. The admiral lighted on my shoulder. It ate honey from Gloria's finger.

Swanson talked to it, fed it, bragged on it. He does not care what the experts say. An encounter with butterflies has changed his life. He sleeps fine now. The world is a different place to him.

His favorite quotation has become this one from Nathaniel Hawthorne: "Happiness is a butterfly, which when pursued, is always just beyond your grasp, but which, if you will sit down quietly, may alight upon you."

Swanson does not evangelize about it, but he has this urge to persuade everyone to find his own butterfly. It requires an extraordinary eye and an innocent mind. But for those of us who have difficulty mastering those, the Swanson story itself is a remarkably good substitute.

Pensacola

Theophilus May
And Restorection

Theophilus May, probably better than anyone else, understands how the common Pensacolan of 100 years ago felt about his life and work. May has an extraordinary sense of historical empathy. With a hammer and nails, he is an instinctive artist.

Out of his head come these bursts of insight he cannot fully explain. Without blueprints or pictures or even markup pencils, he tears down old buildings and then restores and reassembles them from memory.

At this, he has a genuine genius. He does not know how it works, but he knows how to call on it. By studying history and the evolution of tools and carpentry in building, he has extended the range of it. He patiently courts inspiration, and never yet has it failed him.

The Historic Pensacola Preservation Board coddles his efforts to nurture these talents. Although millions of dollars and carloads of blueprints and years of planning have gone into Pensacola's fine historic district, no other single person has contributed a more potent combination of sweat and soul than Theophilus May. What he has done, with a long list of key structures, no one else could do.

May is a tall, deliberate fellow who approaches his work, which he calls *restorection,* with reverence. The historians have come to him, over and over and over, to say that a certain old building is in the wrong place. It needs to be torn down, moved, accurately reconstructed as it appeared in 1890 or so, but in another location. To May, that is *restorection.*

He mystifies architects, confounds historians who have learned to swear by his analyses and dismays younger men trying to work by his exacting standards. He works his own way, at his own pace.

When he accepts a project, he studies it carefully. Sometimes he just sits around looking at it, thinking about it for days, maybe even weeks. Then he will start tearing the building down, piece by piece, laying the parts out. Finally, the whole thing will be scattered across the lot. Then he will put it back together, remaking even the most intricate of the broken or rotten pieces.

Once, on an early project, the parts lay sprinkled about on a slab for six months. May would show up now and then, commune with them, and then go off on another job. "Have to rest my mind sometimes by doing something else," he explained. He also is a Baptist minister. The preservationists began biting their nails.

Then one day, without ever having taken a picture, or written a note or anything of the sort, he began putting the parts together. In a year, or maybe less, an authentically historic building arose. It had previously unknown historic detail, which later research proved accurate.

This baffles the professionals. How can a self-trained, middle-aged man master history and craft in ways beyond their reach? "They get in too big of a hurry," May explained. "Get to going fast and don't know where they going. Get sloppy, that way."

While that might be true, the explanation is too simple. The unhurried May also is a serious student of history and building craftsmanship. By the look of saw-cuts, by the pegs or the nails, by the way the sills are notched or slotted, by the quality of the wood and the precision with which it is fitted and assembled, he can tell you the age of a building. Historians have learned to trust his estimates.

May was atop a scaffold one day, working on one of his *restorections,* when a preservation board official came by. "May, don't you fall off there now," the man said. "Cause if you do, we're lost. Nobody else knows what you're doing."

Another time, an official watched him putting the last peg into a project. The man marvelled at how well it fit. "May, you're lucky," the man said. "That thing fit right back into the slot where the original was." May smiled. "Uhm, hmmmm," he replied. "That's figuring, not luck."

The first time I saw Theophilus May, in 1975, he was standing on a Pensacola sidewalk staring at his current *restorection* project, an old gymnasium called Rafford Hall. His breath fogged and he complained that it was so cold his fingers were stiff.

As we sat in the cab of his pickup truck, trying to keep warm, he poured coffee from a thermos and told me how the preservation board had urged him to train some younger men in his work. It was a craft that should not disappear. But he was having a hard time finding somebody. At the time, he wondered whether one of his sons might do it.

In 1982 he was still looking. "Can't find anybody that's interested enough," he said. "They don't want to take the time. They don't want to do the work. If you're gonna restore a building, first thing you have to do is get under it and replace those rotten sills. Sometimes you have to dig out enough room to work. One place, we had to haul dirt out for half a day before we could get under there. Young folks, they not interested in that."

May has 10 children, four older ones by an earlier marriage, all with college training, six younger ones (the oldest 13) still at home and in school. "My children are too sorry to do this," he said, laughing. "Last one I had working for me, he said, 'Daddy, you work too hard. I'm too young to work this hard.' He left and went to Atlanta."

May's experience has led him to be skeptical of young people and new construction. He has learned to question the quality of their foundations and materials and standards. Too often, he has seen they will not stand up under burden and stress.

Out of this has come that historical empathy. He thinks more like the men who put together those fine old buildings a century ago. He understands the appeal and deep satisfaction of true craft. He thinks this is what led him into the ministry about 20 years ago. Everywhere he looked, he saw a lot of *restorection* to be done.

Miami

The Historic Mosquito Raid On Cuba

Manuel Salvat still looked young, but not quite like the reckless commando whose mosquito raid against Cuba 18 years ago startled the United States and the Soviet Union just as they were stalking toward the 1962 missile crisis.

At lunch, he sipped only unsweetened tea, ate nothing, and talked about his diet. He had lost 40 pounds, and that was not enough. His diet was simple. "I eat nothing," he said.

Salvat, when I talked with him in 1980, was 40, had a wife and four children, owned a bookstore, Libreria Universal, and had heroic status in Miami's Cuban community. The years had changed everything but his red hair, blue eyes and his hopes. Inside, he was still a commando, but to him the situation now was not appropriate for commandos, for terrorism or even for the U.S. blockade.

"I am very pessimistic," he said. "The situation in Cuba is bad, really bad, for Castro. But everything is going the other way. The solution must come from inside and the political conscience is not very good, either here or in Cuba. Most of the people here are not with Castro, but they are not against him either. They are isolated and without spirit.

"Here in Miami, we have changed to a community of immigrants, not exiles. If we were more politically aware, we would not go to Mariel (the Cuban port from which the improvised sealift brought out refugees), but everybody goes. It is a personal feeling that I understand. But if you have a political conscience, that must be first. Once, we would leave our families. We felt we had to. But there is no conscience now."

In 1962, Salvat left a wife who expected their first child at any moment and led a wild, improbable attack against Castro. In the 20-year history of anti-Castro exiles, there have been a lot of crazily heroic strikes, but none topped this.

To understand it, you have to remember how it was during those times. Failure of the Bay of Pigs invasion had crushed the spirit of the exiles. About 1,200 of the invaders were in Cuban prisons, and the United States had begun negotiations to ransom them. This was more bitter medicine.

That August, detailed reports of a Soviet military buildup, including the installation of long-range missiles, had created an extraordinarily high sense of tension and danger.

During all this, a group of young Cubans in Miami — members of the Student Revolutionary Directorate — put together plans for a commando raid. They made a down payment on a 31-foot Bertram boat, painted it blue, bought a used 20-millimeter cannon and 100 shells for $300, picked up some rifles and pistols. Another group contributed a war surplus PT boat as escort.

None of the boys was expert at war. Salvat, who did not know how to pilot the boat or fire the cannon, was military coordinator. They made up for everything with fiery spirit.

Each Friday night at 9, the underground had told them, a group of Russians attended the Chaplin Theater in Miramar, a suburb of Havana. They always returned to their waterfront hotel, the Rosita de Hornedo, about 11 for a party. Castro himself frequently joined them. That was the target.

Their boats left Marathon about 2 p.m., Friday, August 24, 1962, and test-fired the cannon for the first time en route. The gunner never had fired one before. By miscalculation, they came into Cuban waters at Guanabo Beach, to the east, turned right and followed the lights of cars on the *autopista* to Havana. The Bertram carried the eight principal commandos; the PT boat stayed 15 miles offshore. They passed Morro Castle and backed their boat within 200 yards of the brightly lighted hotel. The Soviets were partying. The boys heard a loudspeaker by the pool page someone named Pomarovsky.

The first cannon shots hit the dining room, and the lights went out. The gunner and the others, firing rifles and pistols, used every shell. "If we had rocks, we would have thrown rocks," the gunner said later. They returned safely.

The raid electrified the Cuban community in Miami. The boys were heroes in a way that no one has been since. Radio Moscow, Radio Peking and Castro (who had missed the party) condemned them. The United States officially was horrified at the raid and what it might have precipitated. There was a protest in the United Nations. Three days later, Salvat's wife gave birth to their first child, a daughter. In just a few weeks, the latent missile crisis erupted into a threat of World War III.

The boys became hemispheric figures, courted by politicians in six Latin American nations plus Puerto Rico. Their organization expanded. They planned other raids, but the United States blocked each one. Their mission after that was confined to propaganda and, in time, all the excitement trailed away.

Salvat built up the business of his bookstore, one of the boys went back to school and became an engineer, one became a doctor, others went into business. All were respected men of exile history, remarkably successful except in the thing they put first: defeating Castro.

Salvat walked the difficult line of trying to raise his children so that they had a Cuban conscience, knew their heritage, without becoming alien from their home in the United States. But for himself, he brooded over what could be done for his *patria*.

The renewed exodus from Cuba, the horn-honking parades and the ostentatious resumption of training in the Everglades, did not stir him. "It is not serious," he said. "That is not the way. I am pessimistic because in Cuba they think only of leaving, of coming here, not of settling the problems. It has been our mistake, all of us, from the beginning. We should have stayed."

He sipped his tea, and pointed a finger. "But do not misunderstand me," he said. "I have not given up. In a moment, everything could make things different, set things off. It could happen like in Hungary."

Exile is like that. Even the best of the warriors grow older and wiser, but they never give up.

Lake Okeechobee

Audubon's Cracker Warden

Rod Chandler probably knew Lake Okeechobee and the Kissimmee Prairie better than any other man alive. He identified with the region, merged into it, breathed it and circulated through it. With the eye of a Cracker, he studied everything struggling to survive, human or animal.

"Now you take these people out here on the lake," he said. "The old ones are thinning out but they's still some bunch of people on this lake yet. They good folks. But you don't cross 'em. They got their own ways. When you come up on 'em you say good morning, and if it's late in the evening and it's raining, it's still good morning."

One of the Chandlers, third-generation Floridians from Basinger and Okeechobee, was wildlife warden for the National Audubon Society in this region for more than 40 years. The Chandlers made a family career out of roaming the lake and the prairie with a proprietary eye.

Uncle Marvin had the job first. He started in the 1930s and held it until he died, when Rod's brother Glenn took over. Glenn held it 17 years and turned it over to Rod in 1965. "The society's already asked me if there's gon' be another Chandler ready when I retire," Rod said in 1979. "I told 'em, hell, I wasn't dead yet. But if I was, my boy Russell'd be a good one."

Chandler, 63 then, billed himself as the Audubon's only cracker warden. "They've got other folks, but they're all from Pennsylvania or someplace. No more natural oldtimers like me, that been roaming around the lake and the woods since they could walk. If they didn't pay me to do this, I'd be out there payin' to do it."

Chandler made it sound like a vacation, but he covered an impossibly large territory — more than 80,000 acres — and to be effective used the guile of a raccoon and the caution of a diplomat, and he abided by the code of the Crackers. The code required a priority that put local understanding of justice above the technicalities of law. Chandler, in other words, sometimes did his job in ways that made other people nervous.

"There was a game warden went down there once and kept messin' with those boys on the lake, and I told him, you better let those boys alone, you gon' get in trouble. But he said he was gon' stop 'em from doin' whatever it was they was doin'." Chandler smiled. "He made a run out there to get somebody and they shot his boat about half in two.

"Another time a guy went out there and was gon' jump on somebody, and he just made a mistake. He got over there rawin' and jawin' at them and they beat hell out of him with a damned oar, put him in the hospital. Like I say, don't mess with 'em. Anything that stops 'em from making a living, they get rid of it."

Briefly, Chandler worked for the state. He was sent into an area where some "big-shot" poachers from Miami had been reported. He encountered the big shots. They argued that it was a local custom to poach. "These people born and raised around here they just eat a little when they need it and I don't care, but you fellas know better," Rod told them.

"It wasn't long before it hit the fan. I lasted three months. One thing I'm proud of about my Audubon job is there's no politics," he said, explaining. "I'm real proud of that."

A Chandler preoccupation in later years was the preservation of the Everglades kite, a snail hawk that almost became extinct. "There for years, we only had three left," he said. Its last U.S. nesting place was around the lake. Thanks largely to Chandler's efforts, the bird made a comeback.

Preservation of the kite is an example of how Chandler worked. Following a discussion among Audubon officials about the value of delaying duck season on the lake past the kites' nesting period, word spread that Audubon was trying to close duck hunting season completely.

"I began to get calls from them duck hunters," Rod said. "They was mad. Told me they'd done radioed around the lake and said they was gon' kill every damned kite, every one 'em, if we tried to stop duck hunting. They had me sweatin' blood, but I got 'em to hold off and we got it straight. Those fellas out there on the lake, most of 'em, don't give a damn about the kite, but they know I'm working with 'em and they won't mess with 'em. Without their cooperation, I wouldn't have a chance.''

Once the state leaned on Chandler to act as a deputy game warden on his tours. He refused. ''The impression I got of a deputy, an unpaid man trying to do something like that, you couldn't print it,'' he said. ''I know these people. I was born and raised with 'em. They help me and I don't mind telling ya, I help them, too.

''If I'd go out and see these guys (state wardens), seven or eight big outboard motors, all dressed up, shoes shined and a can of Mace on, it'd burn me up. If you gon' catch a man, catch him in the act, not waiting like that. I'd go out there and get on the point of a reef and just sit there and when those boys (Cracker fishermen) come by I'd just do my hat like that (he waved his cowboy hat) and those boys'd just make a circle and go back. I didn't have to say nothing. They knew.

''I'll tell ya what, between the game commission and the public, those boys never know what they're going to do next. Looks like the whole state of Florida cares about nothing but digging for tourists. They just shove these people out of the way if it's gon' mess up some more damned Yankees coming. It's rank.''

Chandler laughed. ''They still sort of run me across the log every now and then when I talk like that,'' he said. But he kept talking. Kites or Crackers, Rod Chandler knew the survival odds and he would bend every effort — or rule — to help.

Tampa

'A Cigarsmoker, He Don't Give a Damn'

The blonde said she was from Paris, and Mario Puig was entranced. He offered her a seven-inch elegante cigar, and popped a match under it. "That look good, taste good," he said, beaming. She gave it a French puff.

"You can't walk down the street like that," the lady with her protested. Puig intervened. "Sure, sure she can walk. Good cigar. People like." The lady puffed and studied him. Puig continued. "It's OK. They see you with the elegante and they say, 'Where the hell you get that?'"

"No," Her friend said. Puig persisted. "You have woman rights. Can smoke cigars if you want." The lady from Paris blew a puff at him. "I have rights," she said precisely, "but I still choose." She bought a box of elegantes and chose to walk away, a full six inches to go and smoke trailing.

Puig was delighted. "Good propaganda," he said.

He ran a buckeye, a one-room production center for hand-made cigars, in the cluster of tourist shops located in Ybor Square, where Martinez Ybor began the cigar business in Tampa in 1886 and around which the neighborhood called Ybor City grew.

Puig was as much showman as cigarmaker, and tourists loved his act. The short, bronze man with graying hair sold a lot of cigars. He compared cigar-making with poetry and art, and explained that a machine simply cannot do it well, that it must be the work of someone who cares. He suggested, too, that smoking a cigar was a thing of quiet passion.

"Like this," he said, lighting up a nine-inch Rough Rider

($1.50), the star of his Tampa Rico label. "You get it, you look at it good, maybe lick it a little bit, and maybe you give it a little bite and you put it in your mouth like this and get the match. See?"

He puffed a couple of times. Smoke spurted from his mouth and then just floated out while he narrowed his eyes and watched. "Smoke slow, you enjoy it. You do like this," he said, concentrating. "You look at it and you turn it around and around and look at it some more. See?"

With Puig, it is like love. "You have a big dinner, and you enjoy it. Is different, see? Not like cigarets. Cigaret smoker takes one after the other. What does he know like that? Cigar-smokers do it slow, for pleasure."

Though the distance does not appear far, Mario Puig traveled a long way to get to Ybor Square. He was born across the street in 1907, the son of a Cuban cigarmaker, and at 14 entered the cigar business. He worked six and one-half days a week as an apprentice, without pay, cleaning the spittoons and toilets and sweeping the floor.

"They stingy," he said. "When they pass the minimum wage, 40 cents an hour, the manufacturer abolished the apprenticeship. See how stingy they were? Because of that nobody has learned the cigar business here in 45 years. All old men now."

For about 20 years, Mario said he could not get a job in the cigar business because he was a union organizer. "Those that tried to organize, they cut your head off," he said. While his head was "cut off," he became a sanitation worker. When Ybor Square opened up in the mid-1970s, a project to revive at least for tourists the old flavor of Ybor City, Puig came in with his buckeye. In 1979 he had five helpers. The youngest was 70; the oldest, 83.

"But Ybor City ain't like it used to be," he said. Once there were more than 20,000 artisans handrolling cigars in more than 50 factories. Most workers were Cuban or Spanish, but there were Italians and Germans, too. In 1979, there were fewer than 700 cigar workers, most of them employed at a half dozen factories where machines did the work.

Nearly everything has changed. Tampa grew out and around Ybor City. Machines reduced the number of jobs. Urban renewal wiped out some of the old neighborhoods.

Ybor became a typical inner city neighborhood. Revival efforts dug out a toe-hold for the old days, helped by government buildings and housing projects and architectural restrictions. Ybor Square helped and the famed Columbia Restaurant (once called the largest Spanish restaurant in the world by Spain's dictator, Franco) still draws. But a basic ingredient was missing: the swarm of Latins who gave Ybor City such vitality. Without them, the renaissance was a facade erected for tourists.

Puig sold his home in the old neighborhood and moved to West Tampa in 1961. Ybor City was struggling to hold on to its Hispanic tradition. But he was a romantic; he saw opportunity here.

Puig found prophecy in the tourist popularity of his buckeye. He maintained that handmade cigars and Ybor City could revive together. Government edicts about the dangers of tobacco, the price competition of machine-made cigars, the problems of an inner city neighborhood, faded before the Puig faith in a quality smoke.

He endowed the true cigar smoker with the will to pay high prices for quality, suggested U.S. relations with Cuba could bring new cigar craftsmen to Ybor City and speculated that crowds would follow.

"A cigarsmoker, he is different," Puig said. "A guy came in here from Europe and said he paid $5 for a cigar like I make. A lot of money; but a cigar smoker, he don't give a damn. He pay for the good cigar." Puig calculates with his heart, and lights up.

Sebring

Dust, Noise, Money in Sebring

Allen C. Altvater missed the good old summer doldrums, the years when hot months becalmed Sebring and the pressure was off. Everybody hibernated. Citizens padded barefoot about Lake Jackson and nobody honked a horn or starched a pleat.

There are never any doldrums now. The season never ends. In winter, the population doubles and cars spin around the circle in an unending string. The Tourist Club goes into a shuffleboard frenzy and the traffic down at the shopping plaza jams up trying to wedge onto U.S. 27. But it is also busy in summer.

For more than a half-century, Altvater worked to make Sebring attractive. The boom was a confirmation of his faith. Yet in 1979 he had begun to feel a little overrun by the crowds. Maybe trampled would be a better word. "We have all the necessities of progress now," he said.

Many longtime Floridians in all parts of the state share the pride and conflict he felt. Those who have seen the face and lifestyle of Florida altered so swiftly worry whether they can cope with what might come next. Sebring, a gem-like city in south central Florida, is an example of Florida's No. 1 dilemma. It wants to grow and fears to change.

Like so many Florida towns, it began with one man's dream. George E. Sebring, a onetime Salvation Army bandmaster and china manufacturer from Ohio, bought 10,000 acres of lakeside wilderness and envisioned a genteel city which would manufacture nothing but oranges, a process "restful and noiseless." In 1911, he laid it out in the fashion of Heliopolis, with streets radiating from a central park like rays from a sun.

Four years later, while the dream was still raw and fresh, Altvater arrived as a teenager from Indiana. By then, the town had maybe 600 residents and Sebring, with his son Orval, was calling it a "City of Smiles."

With his brothers, Sebring earlier had joined in founding one town bearing their name in Ohio. The real estate blurbs hailed this new town, George's own creation, as "The Consummation of An Idea." He wanted preachers and professors and solid citizens but no saloons (land deeds specified this). It was, the blurbs continued, "The Highest Class Proposition in Florida."

By 1920, Sebring had 900 residents. The Boom sounded and the figure rose to 7,000 in five years. Then the Depression came along, said Altvater, in "a creeping paralysis" that introduced a thread of insecurity that never left anyone who saw it. Sebring, with its own utilities plant, fared better than most Florida towns but afterward the dream was forever affected.

Altvater, 81 then, was one of the few left who had been around since the beginning. "The old man (Sebring) wanted a place that would be high-toned but not snobbish, a cultural center," said Altvater. "He gave land to any church that would build. We've still got more churches for a town this size than you'll find anywhere else."

Altvater himself was a cog in the creation. He had been city manager, fire chief, director of the air terminal where the Sebring sports car race is held, worked with the Chamber of Commerce, the historical society, was involved in every new town project. Around town, they say he never turned down a job that would help Sebring.

"Now we've outgrown just about everything that George Sebring had in mind," said Altvater. He knows, however, that Sebring had an impossible dream. It was like a childhood. The Sebring ads advised, "If you want activity...the dust and noise of making money...do not come to Sebring...."

Nobody seriously objects to that kind of thing any more. The irritation disappeared with the summer doldrums. The oldtime easy grace, the measured pace and serenity, have blended with the dust and noise into the crowds.

A great levelling has taken place. The necessities of progress dominate. The difficult goal of the community was to remain Sebring's town but to underpin the tourism and retirement appeal with clean industry and flourishing businesses that would support a year-round community. In Florida, that was the dominant municipal dream.

"We want to retain the charm and uniqueness that was always here," said Betty Neale, executive director of the Greater Sebring Chamber of Commerce. "But in terms of growth, we're where it's happening and we have to face it. One-half of our high school graduates now have no local job possibilities. We want enough light industry to give them the option of staying at home."

Altvater understood all this perfectly well, perhaps better than anyone else. Florida would grow. It was natural and proper, even if uncomfortable. "A person can't help where he was born," he said. "Don't hold that against him. But when he reaches the age of reason, if he doesn't move to Florida, it's his own fault."

His response was to go down to the boathouse and talk to his little dog, Josie, as he hand-assembled on his old Multigraph, letter by letter, another illumination of the past for the Sebring Historical Society.

While birds splashed in Lake Jackson, and the crowds buzzed down U.S. 27, he mused about how little boys and little towns grow up in surprising ways. "I guess we were pioneers," he said. "But we didn't feel like pioneers. I liked it."

Collier County ★

Corkscrew:
The Cutlips' Camelot

Jerry Cutlip lived in a swamp and considered it Camelot. The natural order, the delicacy and complexity and quietly logical savagery, so bewitched him that the whole of it defied accounting. Corkscrew Swamp gathers a thousand small mysteries into a single big one. Only with imagination can you sense its magnitude.

Inside this sanctuary, Cutlip and his wife raised two children, so steeped them in the priorities of nature that he sometimes wondered whether he had been wise. For the young Cutlips, Camelot had become the way life ought to be.

At sunset, Jerry and his 13-year-old son would walk a mile along a boardwalk through the swamp to the observation tower. Coming back, they might see huge flocks of white ibis flying just over their heads, maybe 500 of them. The boy would get so excited that he ran to get his mother and sister.

Jerry took the children fishing. The girl, 11, sat on the jeep and studied the scene around her. She watched an alligator slide across a pond, clamp his huge jaws on a turtle. She heard the crunching as the alligator ate.

The children saw the wood storks nest in bald cypress trees 500 years old, watched the new life hatch out. They saw the young ones bumping and crowding each other in the nest, awkwardly learning to fly, struggling into the air, crashing into trees, falling back into the nest on top of each other. They saw alligators posted silently in the water under the nests, waiting for the little birds to fall. They saw young ones test themselves, gain confidence and do crazy things, loops and rolls. Finally, they saw the new skills combine with experience to produce the mature, graceful wood stork.

The children learned about the natural forces. They watched flocks of birds circle on the rising thermal currents out of the swamp, going up almost out of sight, and then gliding to their feeding places. They saw a hawk eat a snake, a snake eat a frog, a frog eat an insect. They saw the egret stalking through the black swamp water, freezing before a twitch of life, knowing that if it is to eat, it must stab that twitch before it can escape.

They saw their father pick up a diamondback rattler, swollen with a rabbit dinner, sluggish and vulnerable, and move it out of the parking lot safely back into the swamp. They saw an otter playing on the boardwalk, raccoons scavenging through the garbage cans, on rare occasions a bobcat sneaking through the edge of the yard. They knew about deer, bears, panthers. They knew that the black swamp water, so mysterious and chilling to some, was a clear, harmless, weak leaf tea. But they knew cottonmouths like it, too, and leeches.

From Cutlip, they heard about the 13 plant communities found in the 11,000 acres of swamp, the lettuce lakes, the pond apples, the ghost orchids, the incredibly huge virgin cypresses that were already 300 years old when the United States became a nation. They heard their father discuss the probabilities of what might be here in another 500 years.

Television did not entertain them as much as it did most kids their age. They rarely watched it. Besides their absorption with the life processes of the swamp , they talked a lot, read a lot, worked at projects. The boy read five Shakespearean plays. They went to school in Immokalee, where their mother taught the first grade. "I don't mean to suggest that they are exceptional students, because I don't think they are," Cutlip said. "But their ideas about life might be exceptional."

Would these special beginnings nurture and strengthen them for the life outside, or so sensitize their appreciations and expectations that encountering a crazily disordered world might overwhelm them? That was a question Cutlip pondered in 1980.

"I don't know. It concerns me a little bit, and I don't push it on them," Cutlip said. "But it's here and they're exposed to it and they appreciate it. It's something that happens. This environment is almost a Camelot. It has problems, but it comes close. They're seeing things and understanding things every day that a lot of the people in the world do not have the vaguest idea even exist.''

The National Audubon Society first became concerned with the swamp in 1912, when it posted wardens to stop hunters from killing the birds for their plumes. A quarter-century ago, the society began to buy the 11,000 acres and it maintained them as a sanctuary where the public (adult admission, $3) would sample the terrain (via a mile-long boardwalk and observation tower) that once was accessible only to the most intrepid. A small commune of National Audubon naturalists and their families, including superintendent Cutlip, lived inside the sanctuary boundaries.

The swamp is located in Collier County, on State Road 846 between Immokalee and Bonita Springs, and open daily. But only 36,000 visitors a year come to see this marvel, the Cutlip children's Camelot. On most days, Disney World greets more than that by noon.

The Cutlips are from West Virginia. He went to Marshall University there, joined the National Audubon Society about the time his son was born. He first managed a small sanctuary in New Hampshire, then came here in 1971 while the children were still toddlers.

Among the fascinating things about the swamp sanctuary are the visitors. The mystery of the swamp awes them. Some have a deeply emotional reaction. "Sometimes they'll just lean their head up against one of those 500-year-old cypress trees, and tears'll come into their eyes," Cutlip said. Others are less impressed. One man dropped a note into the contribution box that said, "Donation, hell. You ought to pay people to walk through this slop."

Most of the visitors come from an urban environment. "They are absolutely lost. The whole experience is new. It is not meaningful until we tell them about it, show them how to look," Cutlip said. "They'll walk right by an alligator and not see it. They'll walk directly under the wood stork colony and ask where all the birds are.

"That is part of the natural order, too. In the city, they'd have to teach me. They'd see things I don't." He thought for a minute.

"That's what I mean about the kids. I don't know whether this gets them ready for the disorder and the heartache they'll have to confront some day. I have argued with myself about it."

Cutlip resolved his argument by revising the definition of Camelot. He has decided it need not be just a fleeting bit of time passed in a place of near perfection; it also can be a way, a positive insight, that continues. He does not know yet whether he is right about this, but he is betting the best part of his life on it.

Belle Glade

Into The Migrant Stream, And Out

Wiley Billups was born on a tenant farm in the Mississippi Delta during the Depression. His mother and father sharecropped cotton, and their five children grew up working. "I went to school some, Wiley said, "but not much."

At eight, he learned to drive a tractor. At 10 he drove as well as a man and got a steady job paying a man's wage, $2.50 a day, but there his progress stopped. At 19 he still drove a tractor and did farm chores and he was restless.

"In winter time, there was nothing to do," he said. "Used to snow a lot up there. Me and a bunch of boys got together and decided to come to Florida. Everybody talked like money was growing on trees in Florida. Thought I'd come down and see.

"A bus came to Greenville every year to get workers. Picked 'em up around the fields and all. We got on that bus and it brought us down to Apopka. We cut celery there for a couple of weeks and then moved on here to Belle Glade and worked until the season ended. Then we went back to Mississippi."

Wiley Billups had entered the migrant stream, that current of seasonal workers that follows the crops and the sun and the harvesting jobs. At this point, he seemed as typical as thousands before him. Most would drift into The Stream, get entangled and never get out. Their misery was an old and continuing story.

Wiley followed the crops four years, until the winter of 1960, but there was something different about him. He made a complex dilemma sound simple. "I just got tired of going up and down the road," he said. "It's a hard life. You get a job, and if it rains, you don't work. If the crop runs out, you move on. Piece work don't last, but the money looks good. That's the temptation. Up the road I'd make $11 or $12 a day. If I took permanent work, maybe I could get $6 or $7."

Still single, not yet entrapped by the debts that almost inevitably burden most migrants and lead them to despair, alienation and fatalism, he decided to break away.

He was working in 1960 at the Duda Farms in Belle Glade, just off the southern shores of Lake Okeechobee, an area famed for its black mucklands and winter vegetable crop. He went to harvesting manager Alton Long.

"I just told Mr. Alton I was tired of the road, and asked him if I could get permanent work. He said he would give me a job. I didn't even ask him what it was. When you're looking for a job, you don't push it. You take what there is," Wiley said.

While $12-a-day migrant work was available up the road, Wiley took on field work at $7 a day. With that, the deadend that had faced him since age 10 began to change. He did whatever came up. The pay and work was steady and Wiley was able to send money back home to his widowed mother in Mississippi.

Five years later, in 1965, he met and married Delores. New ambition flared. He decided there might be a better future in sugarcane. This time he approached Ed Duda, a grandson of the original Duda, who was then in charge of sugarcane at the family's Belle Glade farms.

"Mr. Ed told me he didn't have nothing. I told him I wanted a chance, anything. I think it kind of surprised him. He said there wasn't nothing but hoeing cane. That's mean work. The cane's up about four or five feet high and it's August and you get cut and scratched and hot and it wears you out.

"Most of the men who stay and do that are older, maybe 50 or 60. They're the only ones willing to do it. Can't hardly find no young man to do no hard work. I don't know whether it's the work getting harder or the people getting sorrier. But I took it. I think that impressed Mr. Ed."

In another five years, Wiley was field foreman; in four more years, field supervisor; then, a crop superintendent. With the help of five to eight men, plus the use of planes and a variety of machinery, he supervised the growing of 3,000 acres of sugarcane. Imported labor, much of it from the Caribbean, did the harvesting.

"I got a real job now," Wiley said in 1978. At age 41, he had a son, 2, a daughter, 6, owned a home in Belle Glade, had a solid position with bonus incentives based on production (in a good year, his salary reached $17,000) and, perhaps more important, still retained faith that hard work brings rewards. He has come a long way from the Mississippi mud.

Some may argue that Wiley simply was lucky to avoid the entrapment of The Stream, and that could be so. Some might view him as an exceptional worker, not an example, and that too could be so. It is a point that can be argued endlessly if each migrant success story becomes by definition a special case.

Wiley laughed at the idea. Experience persuaded him otherwise. He saw himself as an average man who learned early the realities of life. The most unusual thing about him was his commitment to that belief, that if you work steady, you eat; and if you work harder, you eat better.

Lucky? He was a black boy in Mississippi before anyone there ever heard of the civil rights movement; he was a sharecropper's son who rarely saw a school; he was doing a man's work at age 10. Exceptional? After four years of seasonal work he had to take the meanest job on the farm, at a pay cut, to prove himself worthy of permanent employment.

"Most of the boys I come down here with from Mississippi are still on the road," he said. "Some of 'em had a chance and just didn't take it. Some of 'em took it, and then blew it. Some of 'em turned out to be wineheads. How come I didn't? I don't know — I think about that a lot. But I know this: it ain't always what you got, it's what you do with it."

White Springs

Will McLean:
Black Hat Troubadour

The tales about Will McLean began to take on giant proportion back in 1961 when he rolled up to the Florida Folk Festival at White Springs driving a black hearse. He wore a black frock-tailed coat and tipped a black wide-brimmed hat to the ladies.

His funeral air softened to melancholy poetry when he put a harmonica to his mouth and made near orchestral sounds come out, when he picked a guitar, when he sang quiet songs about the primitive side of Florida and when he whistled like a bobwhite schooled at Juilliard.

After the sun went down, the pace became more lively and the black garb became less noticeable. The legend-building continued with Will McLean at frolic, where his unusual dimensions of character were a match for his music.

Since then he has managed to widen the eyes of many a Floridian and become a colorful and contributive piece in this state's mosaic. He has roamed the state for more than 30 years as "The Black Hat Troubadour," written the book *Florida Sand,* composed more than 1,400 songs, performed at Carnegie Hall with Pete Seeger, heard his music sung on national television and been the subject of an hour-long educational TV special.

Few who follow the folk side of Florida have not encountered him. Many have learned to love him — for his music, his sense of humanity and for the foibles that enrich his story with contrast.

"I'm not trying to do anything," Will always said. He is a tall, heavy man with sand-colored hair who was born near Chipley in the Florida Panhandle. "Just going along, where the wind blows me.

I'm not interested in protests or crusades. I just want to tell about this land of flowers. That's my thing. I live by my feelings."

A man with such sensitive and honest instincts, with an inborn Baptist conscience that plays counterpoint to his Bohemian bent, one with such creative friends, takes a chance when they all get together at a state-owned Stephen Foster Center or at other folk and bluegrass events around Florida. The center is located along the Suwannee River at White Springs about 20 air miles from Georgia.

One special session of his folk music clan was held in 1978 just to honor Will. He had announced he would donate his collection of Florida folklore, music and books to the state for housing at the center, but that was not the reason. It was the week of Will's 59th birthday, but that was not it either. Neither was it a warmup for the annual Folk Festival held here each May. They just wanted to celebrate Will.

The friends met at the amphitheater among the tall pines on a pleasantly cloudy day to rib him and revere him, to sing McLean songs and tell McLean stories. Will came in a somber black suit and open-collared yellow shirt. With dignified manner he set up a folding chair to monitor the praise and dampen the playful slander.

"Cousin" Thelma Boltin, director of the Florida Folk Festival, set the mood. "How wonderful it is to know him," she said. "Will is full of music. He's like Stephen Foster," Smiling all the while, Cousin Thelma abbreviated the comparison before it reached Foster's fondness for booze. "That's Will, and we love him," she said.

Gamble Rogers, one of Florida's first-rank folk-bluegrass entertainers and a McLean disciple, paid tribute. "Will's a man who somehow managed to live in this complicated world and retain the spirit of a poet," he said. Then he exacted his price.

"Will always told me it was pretty quiet up in Chipley. The Chipola River runs through there, but it only runs two days a week.... Will says he grew up in hard times. Everybody used to have their coffee grounds about a month and then they'd bleach 'em white and eat 'em for grits.... People up there used to put fertilizer around the telephone poles to talk over the wires."

Dan Tillinghast of North Carolina recalled putting a song on paper for Will who, his friend C.P. Heaton explained, "knows just enough formal music so that it doesn't get in the way of his playing." Tillinghast wrote down the notes and Will did the words. Pretty soon he asked, "Dan, how do you spell keerless?" Tillinghast spelled careless for him. "Not careless," McLean said. "Keerless." Will always demanded authenticity.

The song was *Wild Hog,* one of his selections for the Carnegie Hall performance. "A critic for one of the New York dailies wrote that this song was an allegory about man's quest to push back the margins of the frontier...and the mythic beast...was in effect a symbol like that of *Moby Dick* or William Faulkner's *Bear,*" Gamble Rogers said. Asked about that, Will replied, "Aw, naw, Gam. It's just a story about a big hog."

Don Grooms, a University of Florida journalism professor and musician-composer whom McLean calls "Florida's best," noted the donation of papers with a word of caution. "He gave me his papers once too," Grooms said, "but then he came back and got 'em. He'll give you anything he's got but next day he's liable to be back after it." Grooms, one-quarter Cherokee, used Indian symbolism to describe his regard for McLean. "To me, he's an eagle."

"Will always had quite a time keeping his guitars," Heaton said. Heaton is a Jacksonville educator and the man who first put McLean's songs on paper. "He was forever hocking them in the old days." Once McLean hocked and lost a guitar given him by Pete Seeger.

Will McLean endured all the praise and selected insult with the tolerant smile of a patient shepherd, and answered in just the way his friends hoped. With harmonica and guitar, he and Grooms became a White Springs Symphony, a pair of folk music blood brothers nourishing their souls by performing their own music for people who understood it. "When I'm playing a club," Grooms had said, "and someone asks me to do *Lucille,* I tell him to put a quarter in the jukebox. That's not my music."

McLean closed the day alone, with that special strain of quiet musical melancholy whose beauty does not have standard commercial quality. It requires listening, not the snapping of fingers or clapping of hands, and does not tolerate accompaniment by babble. Under the pines where there was no such disruption, Will — a burly yet somehow fragile poet of the backwoods who thinks life should be appreciated, not pursued — in his husky voice sang *If Your Wings Be Broken*. His friends knew they had been topped.

Jasper

Mysteries: Sons and Pine Trees

The longer Oliver Hunter lived the more his answers seemed to wear out. He grew up in the north Florida woods, a turpentining man, and the mystery of life grew with him. Two of the things he knew and loved best, pine trees and his sons, always puzzled him.

He had 7,000 pine trees and two sons and he did not profess to know absolutely what to expect from any of them. "You can't tell," he said, "You have to wait and see."

Hunter lived on a dirt road that trailed off the old Woodpecker route outside of Jasper, a few miles south of the Georgia line in Hamilton County. To get there you turned down a dirt road by a tobacco barn, past pine trees gashed to drip resin, between split-rail fences to a comfortable brick home set on 700 acres. His and his wife's families had lived in the area for more than 100 years.

Hunter, wearing a Mack cap and Sears overalls, tended his fireplace one cold January morning in 1980. His wife, a teacher, had driven the school bus to work. He spent the day repairing fences and checking his cattle. He talked about the good deer hunting on his place and how his dogs sometimes disappeared. (He thinks maybe alligators got them when they went down to drink at the Suwannee River, which flows through his place.) He told about giant rattlesnakes and how his Daddy used to refuse to buy land if there was not enough easily available heart pine timber on it to put up split-rail fences.

But mostly he talked about the mystery in life, how the turpentining business he loved all but disappeared, how educational emphasis and poverty programs nearly eliminated the pride and satisfaction in manual labor. He spoke carefully and intelligently, reacting to experience.

"I love turpentining," he said. "I can't explain why, but I love it. I started out when I was 8 years old, quit school in the third grade. I knew it all. My Daddy and uncles taught me to turpentine. I can remember loading them big old barrels of resin, some of them weighed 600 pounds, on the back of a wagon by myself. We'd put poles to the wagon and I'd roll the barrels up those poles. Sometimes the ground would be so slippery with pine needles that I'd take off my shoes so I could dig my toes in the dirt to get better traction."

He remembered the old turpentine stills, the camps filled with workers. "They'd get up every morning and build a fire. Summer or winter, they'd build a fire. And they'd sing. They'd make up a song for anything. I've seen 'em turn those old barrels bottom up and beat on 'em with tree limbs and make music." Each time a worker "faced" a tree, he would sing out his number to a man with a tally book. Workers got paid by how they produced.

Those were the days when turpentining was one of Florida's leading industries. There were turpentine camps all across North Florida, most self-contained units deep in the woods with their own company facilities: a commissary, maybe a chapel and sometimes an entertainment outlet, called a jook joint.

Not only did that old paternalistic system become unecomonic, but abuses in some camps became a scandal. In some, the state leased convicts for labor at the rate of $26.50 per man per year. "Repulsively medieval," author Stetson Kennedy called them. Cases of debt-peonage became common. One worker explained: "Turpentining ain't something you get into; it's something you get out of."

Time passed the old turpentiners by as harvesting methods improved, chemical substitutes took the edge off demand, workers left the farms in the mass migration to cities, the demand for higher wages and better working conditions joined with higher ceilings on welfare assistance to squeeze out the old system.

Hunter held out. He believed turpentining was a good business and that good money could be made at it. He cited the figures and made a convincing case. But he no longer could do the work himself because of high blood pressure and diabetes. Though he offered workers a 50-50 share, with him providing the trees and equipment, few wanted the work.

"To think back and look at the changes that have happened, a person can't visualize what it's going to be like 10 years from now," he said, a bit apprehensively. "Different ideas, different attitudes, they change our lives.

"I was the youngest of 11 head in my family. All of us worked. Each time one left, my name was called that much more often. But today, you just don't know. There's no way to tell. My older boy, he's a hard worker and he loves it here on this place. He will stay and work. We're fixing up my Daddy's old home for him and his wife."

"My younger boy, that's something else. If I asked him to bring in a piece of wood for the fire, he'd think that was the awfullest thing in the world. Yet he wants to go to college and I'll send him as long as he doesn't go to finagling on me, partying all the time." He thought for a moment, and smiled. "I'm just proud I didn't have the temptations these kids do. No telling what I'd a done."

Hunter, an old-fashioned man, intuitively mistrusted a life not based on hard work. Anything else seemed too hit-and-miss. "People gotten to be just like trees. No way to tell. These days, this little spindly one might produce better than this big heavy one. You can raise 'em up, side by side, and one will and one won't. There's no accounting for the difference. It's something inside."

It was a puzzling thing, a mystery. At 52, like many of us, he understood more and felt like he knew less.

★ *Broward County*

Anne Kolb: In Memory

The angry lady of Broward County, Anne Kolb, sat on her living room sofa in a pink robe and spoke softly. She had been out of the fight, distracted by a more personal issue of survival, and it had opened a distance between her and the anger.

With Anne Kolb, the trouble nearly always began because she loved this swatch of South Florida, Broward County, for itself: for its climate and easy style, for its trees, beaches, birds, swamps, even for its role as a kind of ocean which collected and held unending rivers of people.

Those rivers brought an average of 35,000 new residents each year to Broward County, the highest number for any county in Florida, and the surest route to wealth was selling them a place to live.

Kolb understood the natural pull of that market and did not argue with it, though some of her political enemies thought she did. She did not fight the numbers; she fought the high cost of the way the county was exploited to make them pay off.

She did not use the word, but her anger boiled because so many wanted to make a whore out of the land. They would use up its beauty and trample its dignity and destroy life-nourishing qualities to keep the dollars flowing and never worry about tomorrow.

With Kolb, early in 1980 a 47-year-old mother of three and wife, the feistiest of the Broward County Commissioners, it was a crusade; for some others it was a charade. She called commission meetings a convening of Developerville. She loved politics.

On this crisp winter day at her home in Plantation, she was pale but charmingly frank about the major surgery she had Christmas Eve. One day earlier, when I called, she had apologized that she did not feel like talking. "You know how it is with chemotherapy," she explained. "Some days it is very hard." But now she said in good humor, "I should have put on a wig. I'm losing my hair."

She came here in 1954 from St. Louis, when the county population was 200,000 and almost anyone could drive to work in 15 minutes, walk almost any street at night without fear, be kind to strangers without risk of being conned. Wealth, or lack of it, was not a social barrier.

Now there are more than a million. The county begins at the ocean in high-rise opulence, moves west through one-time affluent zones spotted with decay and continues through new towns growing old too soon to frontiers where the Everglades laps at front yards. Its rate of crime draws prominent national ranking, the traffic is Florida's worst, the cost of living soars, wealth has erected privacy barriers for protection and the path up and down the social ladder has pecuniary obstacles — and yet it was the single most popular place in Florida for new residents.

"It really breaks my heart to see what's happened," Anne Kolb said. "It's still a beautiful place, but it's growing so fast. It's so wild, so undisciplined. The developers and their supporters want all this density and all this growth but they don't know what to do when they get it. They don't know how to make a big metropolis operate."

Sometimes, density begins to sound like a profane word. "I'm going to write a book," she said wryly. "Call it *Up The Density*. They amend the county land use plan to add another development and by magic we are expected to widen roads, produce buses, produce schools and all the stuff needed out of thin air. The problem is not just money. It's old attitudes and philosophies."

She cited public transit. Broward County then had 125 buses for public transportation; Dade County had about 600. She said 60,000 Broward Countians worked in Palm Beach and they commuted by car, usually one to a car. Adding Dade Countians who work in Broward, and Palm Beach Countians who work in Broward, she estimated the three-county daily criss-cross at nearly 200,000. She had long advocated a three-county transportation system, which resulted in appointment to Gov. Bob Graham's transportation committee.

She urged higher city and county standards on development that would anticipate and prepare for such things. "The way it is now, the system invites graft, corruption, manipulation and the whole thing," she said.

She lamented a political situation in which some politicians figuratively "get away with murder" in their association with vested interests. She was distressed that young politicians were so pressured by special interest that they confused these with the public interest. She wished the process produced opposing philosophies rather than carbon copies.

She called it a tragedy that Broward continued to spread west toward the Everglades, toward critical water recharge and conservation areas rather than revitalizing and redeveloping inland areas of higher elevation originally developed. "They keep wanting to develop our flood plain. In the last heavy rain, the whole thing was under water. The health department makes them put 9 to 10 feet of fill at the house and so the rains leave the houses sticking up and everything around them — roads and everything — under water. But they keep insisting on putting people out there. And they keep amending the land plan to reduce industrial space because residential land is more valuable speculatively. In 20 years, there won't be any space left for industry that we need."

Above all, she fretted because the county did not appreciate and respect itself.

As she talked, there was a kind of desperation about Anne Kolb. "So many people don't know. They don't know about our vegetation, about our wildlife. They couldn't tell you an egret from a robin. They don't know about flood plains or water problems. To them, if there's undeveloped acreage out there in the water recharge area, why not develop it?"

Audiences responded well to her. Even as a minority voice on most development issues, she had an established reputation as one of the county's most popular politicians.

Enveloped in her pink robe and her troubled, beloved county, she pondered it all and a hint of the angry lady showed in a frustrated question: "How can we educate 35,000 newcomers at a time?" She was a lady who should be remembered.

Sanibel ★

The Father of the Sanibel Bridge

Hugo Lindgren had the instincts of a pioneer promoter. He missed being a hero by less than 50 years. He was the kind of man who built and shaped, who altered history by jumping into it and personally steering a new direction.

By inclination, at least, he belonged in the company of such men as Hamilton Disston and Henry Flagler, those giants of Florida's last century. Disston dredged and drained swamps, made them livable and salable. Flagler pounded railroad beds across scrub sands and sent trains howling down a peninsula wilderness. Disston and Flagler profited hugely from their pioneering, yet were hailed as saviors.

But Lindgren had the bad luck to bob up after World War II, after the stampede had started. By the time he truly began to wrestle with Florida — the early '60s — the frontier had been trampled thin. A reverse thing had started, the age of the environmentalist.

Bird-watchers grew muscles and changed from scattered oddballs into an army of naturalists — the new saviors — protectors of the earth whose wrath made politicians blanch. Pioneer promoters went out of style; wetlands and scrub jays and skinks were in.

Just as all this was beginning, Lindgren made his place in Florida history. Pioneering on a smaller scale but in the tradition of Disston and Flagler, he personally changed the twin gulf islands of Sanibel and Captiva more than anyone else has since Ponce De Leon blundered onto them in 1513.

Lindgren conceived the causeway that in 1963 gave the public easy access to the islands. He paid for early proof of its practicality and compelled, with influence, its construction. He did it for the revered American profit motive that to him (and to many others) fuels political democracy and parallels patriotism.

Environmentalists raged against him, but their numbers then were few. Businessmen scoffed that it would be a bridge to nowhere. But Lindgren campaigned and gathered help and prevailed.

His achievement initiated an immense controversy. It set up a nationally debated test case of developers vs. naturalists and created a city founded on the naturalists' position. Politics there became a simple head-butting of philosophies.

But Lindgren did not like to talk about it. He remembered well the old uproar, the sleepless nights, the lawsuits, the surprise, the hurt. In 1980, he was trying to live quietly in his home at Fort Myers and forget all that.

For three years, I had tried to meet and talk with him about the Sanibel bridge. I called, I wrote, and always he declined by explaining how the subject pained him and his family. Finally, this time, he agreed to discuss it as a matter for history.

He was a tall gentleman in his 70s with a pleasant Swedish accent and a tentative manner until he seized upon a subject. Then he split it open with flat, edged description. "You would not believe what they said about me," he said. "I felt like a wounded dog that someone had tried to kill."

He studied you as he might study a blueprint, watching the eyes, listening to the words, assessing the attitude, asking questions. The thin, straight hair combed down and forward gave him the look of a shy Caesar peering through glasses to see whether this was Antony or Brutus.

He talked about the folly of trying to hold back change and progress. He confessed he did not understand "these people who want to keep things as they are." He compared them to children who did not wish to grow up. Lindgren described lovingly most things new — nice restaurants, big buildings, pretty golf courses, achievements that bring convenience and comfort.

He argued that now the public can enjoy the islands, that the bridge makes money with its tolls, that the state has benefited from the islands' tourism appeal, that the old islanders themselves who fought him so bitterly have profited well, as he has. "The bridge was a good thing. A service. I am happy about it," he said.

While still young, Lindgren left a small village in Sweden, came to the United States and found work in a Jamestown, N.Y., furniture factory. His qualities showed early. Soon he began his own factory, manufacturing metal cabinets. He prospered.

The Lindgrens visited Florida, began to look for investments. He bought a large tract of land on Sanibel, an island in the Gulf just off Fort Myers, and then wondered whether he had made a mistake. It was a remote place reached only by ferry or boat. "Who would want to buy such land?" he asked. "I thought about it, and the idea of a bridge came to me."

Lindgren personally paid for feasibility studies and engineering plans, guided it through state and Lee County political and legal tangles, donated the bridge landing on the island side and a site for the Sanibel-Captiva Chamber of Commerce, lobbied the state to pave a 5-mile mainland approach and nursed a revenue bonds strategy that would pay for this whole thing with $3 bridge tolls.

"The bridge was a bargain," he said. "Not a nickel of county taxes went into it."

The bridge opened May 26, 1963, to island hideaways renowned for leisurely lifestyle and serenity to those hardy enough to endure the inconveniences. A few escapist seasonal visitors and tourists mingled with perhaps 250 permanent residents. Lindgren helped bring water to the islands and built their first sewage treatment plant.

The islands became luxury resorts with condominiums, motels, nice restaurants and shops, golf courses, tennis courts, marinas. The old serenity was traded for comfort. Environmentalists mourn that population pressures have degraded the fragile natural systems, forced them into a decline that will get worse. Developers clamor for more building permits.

Lindgren spent a lot of money to bring the bridge to Sanibel, and he made a lot of money because of it. That this should outrage anyone puzzled him, hurt his pride. "Can you imagine what Sanibel would be without the bridge?" he asked.

Cross City

Everything's OK In Cross City

The editor of The Dixie County Advocate, O.K. Jones, was explaining himself. "Yes, I'm the editor, but I'm not a newspaperman," he said. The office door, without screen, stood open to all of Cross City.

The Advocate office had a look of creative ease, comfortably full of small machines and tables and desks. One wall was lined with pigeon-holes stuffed full of papers. To complete the picture, O.K. should have worn a green eyeshade, but that was another journalism tradition he did not honor.

A patch of wires spread across the ceiling and trailed down the walls behind cabinets. "Don't look up," Jones said, laughing. "It might fall on you. We were thinking about bringing that ceiling down a little, but somebody might think I was making too much money if I did that. Doesn't pay to look too prosperous."

On Fridays, O.K. Jones takes it easy. The other days are not bad, either. Some weekly editors in rural communities literally work themselves to death. Jones, 59 when I talked with him in 1980, avoided that. The Advocate appears each Thursday without a lot of sweat and strain.

"I knew how to organize before I got into this business," he explained. He had four assistants, including son Skipper, who concentrated their work on the first four days of the week. "I think I can sit around and watch things and keep it going, and do better than jumping in and trying to be a part of it. I'd only get in the way."

Eighteen years earlier, after a job as a Standard Oil agent withered away before consolidation of service routes, he walked into The Advocate office and offered to buy it. "Looked like a business I could handle. The sheriff owned it. All I really knew

175

about it was that the paper cost a nickel. When I raised it to a dime, nobody complained.''

"What we do is try to get all the local stuff in. That's all," he said. "We stay out of conflicts. We don't do any editorializing. I did at one time. I editorialized about garbage, and I got a little garbage thrown in my yard. I wrote considerably about hunting, and I got a doe (deer) head in the yard. I haven't written too many editorials since then. I got tired of cleaning up the yard.''

O.K. was a friendly, pacific fellow. He believed this Gulf Coast rural county, 80 percent taken up by swamps and timber lands, where Cross City (pop. 2,312) was the only incorporated town with more than 300 population, looked after itself. He did not think it needed an editor to set it straight. "I go to the meetings and sit in there and I don't see them doing anything to get upset about. Those fellows know they're in a small town. Everything they do and say is watched. The auditors check on 'em, too. They can't get away with things. At least I don't think they can.''

Jones took whatever came in the door, and enjoyed it. He made notes on wedding anniversaries and church news, arranged for written accounts of other events to be brought in, exchanged pleasantries with each caller.

The Advocate usually came in two sections, eight to 12 pages each. It was a community billboard. One or two small news stories made page one. The rest of the front and inside filled up with items announcing scheduled events, club and social activities, the minutes of county commission meetings, reports from officials such as State Rep. Gene Hodges, advice on insurance, cooking, Social Security.

Jones composed the ads himself, and there were plenty of them, including all the city's and county's legal advertising. In one issue an "ear" at the top of page one noted. "It brings tears to my eyes to bring to your attention that subscriptions are now due." At the bottom of that page a headline urged, "Get Your Carnival Tickets Early.''

"This community's small enough that we all know each other. Everybody knows everything that's going to be in the paper, but they want to read it anyway, just to be sure. They just let me put it all together for them," he explained. O.K. was like a successful doctor who rarely made house calls. Dixie County brought him its pulse to be felt.

Jones' father was an Alabama sawmiller. The family moved to Perry when O.K. was 5 and, except for a stretch in the Army, O.K. never left this area of Florida. When he bought the paper, the circulation was 350; it rose to 2,150. He had no local competition for advertising. The nearest possibility was a radio station in Chiefland, 21 miles away in Levy County. Daily newspapers from Gainesville, Orlando, Tampa and St. Petersburg sold in coin boxes at businesses along U.S. 19, which served as Cross City's main street.

Since 1970, the Dixie County population had increased by 2,176 persons to a total of 7,656. Eighty per cent of that increase came from migration, people moving in. Among them were 17 Republicans, making a grand total of 29. "We get a bunch coming up this way from Southwest Florida and around Tampa Bay," Jones said. "Funny thing, they haven't changed the county much. They blend in. But in another 10 years, if they keep coming, we'll be different."

Presidential year politics do not rouse The Advocate to any fever of advocacy, but Jones alway looked forward to the campaigns. "It means a big year in advertising," he explained.

The phone rang again. It was his wife. "You are talking direct to the editor," he told her. Lunch was ready. "I will try to break away," he said. He hung up and turned back to the subject of Dixie County journalism.

"One thing I forgot to mention," he added. "I always advise people, when they're talking about weekly newspapers, that the first thing needed in a small town like this is to get yourself a wife who is the postmaster, like mine was. That'll get you through."

O.K. Jones walked out the door, blinked in the sunshine and began to close that open door. He stopped, pushed it back open. "Better not do that," he said. "Might be something in there somebody wants." The editor may be out to lunch, but not The Advocate.

Estero

They Lived Inside The World

For years, Hedwig Michel had been explaining to skeptics, "We are living in the great egg." She never quailed before the burden of being trapped inside there with so many disbelievers. In that gentle, precise, German-accented voice, she sketched out the way toward heaven that Koresh revealed: Give up sex and all worldly goods, and try to understand that we live inside the egg, a finite globe.

Though sex, money and the theories of Copernicus remained popular, she did not let this roil or even distract her. She was a grand, forgiving lady of the Old World. Until her death, she continued to pursue Koreshanity, a Utopian philosophy described as embracing all science and religion. However, in later years she began emphasizing intermediate stages in the route toward heaven that permitted marriage, property and honored women's rights.

Despite what others might see, she always found reasons for optimism. A new membership drive and the opening of the first "season" of the World's College for Life were the reasons at the time I met her in 1980. The college, a hall-library-museum housed in a new, symbolically circular building, was the product of the organization's educational arm, the Pioneer Education Foundation, Inc. Subjects for its workshops varied from conservation, folk art and gardening to Koreshan Unity itself.

Michel understood clearly that most visitors to the Koreshan Center at Estero, on U.S. 41 between Naples and Fort Myers, considered the whole thing at least an oddity. She was remarkably tolerant as she tried to enlighten them with the tale of Koreshanity. It began in 1869 when a New York Baptist, 30-year-old Cyrus Teed, married, father of one son, experienced an "illumination" which he said revealed his divinity. He called it "a spiritual ecstasy." An

178

exquisite woman emerged from a sphere of purple and golden light and told him his mission. He suddenly found he could speak Greek and Hebrew. He changed his name to Koresh, a Biblical version of Cyrus, and Koreshanity began to evolve.

He preached Universology, based on Cellular Cosmogony, which concludes that we do not live on the surface of a world that revolves around the sun in a universe that stretches endlessly outward, as the Polish astronomer Copernicus theorized in 1543. Instead, Teed said, we live on the inner walls of a globe which contains the sun and the stars in its middle. The theory states that the universe and all of us in it are cells within cells within cells.

Skeptics called him a crackpot, a reaction that bedeviled him as he propounded his beliefs in four New York cities without notable success. He moved to Chicago, where he had better luck. He established the first College of Life there and a commune which members could join by pledging celibacy and donating all their worldly goods. The controversial cult grew to nearly 200, was successful enough to attract wide attention, and to inspire several branch operations in other cities. By 1891, Teed was confident enough to predict that within 10 years his system would prevail in the United States. In 1894, the cult moved again, setting up its headquarters, called the New Jerusalem, on land at Estero donated by a disciple.

But attention and success created an opposite force to Koreshan practices. Old accounts of those days mention disgruntled (and disinherited) relatives of commune members, police raids, political troubles stemming from being so messianically purposeful, from the lifestyle, from the religious communism. At one point Teed, described as a short, sturdy man with piercing eyes, a man sometimes accused of using hypnotic influence, was assaulted on the streets of Fort Myers. After he died in 1908, the organization began to flounder.

By the time 40-year-old Hedwig Michel arrived in 1940, a Jewish refugee from the Nazis, there were only 12 celibates left in the Estero commune. The youngest was 57. Michel, grateful for this peculiar haven, became the newest, the youngest and the 13th. A friend in Frankfurt, interested in Teed's theories because they were reminiscent of 18th Century Swedish mystic Emanuel

Swedenborg's similar visionary experience and founding of a new religion, had written a letter to Estero in her behalf. That, plus this climate more suitable for her interest in tropical botany led her here.

In 1961, after having been president of Koreshan Unity for one year, she transferred 305 acres of its land to Florida as Koreshan State Park, where the relics and history of the organization would be preserved. Many interpreted that to mean Koreshanity had ended, but Michel persisted.

She found mention in the charter of three Koreshan orders of ascending status: inquirers, the noninformed who were curious and asked questions; a marital order which belonged but was not required to join the commune and give up sex, wealth and family life; the leadership order, the celibates, the commune members. Until then, she said, only the celibate order had been emphasized. She found further modern appeal in passages that dwelled on equity for women.

To offset the holes that space exploration appeared to be shooting in Cellular Cosmogony (Koresh once had declared the sun was only 4,000 miles away, not 93 million, and the moon only 1,000, not 240,000), she placed more stress on the open, iconoclastic philosophy of Koreshanity.

On these new emphases rested Koreshan hopes for a revival. Michel cited Gerard C. Wertkin, New York City attorney, husband and father, lecturer at the College of Life on the American Utopian Experience, as an example that it was possible. He joined in 1970 as a member of the marital order and she regards him as a significant link to Koreshan beginnings in New York. Wertkin, visiting Estero, said the apparent conflict between Cellular Cosmogony and science did not bother him. "I accept Cellular Cosmogony as a born-again Christian accepts Jesus walking on water," he said.

In 1980, three Koreshan celibates remained in Estero, including Michel. A mailing list of 800 other persons got the Koreshan literature. Among these were the marital and inquirer orders. "But we don't know exactly how many belong to which. Get yourself away from the numbers," she advised. "The thing to remember is that the system is active. The commune is still here. Anyone who wants to join and live in harmony will be placed."

After 111 years, Koreshanity still had a pulse. An elegant old lady out of another world deliberately, confidently nourished it. Science, skeptics, numbers did not cloud her serene sense of the inevitable at work. "It is very complicated. I remember how green I was. I had to walk the road from zero," she said. "Everyone begins in ignorance."

Graceville

Up Yonder, Williamses Call The Roll

*When The Roll Is Called Up Yonder,*it will be a big surprise if there are not a lot of Williamses present. They sing the old hymn as if it were written for them. They pat their feet in the red dirt, tilt back their heads with mouths open wide and belt it out for the Lord. *When The Roll Is Called Up Yonder, I'll Be There.* From them, it sounds like a promise.

On a cool fall day each year, the Williamses hold a family reunion near Graceville, just a loud you-all from Alabama. It is Florida's longest running, most honored family event. If the sociologists who preach doom for the family as a lifestyle ever could attend, they would flat out faint, and revive to the tune of *Love Lifted Me.*

The Williams clan dates its beginning from their early 19th Century patriarch, Andrew Elton Williams, who with two wives (the first died after 10) sired 23 children. By the time those produced 145 grandchildren for him, the seed scattered. Family historians by 1980 were swearing (gol-ding, con-jimn and shoot) the numbers had reached into the neighborhood of 25,000, flung across all 67 Florida counties and the United States and still sprouting.

They gather under the big oaks by the red-brick Galilee Methodist Church, which some of them helped found, next to the cemetery where many of them are buried, and what follows is an orgy of platonic love, enthusiastic praying and no-hold-barred feasting, Panhandle style.

They begin politely enough. They arrive fancied up, most of the ladies in dresses and most of the men in coats and ties, all of them proud to be here and wanting to impress. But pretty soon the formality melts away and they become, as the family describes it, Williamsey.

They hug and kiss everybody in sight at least once. The ladies squeal and the men pound shoulders. They register in the family book, pick up bumper stickers, decals, name tags, subscribe to the family newsletter. The children get a lesson in family history during a guided tour of the cemetery, where the honored ancestors lie.

By midmorning it is time to gather under the open-sided tabernacle, built by the family just for this annual occasion, and used in other days for church socials and as a fresh-air, sand-bottom basketball court. In the tabernacle, the praying and singing and storytelling become serious.

In his invocation, the Rev. Bud Williams of Jacksonville cited the Biblical families of Abraham, Isaac, Jacob and David, and rang in the Williamses at the end. Jimmy Williams paid tribute to the deceased. The Asa Williams family played the guitar, the accordion and led the clan in a swinging version of *Amazing Grace*. Buddy Williams introduced officers of the family organization. D.V. Williams recognized the oldest, youngest, and the most this or that, among the Williamses present.

At the 78th consecutive family reunion, there were six who attended the first. Joe B. Williams spun a tale of old Williamses, of his grandfather, of the patriarch Andrew Elton, of uncles and aunts and cousins. Earl Williams took up a collection, Alton Williams gave the benediction, and all the Williamses sang *God Be With You Till We Meet Again*. Then, hardly taking a breath, D.V. Williams said grace for the coming feast.

All the families had brought covered dish lunches. Strung out on the other side of the church were long tables constructed by stretching wire fence on its side between trees and posts. The ladies threw tablecloths over the wire, and nobody worried about spilling the iced tea.

Sampling the fare was an awesome task. It ranged from cheese sandwiches and pickles through fried chicken, venison, ham, varieties of salads and casseroles and vegetables, assorted pies and cakes. Through the benign intervention of Nellie Wood O'Riordan, the family treasurer from Fort Pierce, we non-Williamses over-ate just as though we belonged.

The 78 family reunions had stretched mostly unchanged through four wars, the Great Depression, the popular arrival of radio, movies, television, the automobile and airplanes. Not even the exploration of outer space altered their celebration of the search for the elemental good that can exist inside one man or woman.

The Williamses tell the same stories, sing the same songs, offer the same prayers, have the same good and wholesome time each year, and it has rained on them only once. Politicians flock to this gathering, just to be seen, hoping some of that family glow will rub off, but they are not allowed to spoil the occasion by speaking.

There have been small upsets. Once, a moonshine still was discovered near the first site, and they moved. Once some children raided the picnic baskets during the praying and singing, and they moved again. Once Gov. Reubin Askew's helicopter set down in a nearby field, spraying dust over the tables. Once a critical situation of form developed because there was a misunderstanding about the difference between a third cousin and a second cousin once removed. Definitions were established and issued. Through all this and more, the Williamses have prayed on, celebrated on, missing neither a kiss nor a bite.

They have become a live memorial to the days when necessity created families, interdependence held them together, and out of it all grew a cementing love. It is different now. The necessity and the interdependence are not so strong, and love therefore has not so fertile a ground.

The Williamses are the biggest family in Florida, a treasure in what they represent, and it seems a pity that no family beginning today has much chance of creating what they have.

Okeechobee

Pogy Bill: Legendary Sheriff

In a cemetery north of Okeechobee, among the flatlands not far from Taylor Creek, the town folk paid their permanent respects to a beloved bootlegger, an old sheriff who became one of Florida's most intriguing legends. His tombstone bears a shiny badge, a ceramic picture and an engraving of the courthouse.

Neither Okeechobee nor the old sheriff, William E. (Pogy Bill) Collins, ever liked to let convention upset the rule of human instincts.

Pogy Bill's life ran over with civic lessons. His 14-year sheriff's career could fill a law enforcement textbook with both do's and don't's. With him, justice never was blind, although it might occasionally sport a black-eye.

Pogy Bill was a Robin Hood who became the sheriff of Nottingham. In hell-raising frontier Okeechobee, he could whip any man. He was a barefooted, cigar-smoking terror until he joined the law. After that, he put on shoes and a white shirt, took a teenaged bride 22 years his junior, and reformed — somewhat.

He became president of the Boy Scouts and lectured youngsters on the evils of tobacco and alcohol but deplored Prohibition laws which denied a man a legal drink. Some say he continued to enjoy a private toot now and then, but many insist he stayed dry.

He came to Okeechobee in 1910, and told everyone he had been born of American parents aboard a ship in an Australian harbor. He joined the catfishermen, considered then to be the wildest element in a town that included cowboys and sawmill workers who would argue the point, and quickly asserted leadership with his fists. Most stories attribute the nickname Pogy Bill to an embarrassing incident as a rookie fisherman when he caught and tried to sell

185

a load of near worthless baitfish, called pogies. Some oldtimers scoff at the suggestion he would have made such a mistake, but they offer no other explanation.

During his rowdiest days, he threw a Circuit Judge into the creek; took over a courtroom and administered mock justice to real defendants, fining each a bottle of booze; befriended children, especially orphans, and the needy; literally knocked the walls off a cypress shanty during one fight; corrected injustices, especially to friends, by making the catfishermen pay handsomely for damages their frequent fights caused.

The good folk of Okeechobee, encouraged by Pogy Bill's sunny side, recruited him for the local police. His benevolent influence won him election as sheriff in 1918 and he held the job until scandal forced his resignation some 14 years later.

Not only did Sheriff Collins take on the job of taming a frontier town in the classic manner of a Matt Dillon or Wyatt Earp, in two years he faced the complicating burdens of being called upon to enforce unpopular Prohibition.

Prohibition, said Pogy Bill, was "the bunk." Moonshining and bootlegging were widespread, and almost everybody knew it. As the Depression hit, many depended upon one or both of them to eat. He could control it, but could not stop it. His law enforcement formula evolved into tolerance for the local entrepreneurs as long as they, as he put it, did not "run wild and try to sell the stuff in the post office."

Bootleggers regularly put illegal booze aboard fast boats in the Bahamas, and ran it into secluded spots along the Florida coast. It became customary to truck it inland to a rail depot like Okeechobee, load the booze inside box-cars that appeared to be stacked with lumber and ship it north. One desirable gambit was to recruit sympathetic local law officers to guard the booze across their jurisdictions to the railroad. If federal agents appeared, the local officers could step in and declare priority.

Pogy Bill's fall came, oldtimers believe, because of the bloody rivalry among bootlegger groups. Late in the 1920s, for example, henchmen of Al Capone approached him for cooperation, and he refused. Some say Bill was under investigaton constantly after that.

In 1929, Pogy Bill and one of his deputies were charged with guarding the road while box-cars were being loaded with booze and lumber. He denied it and accused three witnesses against him of lying. The first trial, in Miami in 1931, ended with a hung jury. The second convicted him on three counts, each carrying two years' imprisonment. He got probation, and resigned as sheriff.

Despite probation, Pogy Bill ran for sheriff again in 1932 and — to his shock — lost. One of his old deputies beat him by three votes. The trials had taken all his money, even his car, and he had campaigned on foot.

Unhappy, he worked briefly in Indiantown, but his statewide reputation rescued him. Frostproof, a citrus community in Polk County, offered him a job as police chief. He served there until February, 1935, when he died of pneumonia after a fire truck overturned in the rain and pinned him underneath.

Although several organizations and individuals vowed to honor him, he lay for 42 years beneath an unmarked cement slab up on Cemetery Road. History buff Gordon Leggett and the Okeechobee County Historical Society stirred memories and corrected that oversight. Among those who responded was the grandson of Pogy Bill's old buddy, neighboring St. Lucie County Sheriff J. R. Merritt. Young Ed Merritt donated the monument.

Legend and time obscure Pogy Bill's full story, but the picture emerges of a humanly flawed man of giant character dimensions. "He was like the old lady's mule," said a lawyer who once represented him. "When he was good, he was mighty good. But when he was bad, he was hell."

Okeechobee understood, and loved him anyway.

Duette

Miss Ada's
One-Room Schoolhouse

Not a single strand of Miss Ada's graying hair was out of place that morning in 1979, and she barely raised her sweet voice two notes on the scale. Maybe from "do" past "re" to "mi", but no more. It was a soothing, commanding tone that banished impish impulses.

"You want to keep your head down a minute?" she asked declaratively. "Your mind not working good? We forget how to act and we have to rest our minds. Put your head down and rest so your mind will work for you. You know, your mind gets tired and you forget what to do."

At the little desks and tables down a long room with shellacked wooden floors, 21 little mops of hair went down. A few eyes peered up furtively at Mrs. Ada Bilbrey, a trim 59-year-old in a red pants suit. Was she angry because they had been talking too much? It was hard to tell.

Miss Ada ruled Florida's only one-room school — one of approximately 1,100 like it in the United States — with loving authority. One room, one teacher: six grades, kindergarten through the fifth. A small stenciled sign, black on white, at the edge of an 11-acre yard identified the schoolhouse.

Duette is an isolated speck on the Manatee County map along SR 62. The highway slices through the farms, cattle ranches and phosphate mines between Bradenton and Wauchula. The school and the Dry Prairie Baptist Church make up the only structural signs of a community.

Duette opened in 1979 with 12 students, the same number it closed with the previous June, but enrollment climbed to 21. One reason was that the fifth grade was added, but the figure always fluctuates with the coming and going of seasonal workers. The fifth grade, for example, tripled one day in February when two new boys showed up. That was only partially and temporarily offset when chicken pox cut kindergarten attendance by half, or one.

Overall, the enrollment trend appeared upward, however, and Miss Ada worried that the school was getting too big for her. "It's grown so," she said. "I have seven in the first grade and seven in the second and it's too much for individualized teaching. To me, five in a grade is ideal, and no more than 15 in all. If we keep growing, I'm going to want another teacher."

The number may seem small but she served as teacher, principal, guidance counsellor, practical nurse and maintenance supervisor as well as coach, umpire and frequently scorekeeper for the kickball game. For assistance she had one teacher's aide plus a cook who prepared hot lunches, including fresh bread, every day in the school kitchen. The children say a blessing before eating.

Arguments that kept Duette going involved distances, the age of the children, local pride and a general belief that the population boom around Bradenton one day would spread east and nudge Duette.

"The nearest other school for these children would be 35 miles away," said Miss Ada. "That is too far. They are so very small. We need the school. For a long time people wouldn't sell any land out here, but they are beginning to sell now. We'll have more and more children."

Other arguments for Duette were less specific, but perhaps stronger. Miss Ada's school represented a faint counterpoint to education which strives for efficiency in learning and elegant book-keeping. In large school systems, with superior facilities and staff and varied student bodies, the proper educational and social diversity are guaranteed.

As desirable as that is, some educators still believe that the benefits of individual attention in a one-room or one-teacher school at the elementary level make it an attractive if not preferable alternative. The different views do not develop into much of a debate, however, because the small school is not considered practical.

Manatee County, for example, then paid about $2,000 per pupil to keep Duette open, as compared to an average in its other schools of $1,200. Beyond that, Duette had no Hispanics enrolled and never had a black student — failing the test of social diversity. "But I assure you that if any lived out here, they would be welcome," Miss Ada said.

Miss Ada, born 18 miles west of here in the community of Parrish, did not attempt to duplicate the program of a larger school. Her work was tailored to Duette. "If we learn to read and write and spell and do arithmetic, then we do other things. We don't have time for everything," she said.

She had been there 25 years and had seen most of her pupils go to work and marry and begin to raise families. In assessment tests, Duette met all state standards, but she had not detected any pattern that proved the school superior by the results of students' work in higher grades. "It's mixed," she said. "Some students have done well, and I'm sorry to say that some have not."

That did not dismay Miss Ada. She did not need statistical reinforcement to continue believing strongly in her work. She was an extension of the family, tutoring the children for life, not just for tests. She imparted basic values with a basic beginning to education.

Miss Ada tried to give her children a sense of individual identity, a sense of responsibility and — most important of all, she thought — love. If they missed some science, or some other subject beyond the financial reach of Duette, she hoped these other things would make up for it.

When her students entered the world of the sixth grade and beyond, the formulas would begin to correct these omissions of diversity, as they should. But once in the crowd, the children might never get the other things unless Miss Ada saw to it.

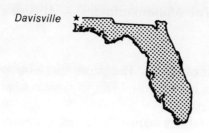

Davisville

Fiddling: Heartbeat of Better Days

Around Davisville, as far west and as far north as you can go in Florida, they value a man who can play the fiddle. A fiddle brings back the old days. It makes a fine party out of the cakewalks, uplifts the square dances, puts spirit into the Wednesday night prayer meetings.

The instrument is a fiddle, not a violin, but the difference is in the player. Genuine freestyle fiddling cannot be gleaned from a book or synthesized with bought lessons. It depends upon blood and experience. At least, that is how they felt about it around Davisville.

Fiddle playing in this part of the south ranks as a kind of folk art, and involves not only a natural ear for music, but a soul-bred conviction that this particular music represents the heartbeat of better days. Done right, the feet will begin to pat, the faces to smile and the hard facts of life will stand aside for defiant celebration. But not many do it right any more.

"It's an inherited thing," said Mike Thomley, who got it from his mother's side of the family. At age 6, his grandfather gave him the family fiddle and a charge to carry on the tradition. "My Daddy, now, he couldn't play nothing. Wasn't in his family," Thomley explained. "Didn't have the blood."

Thomley, a Cracker leprechaun whom I visited in 1980, still remembered the night he got the fiddle. It had belonged to his great-grandfather, too. "Two weeks before Grandpa died, me and him went fishing and we come on back and went to his house for supper. He got out the fiddle and had somebody play *Black-Eyed Susan* for him, and he went to buck-dancing."

191

That is another of the old skills. The music stirs a buck-dancer's emotions, and he moves his body and feet to express what he feels. It can be poetic or athletic.

"Grandpa, he could buck-dance," Thomley continued. "It seems like he could just knock a tune with his feet. He'd go down and bump his knees on the floor, and then he'd just hop out. That night, he got me up there buck-dancing with him. I did the best I could. Later on, he give me the fiddle."

No instructions went with the instrument, which Thomley insisted was a valuable Stradivarius. "I learned it by myself," he said. "I just started in on it. We'd build them old wood fires out in the yard and everybody'd get around and play and I'd watch them. After awhile I'd pick up that old fiddle and begin to seesaw on it. It went on from there to where I'm at now."

Thomley and his fiddle kept alive in its pure form a tradition being diluted by the influences of an array of other amusements for the young. "I'm the onliest fiddler left in Davisville," he said. He played at church, at square dances, folk festivals and family reunions. He played at a series of cakewalks being held to raise money for converting Davisville's old schoolhouse into a community center.

A cakewalk involves a large, numbered circle chalked on the floor. Entrants pay a small fee. When the music starts, the players begin walking around the circle. When it stops, they stop. A number is drawn from a hat. Whoever is standing on that number wins a homemade cake.

Thomley's fiddling draws enthusiasm wherever he goes. "I don't mean to brag on myself, but I've had people tell me that I can just make that fiddle talk," he said. "It ain't fiddling if you can't make it say the words.

"I tune my fiddle to *Cotton-Eyed Joe* for nearly everything I play. I have to let the little string down when I play *One-Eyed Gopher* but outside that I keep it tuned to *Cotton-Eyed Joe*. That's an old-time fiddling piece. "He also likes to play *Leather Britches, Black-Eyed Susan, Going Up Crippled Creek* and *Slow Train Through Arkansas*. "I could get started and keep on fiddling to sunup without repeating myself. And I did, when I was younger," he said.

Thomley learned a new song every time he heard a new one he liked. "I don't know one note from another and I don't want to know," he said. "But if I get a song in my mind, I can play it. I play by ear. It sounds different from playing by notes but lots of folks will tell you they like it better. Seems like it just suits 'em better."

Thomley and his wife were born in Alabama, grew up on farms across the creek from each other, married and moved to Davisville, an unmapped community on SR 97 just south of Atmore, Ala. in 1950. They had six children and a bumper crop of grandchildren.

He worked as a turpentiner and a barber. He started cutting hair when he was 12, and when he began turpentining, took his scissors into the woods with him and gave what he calls "stump" haircuts on his "dinner" hour. Nights, the fiddle made it all seem worthwhile.

"I tell you, it looks like the good Lord's just been blessing me all the way through," he said. "I get down to the church and get to playing that fiddle and the Lord gets to blessing me and cold chills run down my back. I mean, I'm getting some help then."

For Thomley, fiddling not only fulfilled the mission laid on him by his grandfather, but it brought in a little money. "I don't charge the church. That's for free. I'm a deacon," he said. "But I get a few dollars when I go out on something else. I sing a little, too. Have to be careful what I sing though because I ain't got a tooth in my head.

"You hear of anybody needs a fiddler, let me know. But tell 'em I don't play no dirty pieces, them that's got dirty words in 'em. I know some real dirty ones I used to play but I don't do that any more." He chuckled, "Mama always says I'm too plain-spoken."

He had begun fretting over whether it was time for him to pass on the family fiddle, as his grandfather did. It was a problem. There were several fiddlers among the children, who were scattered across the South. Who should get the Stradivarius? All of them wanted it.

"I about decided I ain't going to pass it on to nary a one of them," he said. "When me and Mama die, they're gonna have to fight over it." All of them have the blood, and it grieves him that only one can have the fiddle.

But for Davisville, and all the cakewalkers and buck-dancers and square-dancers, it was a piece of luck. Mike Thomley kept on fiddling, just as long as he could for that defiant celebration.

★ Ft. Lauderdale

The Old Man And
The New River

In Fort Lauderdale in February traffic on the interstate moves like cold molasses. At the beach, hotels stand in line behind the public. Waterways create the variety of old Venice in a youthful ambience. Everything seems a little mixed up, and a little better.

To the West, you can eat Georgia barbecue and smell cows; men wear wide-brimmed hats to keep the sun off. Along the water, it may be crepes and wine and perfume that wreathes bare faces appealing to the sun for a burn.

One late afternoon in 1979 August Burghard sat in his living room at Pinar del Rio, a cloistered patch of houses near downtown, and sipped wine in defiance of his doctor who advised something stronger. He had 27 pine trees in his yard and paintings of snowy egrets on his walls. He was the first lifeguard at the beaches, became a prominent civic figure and the most noted local historian.

He was old Fort Lauderdale but he loved the new. He came from Alabama, met his wife Lois while going to school in Georgia and adopted Fort Lauderdale in 1925. He was a soft-voiced gentleman, and she a gracious lady. Around them swirled a conservative city jammed with swingers from the North foraging for physical delights. The strangers did not know, most of them, what life was like here last week and think history began the day they arrived from Chicago.

Burghard, gentleman that he was, wanted to do something for them. He wanted to sugarcoat a little of old Fort Lauderdale and spoon-feed it to them.

Burghard wanted Fort Lauderdale to put up what he calls a front

194

porch along the New River. It was kind of an old-fashioned idea that would emphasize the special qualties of life here: flavors contradictorily piquant and subtle that require cultivation, like the tastes of shocking kumquats and delicate avocados. To go with the public beaches created long ago by remarkable civic foresight, he wanted a public river front. It was not just a dream. Sentiment for it already fermented among many old-timers, and a legal foundation for it was established more than a half century ago.

"New River is the number-one attraction of Fort Lauderdale," Burghard said. "It represents better than anything else why it all happened. It should be our front porch, not our back door. We need to protect it, beautify it, let people enjoy it. We need a New River Authority to create the means to celebrate it."

New River uniquely explains and nurtures Fort Lauderdale. It begins with sweetwater seeping from the Everglades into a deep channel and flows a winding course through beautiful neighborhoods and under bridges and over the U.S. 1 tunnel to the ocean.

Where the river intersects the Intracoastal Waterway, a traffic cop is needed for the yachts; and it is called the World Crossroads of Pleasure. Everywhere, there is bared flesh bobbing in opulence, golden ones waving to the dryland poor folk. There are tour boats to slake their envy.

At one end, Gov. Napoleon Broward who vowed to drain the Everglades for agriculture and make it another Holland (sometimes, he said Egypt), in 1905 sent dredges to cut a canal through the Everglades, linking New River to Lake Okeechobee. At the other, the opening of Port Everglades in 1928 gave New River for the first time the set of a permanent mouth.

New River historically has fascinated nearly all who saw it. Lawrence Will, the Cracker historian of Lake Okeechobee, called it the deepest river for its length in all of Florida and in typical understatement, "A right pretty stream, for sure." In her *River of Grass,* Marjory Stoneman Douglas spoke of "the lovely river," and its "bright white bottom sands."

Robert (Believe It Or Not) Ripley once cited a legend which told of a river appearing overnight and how Indians called it Himmarshee or New River. (Spoilsports attributed the sudden new river, if that is how it occurred, to the collapse of a limestone crust above an underground stream.)

Along its banks, Major William Lauderdale of Tennessee set up a fort during the Seminole Wars in 1838. Pioneer Frank Stranahan settled there. After the canal to Lake Okeechobee opened, a series of fish houses strung out there, peddling barrels of Okeechobee catfish. Their stench helped persuade the city in 1913 to file a suit against Mary Brickell of Miami, who owned property along the river. The controversial action established a municipal claim to riparian rights. From that, city docks and seawalls and the present public section of the river grew. On that, the Burghard proposal rested, and not without its own controversies.

He liked to compare its possibilities to the San Antonio River which winds through that city's downtown. Once, that river was so poorly regarded that there was a serious proposal that it be paved over to provide an underground sewer. But, like New River, there were historical and legal grounds for developing it. San Antonio began with a River Walk Commission in 1962, then attracted local, federal and private funds. The river became the feature of San Antonio's Hemisfair '68 and a nationally renowned showplace.

He told a gentle story, an old favorite of his, to explain how he feels about the honoring of New River. An Ordinary Man asked a Poet, "When is the best time to plant a tree?" Replied the Poet, "Thirty years ago." The Ordinary Man moaned, and asked what would be second best. "Today," the Poet advised.

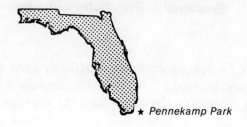

★ *Pennekamp Park*

John Pennekamp
Visits His Park

As the car pulled up to the gates of John Pennekamp Coral Reef State Park in Key Largo, John Pennekamp leaned toward the driver's side to hail the ranger.

"Let me talk to him," he advised me. "I know most of these fellows."

The ranger walked over, propped his hands on the car door and stared inside, seeing only strangers. Pennekamp was embarrassed.

"I **AM** John Pennekamp," he said, stressing the present tense. "I want to see my park." The ranger smiled and waved us through.

Pennekamp lived with that kind of thing. His name passed into Florida history long before he did. Nobody expected John Pennekamp to spend the day at John Pennekamp Park. Once a man's name is engraved into stone, people do not think he will come calling.

Pennekamp, a gentleman of Germanic leadership tempered by the kindness of a grand-dad, won his way into Florida legend as a forceful editor at The Miami Herald.

During the 1920's boom, Pennekamp followed his sweetheart from Cincinnati to Miami. He stayed to make a significant impact on all of Florida.

Out of the wreckage of many an editorial fight, employing a writing style that used words like hammers, Pennekamp emerged as the man responsible for the realization not only of the park that bears his name but Everglades National Park as well. The entire state parks system in fact owes much to the Pennekamp vigor.

On my visit with him in 1974 to the park that bears his name, Pennekamp was moved to reminisce about how it all happened. During the day, showing proprietary courtesy, he had complimented each ranger he encountered, each official, each guide. Graying and heavy, he pointed out each facility, explained how it got there and began recounting the names and the situations that brought it all about.

Pennekamp˜ Park is both a remarkable monument and an unusual public asset. It was the first underseas park in the United States, and it covers 178 nautical square miles. It sprang from the dream of marine scientists who wanted to preserve the incredible beauty of the Florida Keys' coral reefs.

The park makes that beauty accessible to the public with camping facilities, picnic and playground areas, glasspaneled boats, scuba and snorkeling tours, rentals for boats, canoes, underwater diving and camera equipment.

"I never was much of a conservationist," Pennekamp said after a while, as though he were confessing. "That's all synthetic stuff. I don't kill. I never shot a gun in my life. But I was a newspaperman, not a conservationist. That's what got me involved in the parks system. I just got interested."

In a reminiscent mood, Pennekamp repeated one of his favorite stories for me, the one about a $2 million poker game. He always said it was the pivotal event in persuading the state to put up money needed to clear the way for the creation of Everglades National Park (dedicated in 1947).

Park enthusiasts needed state money in a hurry to buy one critical tract of 200,000 acres (of the total 1.4 million needed). The old Pork Chop gang, or rural legislators, controlled things then.

Friends arranged for Pennekamp to have lunch with key Pork Choppers at a camp near the Ocala National Forest. After a meal of collard greens and cornbread, they settled down to a game of nickel and dime poker.

"I was a pretty good player in those days but not as good as I seemed that day," Pennekamp recalled. "I couldn't lose. I won hand after hand. Made uncanny draws." Bill Pearce of Palatka, chairman of the Senate Finance Committee then, finally laid down what he thought should be a winning hand, muttering about the Pennekamp luck.

Pennekamp topped him with three kings. "Just how much money

do you need for that goddammed park of yours?'' Pearce asked grumpily.

Until that moment, Pennekamp had hoped for $400,000. Gambling again, he replied, ''Two million dollars.'' Pearce suggested, ''Why don't you come over to the legislature and get it instead of taking it out of our pockets?''

Pennekamp said that clinched Everglades National park. ''From that point on, we were in,'' he said. ''That was a commitment. That was the way with the Pork Choppers. When they said something, that was it.''

In those days there was no mass, organized conservation movement, and little interest compared to what developed later. Many had scoffed at the idea of an Everglades National Park. To some, the underwater park idea that came later seemed even more ridiculous.

''The attitude was, 'Why do you want that? You can't stand on nothing to see nothing from nowhere,'' Pennekamp said, smiling. ''At that time, it was a tough argument.''

The coral reef park at Key Largo became a Pennekamp project after a 1957 biological conference. Marine biologists passed a resolution petitioning the National Park Services and the U.S. Department of the Interior to save the area.

Pennekamp, remembering that plans for Everglades National park once had included a corridor across the Keys to a tract of reef, picked it up.

In 1959 the state agreed to give control of the ocean bottom out to the three-mile limit to the Florida Board of Parks and Historic Memorials (Pennekamp had been its first chairman). The federal government agreed the next year to place control of the ocean bottom from the three-mile limit to the edge of the continental shelf in the hands of the Secretary of the Interior for a permanent preserve.

After that, the future of the Key Largo park was guaranteed. At its dedication, Gov. LeRoy Collins surprised Pennekamp by naming the park for him. Toward the end of his speech, the governor said:

''There may be those who have loved Miami and Florida more but none have I known who has proved it through service more dedicated. We owe him — and future generations will always owe him — a great debt.''

Pennekamp had not known the park would be named for him. Typically, his only thought at the time was that Collins' choice of names might have spoiled any chance that the state legislature would put up the necessary money.

Pennekamp as an editor and a man was impatient with distractions, even if he were one of them.

On this day at his park, he still seemed surprised at it all, grateful, proud in a quiet way. The ranger who greeted us at the gate would never forget him, and neither would any of the rest of us. He represented a special part of Florida's history.

Former Gov. Collins said it best: "To see his living monument, you have only to look about you."

John D. Pennekamp

Interlachen

Art Marshall's Magnificent Obsession

Art Marshall, South Florida's famed environmental zealot, lived beside a lake deep in the Putnam County woods where the closest thing to a Babbitt was the sound that frogs made at night.

Marshall, a Cracker Quixote, was a man with a magnificent obsession. He had been called a heretic, a raving idiot, a wild man who was anti-progress, anti-patriotic and even anti-human. All of that was nonsense. He was simply an intuitive biologist steeped in the ways of natural Florida, one willing to pay a high price for being true to himself.

Some said the fire had gone out of him after a quarter-century of plunging into every major environmental issue to touch Florida — the dredging and filling of bays, the jetport in the Everglades, the cross-Florida barge canal, the Biscayne National Monument, the Big Cypress preserve, the Sanibel causeway, the Kissimmee Ditch, the degradation of the Everglades, all of them. But when I met him in 1981, he was still tilting at every despoiler that moved. He had to his credit a vast array of friends and enemies.

Growth advocates persisted in picturing him as a heretic burping in the chapel, but environmentalists saw him more as an Old Testament prophet raging at a bacchanal.

In the esoteric science of environmentalism, most answers come in the form of ragged prophecies, but overriding his arguments carried the risk of being embarrassed on the record tomorrow. Marshall himself estimated his environmental assessments have 85 per cent accuracy.

After living most of his life on the Gold Coast, from Vero Beach to Miami, he moved in 1974 to these North Central Florida woods near the village of Interlachen. Here, the three of them, Marshall and his wife Kathleen and his obsession, enjoyed the comfort and ease of natural surroundings.

He was a tall man with thin gray hair and glasses, and a deliberate manner. His speech had the slight flavor of cornbread in it. At home he wore jeans, a free-flapping shirt and had the patience to pet a dog and smoke a pipe. All of that created a reminiscence of LBJ presiding at the ranch. He looked peaceful, but at any moment he might turn on the power. His vision of Florida had been consistent. It would wither the trends off an old-time Chamber of Commerce booster. For years he had been prophesying slow-motion disaster for Florida if we did not change our profligate ways. Enough has happened over the years to earn him a more attentive audience.

"In Florida," he said, picking up the sermon, "it has always been said that if we can just get a bigger population, we'll get more businesses and more dollars and it will solve all our problems. That's a bunch of crap. It doesn't work that way.

"Every city in the United States that has more than three-quarters of a million population is in financial trouble and they're also in quality of life trouble. The reason is, once you get beyond the optimum size of a city, which is determined by its local resources plus the energy input, the per capita costs rise dramatically. Then, the bigger it gets the broker it is."

By Marshall's reckoning, the Gold Coast, the Florida Keys, the Tampa Bay area and Orlando already were overbuilt. He gauged Fort Myers and Jacksonville to be nearing overgrowth.

"I have examined every living system that you can think of on this earth and I can't find one that doesn't work that way. It's the nature of things, the way this earth was created. Not only do wild systems work this way, but so do farms and cities and institutions and mechanical systems and almost everything else.

"There's always that curve that rises until the optimum size is reached, and then it declines. From that point for the city, it's catastrophic in terms of the citizen's ability to pay the taxes and the government's ability to deliver services. The burdens rise geometrically."

Marshall was born in Charleston, S.C., in 1919. His parents moved to West Palm Beach in 1925. After military service, he earned degrees at the University of Florida, where he was Phi Beta Kappa, and at the University of Miami, and went to work for the U.S. Fish and Wildlife Service. He developed a special interest in the Everglades and began warning in the 1960s that the fates of the Everglades and South Florida were inseparable. He quit his job in 1970, taught at the University of Miami and the University of Florida, served on the governing board of the Central and South Florida Flood Control District, shifted in 1974 to work as a private consultant and served as chairman of the St. Johns River Water Management District.

Three Florida governors sought his counsel and assistance. He helped write many of the state's environmental laws. He has been peppered with state and national conservation awards. Yet controversy always dogged him, for he was doggedly faithful to an upsetting vision.

That vision included a special fixation about repairing the Everglades to save South Florida, and he had formulated The Marshall Plan to do that. The plan began with the Kissimmee lakes and stretched all the way to Florida Bay. He predicted a variety of rejuvenating spinoffs from it, including an improved supply of fresh water and an easing of drought and flood vulnerabilities.

"I am frightened by the water prospects for South Florida," Marshall said. "We have much to do and it is all obstreperous." No, the fire had not gone out of the man. The bacchanal had begun to produce hangovers and the prophet seemed less heretical. A few amens had started.

Orlando

The Celebrated
Disney Doubter

Paul Pickett appeared to be normal in every way, except one. He refused to visit Disney World. Even when especially invited, he refused. Maybe almost everybody else in America was charmed by the determinedly cute Mickey Mouse, the stupidly whimsical Goofy and the eternally virginal Snow White, but not Paul Pickett.

He had lived in Orlando for 30 years. He loved it before Disney came. He loved it even after Disney came, when he said the traffic jams began to look like the roads out of Pompeii. But even so, Disney World, which grew so hugely that it wags Orlando like a tail, had no personal charm for him. His wife and children went, but without Daddy.

He did not hate Disney World. He thought it was a fine entertainment complex. It made him affluent.

He praised Disney World as a sly Marc Antony would have. But as the praise wound down you noted the rise of counterpoint. By the time he gets through talking about the old days, you might worry that Mickey Mouse and Goofy and Snow White had run away from their manufactured home and fallen into the clutches of a show business Fagin.

Pickett laughed. Of course he would not suggest anything about Disney World except that it is a giant corporate good citizen, he said. What he meant is that when he was a politician, back in the days of Disney's arrival, that as chairman of the Orange County Commission the people he dealt with were neither Goofy nor Snow White.

"They were a bunch of hardheaded bastards." Pickett said. "They had the public image of Snow White but you went to a meeting with them and suddenly you were talking to a whole different type. Probably the hardest driving business people I ever had to deal with.''

Back then, in the late 1960s and early 1970s, Commissioner Pickett said he tried to treat Disney World with the same fairness he would treat a new hamburger vendor coming to town. Disney officials were appalled.

He had some terrible scraps with them about this, and with a lot of other people in the county, who felt he was being insensitive, unimaginative, and imperceptive. Pickett became celebrated as a Disney Doubter.

All this was history, when we talked in 1982, but it was a period of Florida history whose classic dilemmas were being repeated as the state urbanized. Disney World was a benchmark in development. It realigned tourist patterns, changed central Florida and affected all of Florida. Pickett was the historic dissenter.

He moved here from Ohio in 1951, managed a printing plant until 1965 and then formed his own printing company. He first was elected to the commission in 1966. The county had no administrator then and, as chairman of the commission, Pickett became its chief spokesman. His differences with Disney World occurred in the years leading up to its 1971 official opening and stemmed from the state law that gave it extraordinary powers over the 27,000 acres it owned.

"It was a horrible law philosophically," Pickett said."They and God are the two highest entities and nobody knows for sure which is first. It's the most amazing piece of legislation I've ever seen. I think it's unconstitutional.

"It is exactly the same as if the state of Michigan passed a law and permitted General Motors to buy the city of Detroit and exercise all it's powers. It's unheard of.''

While most of the rest of Florida was euphoric about Disney, Pickett fumed. He kept making the Disney folk mad. "I simply maintained that if Disney created any additional expenses for the county, Disney should pay for them. Everybody else had to pay. But Disney paid nothing, because they had a law that said they didn't have to.

"The year Disney opened (1971), they cost the county $8.25 million. That much expense was added in services of all kinds. The only place we could get $8.25 million was to pull it off scheduled projects. We moved 'em back a few years. Some still haven't gotten done. It was grossly unfair to taxpayers in Orange County," he said.

Pickett did not waver before the argument that Disney World was worth it because it created a boom economic climate that benefited almost everybody in the county. "It helped some people with property, and some of those catering to tourists, but for the average person in Orange County who owned nothing but his home the only thing he got out of Disney World was traffic congestion, taxes and one helluva lot of Yankee relatives," he replied.

As for the tax benefits of growing bigger, he added: "If bigger was better, New York City and Cleveland would have a lower tax rate than Pahokee."

Pickett believed Disney World paid its full share of taxes, but doubts whether the $8.25 million in startup expenses for the county ever were made up. His personal benefits came in appreciation of some undeveloped property he owned, some of which increased in value as much as 50 times.

"I always said that I would have given $10,000 of my own money to bring Disney World here — IF it went to some county about 45 miles away, not this one, "Pickett noted.

There were great flaps in those days, and Pickett lost many of them. "I was an 18th Century Whig who didn't have sense enough to understand progress," he said. Pickett persisted, even raising the issue of unconstitutionality as a threat. He thinks that, and a meeting with California stockholders who flew to Orlando to ask him what the fuss was about, helped ease the early antagonisms.

All of that was why he would not visit Disney World. "It got to be a thing," he explained. In the landmark case, the coming of Disney World, Pickett either was too farsighted or too nearsighted to take the public with him. The question of which was still open.

Baker County

They Fear God, Women and Electricity

The Crews brothers, born, raised and grown elderly among the gray sands and black puddles of Moccasin Swamp, once told me they feared only God, the devil, women and electricity.

That was 1976. Since then, they have become the most famous men in Baker County, and I called on them again in 1982 to see how celebrity had changed their lives.

"No different," said William McKinley, at 71 five years younger than his brother, Daniel Lucas. "Still ain't got none of 'em."

About 80 years earlier, their Daddy hacked a 160-acre homestead out of the thick palmettos and pines and sweet bays, making a home and a haven in this extension of the great Okefenokee Swamp that straddles the Georgia-Florida border.

McKinley and Daniel, bachelors, changed nothing. Almost everything was handmade, just like their Daddy left it when he died in 1931, and still handrun.

After their mother died 30 years ago, McKinley and Daniel had the place all to themselves. That year, McKinley bought a new Chevrolet pickup. He would drive it to Jacksonville to buy feed for the cows.

The brothers persistently refused to accept electricity. They didn't trust it. They got water from a hand pump, had no telephone, no screens or windowpanes, read only the weekly Baker County Press mailed to them out of Macclenny.

Their views of the world, and the world's view of them, were ones of curiosity and uninformed fascination. The mutual perception was through a time warp, an open door with history on one side and the present on the other.

The weathered frame house, the split rail fence, the yard beaten bare by cows' hooves and festooned by fragrant cow droppings, lie about 4 miles north of a crossroads called Baxter, far off the paved road, not far from the St. Marys River.

"We got worried out with farming," said Daniel, siting on the front porch, swatting at swarms of flies, filling me in on the news. "Don't plant nothing but a garden. Eating mostly 'maters and roastin' ears, right now. Planted Irish potatoes but it was too wet and they ruined."

They quit farming because of age and health. Daniel had arthritis and walked with a cane. McKinley sometimes faints or, as he put it, "I lose my knowing." Yet both get along fine.

When word spread about the Crews' brothers' lifestyle, and their innocent gentiality with strangers, various emissaries from the outside world began to make pilgrimages.

So many came that the Crews, in their courteous way, began to express weariness with strangers dropping in unexpectedly, disturbing the afternoon nap, breaking peaceful routines, arriving with shiny cars and flashing cameras, staring, exploring, laughing a lot.

"Sometimes, it gets too many," admitted McKinley. "Just a few, you know, is all right. But too many gets kind of aggravating."

"Yeah, people's always coming up here," Daniel said. "Biggest bunch came up from a college. Must of been 50 head of 'em. They kept drawing pictures of the house and counting the boards. Went up in the loft, one of 'em did. I never hear tell of such things. Went all over the kitchen and everywhere, measuring everything."

"Yessir," said McKinley, "we thought they was going to break the lamp shade a-measuring one day, but they didn't. Even went all over the chicken house. We didn't know they was going to do all that, till they done it."

Television crews came calling, newspaper people, groups of schoolchildren, historical groups and some just plain, curious folk. "They like to see it," said McKinley, understandingly. "They say they can't find nothing that looks just like this."

Even the governor's wife, Adele Graham, visited the farm. She sent them á nice letter and an autographed picture of her and the governor. The brothers are proud of that. "That was the first governor's wife we ever seen,"said Daniel.

Most strangers almost instantly felt affection for the shy brothers, and some showed it. "One woman come up here and asked would I let a couple of 'em spend the night with us. I said, 'no, ma'am,' " McKinley recalled. Visitors always joke with them about their bachlorhood. The brothers have to explain that they like women but, as McKinley puts it, "We was always skeered of 'em."

He teased Daniel. "One of 'em hugged my neck but she kissed Daniel." Responded Daniel, "I told her it wouldn't do me no good for her to kiss me but she said, well, it would her." They laughed.

In their overalls and with their country hospitality, they offered each visitor a tour. They learned how to talk with strangers, how to look straight into the TV cameras, how to pose.

There had been suggestions that they should charge admission. They considered the idea and rejected it. "I don't 'spect it's worth nothing, these messings we got," Daniel said. He seemed embarressed.

Not much outside the county interested them. They had investigated television as entertainment. "Nonsense, to my mind," McKinley said.

A friend gave Daniel a small portable radio. He called it "the little thing that talks," and he rarely listened. "Start it up and it'll just go to raring," Daniel said. "It just carries on something all the time."

Fame had not changed the Crews brothers. They remained primitive innocents, skeptical about the world, tolerant of its strange ways, polite when it intruded, ever beguiled by the odd way that an honest life delights the city folk.

Indiantown

Indiantown: Older and Wiser

Just in case he needed them, Cecil Pollack carried his teeth around in his shirt pocket.

"Do they hurt?" someone asked.

"Only if they bite me," he said.

Pollack, orphaned at 7, grew up in the cow camps and prairies around Lake Okeechobee about the time Okeechobee City on the north end of the lake was beginning to sprout civilization.

He was one of those pioneer Floridians who speaks of the old days with more glee than nostalgia. He would smack his unfettered gums and tilt his cowboy hat and savor the whole thing as a great joke.

"I didn't have no home. I grew up in the cow camps all around out here. I was a cow-hunter. All I owned was a horse, a rope and a .22 pistol — to use on snakes," he said.

"When I went to town, I'd stay with somebody I knew. The rest of the time I was in the woods. I didn't go to living in a house until I was 17, when I got married."

As a fresh and still-to-be-tamed bridegroom, Pollack in 1928 moved here to Indiantown, 20 miles west of Stuart (along the St. Lucie Canal at the junction of SR 76 and SR 710).

The town formed when the Seaboard Air Line railroad built the Seminole Inn during the Boom, planning to make its southern headquarters here. When the Bust came in 1929, most of the early, grandiose dreams for the town vanished.

Pollack arrived when it was citrus and cattle and moonshine country. "There was a lot of Indians scattered around here then," he said. "That's where Indiantown got its name, you know. They camped all up and down the swamp.

"They liked whiskey right well and in those days so did I. There used to be a moonshine still right over there," he said, standing in front of the Seminole Inn and pointing.

"It was Prohibition then, you know, and they used to fly in liquor from over there at Bimini in the Bahamas. Those planes would light in the ponds around here, and then they'd try to ship the stuff out on the railroad.

"Some government men caught a box-car full of liquor on a sidetrack one time and they started busting it up with axes. Wouldn't give us any.

"So some of us boys got a water bucket and a dipper and as they'd throw it out we'd dip it up and first thing you know we had us a 10-gallon bucket full.

"Then we walked up and down out here and whenever we took a notion for a drink, we'd just dip one up. Wasn't long before that bucket gave out."

In 1976, four generations of Pollack's family lived in Indiantown, and he boasted then more of his five great-grandchildren than his cow-hunting days. A son-in-law, Homer Wall, had bought the Seminole Inn and was restoring it.

Wall, a practicing Southern Baptist, had the old bar torn out as one of his first actions. There would be no alcoholic beverages served. Pollack took it philosophically.

"I don't use the stuff any more anyhow," he said, "My wife beat it out of me. A long time ago somebody asked me why I lived so far out in the woods and I told them it was so nobody could hear me holler when she started beating on me."

Pollack and Florida, in a way, grew older and wiser together. It was fun then but they grew too old (he was 65) for that sort of thing. The memories remained, though.

Indians taught him how to barbecue a turtle without removing its shell, and an oldtime Okeechobee sheriff — William Collins, called Pogy Bill — taught him to beware of entanglement with the law.

"I was just a boy, but he took up time with me. He was the meanest good man you ever saw. He had a tender heart, but when he went after you, you didn't want to give him no backtalk. He could slap a man around. He was just a natural man."

Collins, once a catfisherman on Lake Okeechobee, was made sheriff because of his fighting prowess. Pogy Bill took on the job of controlling the regular Saturday night fights between the cowboys and the catfishermen.

On Saturday nights in the old days either the cowboys or the catfishermen would pay Pollack to keep them supplied with ice water for their drinks. "They'd give me a quarter or 50 cents, and when the fighting started I'd get under a table," he said. "Whenever they'd drop any money, I'd reach out and get it. They wouldn't pay me any attention."

Pogy Bill was a hard but understanding sheriff, according to Pollack. Once he arrested a moonshiner and told him to post $50 bond to stay out of jail. The man handed him a $100 bill.

"I can't change that," said Bill.

"Just keep it then," the moonshiner said. "You can put it on the next one."

It was a friendlier time, and it took a lot to discourage a good moonshiner. "They'd make a little shine in spite of all," Pollack said. "Pogy Bill would catch 'em and they'd keep right on at it. That was the way of things then."

Not now. Like Pollack, who walks around with his teeth in his pocket, Indiantown changed and reformed and lost its bite except on special occasions.

"I don't even ride much any more," Pollack said, emphasizing the transformation. "Got where it makes my (bleep) sore."

★ *Jupiter Inlet*

The Duboises: Holding Fast For Florida

Bessie and John DuBois, two very special Floridians, had the luck to call one sandy spit of Florida home all their lives. The history of that speck of land at Jupiter Inlet has been grafted to their family tree. They live on DuBois Road at DuBois Point and part of the old homestead has become DuBois Park.

Only the Jobe Indians before them left any lasting mark at this one spot and the DuBoises adopted that. The oyster-loving Jobes constructed a 600-foot long shell mound, and in 1898 John's daddy built a house on top of it. John grew up there and can remember being able to see the Gulfstream from the front porch before Australian pines blocked the view.

DuBois Point, jutting into the Loxahatchee River where it flows into the Atlantic Ocean in north Palm Beach County, became a public haven in an area where the natural lust of the developer has roughed and spangled the natural beauty of the land.

Tall condominiums and hotels throw shadows on sand dunes where the DuBois family once dug coquina to frame a fireplace. Saws whine and bulldozers make monster tracks across the few undeveloped gaps still left, preparing them for the implanting of steel and concrete vertebra to support plush new shelters where The Swells can escape winter. More dunes are being saturated with mulch and fertilizer and water until sod can take hold and turn them into grassy, carpet-smooth lawns with little hills that make pitch-and-putt more interesting.

Even the park had its own dose of asphalt for convenient parking, and when the public crowds in on weekends — while the saws and bulldozers are quiet — the spaces filled up. Cars spill out and line DuBois Road past where Bessie and John lived in a house where an ancient Indian canoe sat in the front yard. Sometimes, it seemed there always was a clatter coming from somewhere.

But the DuBoises (like good Crackers, they pronounce it Dooboys) did not complain seriously. They were the hardy sort who smile and shrug rather than getting upset. They are rooted in history and appreciation of things natural, but they do not rail at the inevitable tomorrow.

"Sometimes it's a little discouraging to see all this development," Bessie said in 1980. "But you know John and I ran a fishing camp on the point for 45 years. We were constantly meeting people and having crowds come in and all that. We enjoy people. And, after all, why should we worry? John's 80 and I'm 77."

Both Bessie's and John's families came from New Jersey. John's daddy moved to Florida as a teenager to work in a friend's orange grove. John was born in the house that is the historic centerpiece of the park. Bessie's father was a florist looking for a warm spot to grow flowers. A man in Washington ran his finger down a map and pointed to Jupiter Inlet as the place where the Gulfstream ran closest to the mainland. Her family, the Wilsons, moved here in 1914.

The DuBoises, married in 1924, learned the peculiar truths of Florida history and environment long ago. Bessie wrote two histories of the area and many historical articles, trying to spread the word. But it did not always spread.

If you can muster historical perspective, some of it has been funny. For example, a development just across the river was named Tequesta, for the Tequesta Indians, but Bessie pointed out to them that the Tequestas lived farther south, not here. It made no difference. One developer launched a search to see whether anyone had pictures of the Jonathan Dickinson shipwreck which he could use in promotional ads. It happened here, but in 1696. Still another tried to pass off a Yankee colonel as a symbol of the Florida Heritage.

The DuBoises enjoy a good laugh, but do not wish to see the distinctive history of the Jupiter area distorted. It needs only accuracy to generate fascination, not embellishment.

The name Jupiter comes from an anglicized version of Jobe. The Spanish pronounced it "Hoebay" but the English thought the word was "Jove" and altered it to Jupiter.

Ponce De Leon came to Jupiter Inlet in 1513, Pedro Menendez about a half-century later, and the Jonathan Dickinson (a park north of here is named for him) expedition survivors were held captive by Indians on what is now DuBois Point. During construction in the 1850s of the landmark Jupiter Lighthouse across the river from DuBois Point, some of the workers raided Seminole Indian Billy Bowlegs' banana patch. He retaliated by harassing the workers and delaying completion a couple of years.

The Barefoot Mailmen started here and walked the beach sands 88 miles to Miami. The narrow-gauge Celestial Railroad (called that because it served Jupiter, Juno, Venus and Mars) relieved the mailmen in 1888 with an 8-mile run to Lake Worth and in turn was replaced during the 1890s by Henry Flagler's railroad.

The DuBoises were like anchors in a state renowned for having few. Even in 1980, with Bessie legally blind, they held fast to a good life and good memories. Their own four children grew up at DuBois Point. They remembered the rum-runners in the inlet, the Nazi subs off the coast sinking freighters during World War II, the toll of growth beginning to be felt by 1963 when they had to quit eating local oysters, being forced by high taxes to decide in 1972 to sell the point to the county for a park.

They watched DuBois Point go from an isolated island to a playground for Swells who live in 8-story filing cases and work at fun as though it were a job. They smile at the new Floridians but have no envy.

Gulf Hammock ★

Lillie And Johnny
In The Hammock

Lillie Strawn worked hard all her life. In a home where she had nine brothers and sisters, most of them self-delivered into the world by her Ma, everybody worked. "I worked my whole life. Worked myself to death, practically. I'm still a-working," she said.

At about age 60, the modern bent for pleasure finally corrupted her. After her children grew up — "I only had four myself," she said apologetically — she turned to the frivolities she never before had time for. She fished some, but hunting became her passion.

That was 15 years before I met her. By then (in 1981), she owned three double-barreled shotguns, a .410 gauge, a 12-gauge and a 16-gauge, plus what she called a doubleheader, a single-shot .22 rifle mounted above a 20-gauge. Her son built a deer stand for her in the woods where she sometimes sat all day with a gun cocked and ready.

"Ain't got a deer yet," she said, laughing. "But I will." Her son took her out to kill some squirrels. She refused to shoot the ones around the house. They were pets. "I just put that .410 in the truck and me and him went down to the hammock. Time I got there, a deer run up behind some bushes. His head was sticking up so I could see the horns. I shot, and the thing never moved until I shot again. It run off. That boy of mine shore gave me the dickens about that. He said, Mama, I told you not to go out there with that little thing (the .410)." Other times, fascinated by the deer, she froze and would not shoot. "He's always after me about that," she said.

Lillie Strawn was a woman of character, spirit and humor. She had a depth and fiber that was among tourist-catering Florida's

216

scarcer human qualities. She had no complaints, even though her first half-century or more was pioneer stuff with no Mickey Mouse and no plastic fantasies in it. "People don't understand it, but to me they was good times even if they was hard," she said. To those who thought her an aging wonder, she smiled and referred them to her mother, still alive at age 114.

Lillie had a pioneer's life. When she got big enough to hold a hoe, it was her duty to help weed the rich, dark dirt in the family garden. By the time she was 11 and in the fifth grade, she could hold an old Dixie Boy plow steady as the horse pulled it between the rows of corn. Then she quit school and worked fulltime until she was 16, when she lied about her age and married Johnny Strawn, a hammock boy.

The family slept on mattresses stuffed with corn shucks or Spanish moss and, finally, after her Pa started growing it, with cotton. They took baths in the tin washtub, sometimes in the water left over from washing clothes. They preserved enough vegetables, canned them in glass jars, to last through the winter and beyond.

They killed farm animals, mostly hogs, and smoked the meat and made sausage and bacon. They made quilts to keep them warm in winter. They made syrup of their sugar cane, took corn to the grist mill to be ground into grits, grew rice.

"We even made vinegar," she said. "Pa made a pile of it one time and they come out there and tried to arrest him and put him in jail for it. Don't know what they thought it was. We'd make it out of peaches or anything like that. You just put it in there and sweeten it and let it set until it vinegars. But I ain't made none in a long time."

The family raised everything it ate except sugar, coffee and flour, and sometimes the flour was so short the only time they had biscuits was for Sunday breakfast. "It was hard times then to get anything," Mrs. Strawn said. "We had to go clean to Dunnellon (23 miles) to get the sugar, coffee and flour."

For six generations, probably beginning sometime after the Civil War when her grandparents moved down from Alabama (the family stories are uncertain) and homesteaded land in Levy County at a place that would be called Gulf Hammock, her family stayed put. "I went to Tennessee one time. I went to Sarasota one time. That's as far as I've ever went either way," she said.

Five of the brothers and sisters still lived in the hammock, with most of their children and grandchildren, and the farthest any strayed was Ocala or Jacksonville. Nobody ever sat down to count them, but they reckon the family might number as high as 100. They still grew most of what they ate, but they bought their sugar, coffee and flour at a Jiffy store two miles to the west on U.S. 19-98 or waited for the "rolling store" that came calling once a month.

Gulf Hammock was a world almost to itself, remarkably little changed by time. Tractors replaced horses, store-bought goods were more tempting, the road was paved about 20 years ago and Social Security put leisure into old age, but many customs and attitudes survived. Wildlife was plentiful. They saw bears in the woods, said they heard panthers screaming at night. The hammock on maps is a low, wild patch of Levy County near the Gulf Coast stretching from the Suwannee River to the Withlacoochee River. The community itself, also called Gulf Hammock, is located on a bend of SR 326 not far from the origins of the Waccasassa and Wekiva rivers.

Midday, as two strangers wandered into the Strawns' yard about a mile off the paved road, the door was open and a friendly voice hollered, "Y'all come on in." Lillie was in the kitchen, cooking and talking. She brushed her hair back and wiggled the frying pan. "I feed a lot of people," she said. "Anybody that drops in and wants to eat. I'm bad as Mama used to be. Always somebody around. I remember when she used to get up and fry chicken for breakfast. I been a-canning stuff. My Lord! Now it's time to make syrup and dig potatoes."

Johnny, her husband was in the living room reading the Bible. He had dug some sweet potatoes in the morning. Lillie fried some fatback, cut the potatoes in strips and was frying them in the drippings. There was a hoecake of cornbread on the table and some grits. Maybe it was not dietetic, but it certainly was fragrant.

In relaxed, colorful, precise language and good humor, she told the story of Lillie and Johnny. It was like a glimpse into the good, solid history of Cracker Florida and, for me, a treat to hear and a privilege to understand.

Apalachicola

Heidi: Champion Oyster-Shucker

Heidi Harrelson loved it when winter began poking its way into the Panhandle. It was her time of the year. The oysters got plump and firm, and when she was working she popped down a gallon or two a day in sheer delight. She was the world's fastest oyster shucker. Not the neatest, maybe, but the fastest.

The chill fall winds sweeping off Apalachicola Bay soothed her warm French-German blood. Many nights, she lay in bed with the covers off and a fan blowing, exhilarating in the cold freshness.

Back in Germany, Heidi had married a U.S. soldier. He and her son came to Apalachicola, where workers at an oyster house raised money to bring her over. The marriage did not last.

Heidi's life had been shadowed by one tragedy after another, yet each time she came smiling through, conquering all. During the grim days of World War II, she ate backyard grass for breakfast and begged at doorways for other meals. Except for oysters, rich food made her ill.

Her father, a German, lost a leg as a soldier in World War II. Her mother, a Frenchwoman from Alsace-Lorraine, worked as a farmhand. As a girl, Heidi plowed crops behind a horse, and developed biceps that measure 17 inches.

She was a large woman — as large as life. At 43, she stood 5 feet 5 inches and weighed 220 pounds. That included a lot of heart and soul.

She waded into life the way Rocky Marciano fought, swarming all over it, taking heavy punishment, paying the cost. She faced life in Apalachicola head-on, unable to speak English and heavily indebted. She became an oyster shucker, waitress and a newspaper carrier. She paid her debts, including the mortgage on her house.

By the end of her first week as an oyster shucker, she was pronounced the fastest ever, eventually shucking as high as 42 gallons a day, not counting what she ate. "Two in the bucket, one in the mouth," she laughed.

But, alone and unhappy, she began drinking. She was a champion at that, too. "I call me an alcoholic. When I left Germany, my Mom told me I would forget her. I said no, I would send her a present every Christmas. But I was drinking for three years and I forgot her.

"You would not be a friend to me then because I go around drinking and beating everybody up. Yep. I looking for fight. A woman did me wrong and I start hating everybody, beating everybody up." She laughed. "Men, too."

Then she joined the Baptist Church. She knitted a present for her Mom. It would make up for those Christmases she had missed. As she was mailing it, a telegram arrived saying her mother had died. Heidi was staggered by grief and remorse.

"I said, every year I was going to make a Christmas party for the old folks to make up for the gifts I didn't send. That's what I did. Every year I made 229 gifts. I knit and crochet and sometimes we have to buy things. We have a party for them."

Her life set right, at least temporarily, Heidi became the queen of Apalachicola, a success symbol. She showed them what was possible. She won the shucking contest at the Apalachicola seafood festival two years straight, and they retired her from competition.

At a national contest in Maryland, she became the U.S. oyster shucking champ. She was the first Floridian, and the first woman, ever to win.

She began wearing bright red T-shirts that proclaimed "In Christ I can do anything." She sold T-shirts celebrating her national championship, using the proceeds for her Christmas party. When she visited her son and grandchildren in Savannah, the mayor gave her the key to the city. Gov. Bob Graham and other Florida officials posed for pictures with her.

She went to the world championships in Ireland and finished first

— but in her excitement, she overlooked one oyster and drew a penalty that dropped her to third.

She went back to Maryland to defend her national championship — and finished ahead of everybody again. However, the judges said her half-shell tray was not neat. There were some chips, a spot of grit, and some oysters not sitting perfectly in their half-shells. She placed second in the women's division.

Penalizing Heidi for neatness is a little like disqualifying the first racehorse because the jockey's shirt-tail fell out. In the excitement of a contest she cuts loose. Naturally, a few chips fly.

But Heidi was the fastest shucker of them all, and they knew it. Her nimble fingers put the knife into the oyster, her strong right arm jams back using the stomach like an anvil, and the oyster pops open. Nobody could do it better.

Each day as she cracks the oysters she figuratively curls her little finger, straining to be neat, flicking off the chips and the grit and making the oysters sit up just right.

Heidi wanted to be the world champion one day. She told me when we talked in 1979 she would keep trying, that it would not be as tough as eating grass, or having her Mom die feeling forgotten, or beating the bottle.

Heidi never gave up, but for her always there seemed to be one more battle before that final victory.

Sanibel ★

Sanibel:
Uncle Clarence Rutland

Clarence O. Rutland slapped a mosquito feeding on his bare belly, and pondered the costs of progress. "Trouble of it is," he said, "we shouldn't of killed off the mosquitoes."

Rutland came to Sanibel Island in 1895, when there was little money and only a few people — all farmers or fishermen — but rich living. Deer roamed the island, and rabbits, and raccoons. He could pile his skiff full of oysters or clams in an hour. The fishing was easy.

But mosquitoes thrived, too, a kind of tax put on by nature.

In those days, he would wake up mornings to find them so thick on his windows he could not see out. "That don't sound right, but that's the way it was," he said. "You could just swing a bucket around in the yard and get a gallon of 'em."

In later years spray planes thundered overhead, laying down blankets of spray and killing the mosquitoes. Instead, people swarmed and the island became financially prosperous. "Everybody's making money over here," Rutland said when I visited him in 1973.

But the deer were gone, and the oysters and clams inedible. To catch the kind of fish he liked, he had to take a boat out into deep water.

In the years since a bridge connected the island to Florida, people have overrun the place. Rutland preferred the mosquitoes. "We was different as long as we only had the ferry," he said. "When they put that bridge in, we was just like the rest of them."

Rutland, before he died, became the most popular as well as the oldest man on the island. He was known as Uncle Clarence, and spent his days fishing or ambling shoeless and shirtless around his pine house and 18-acre nursery. In the evenings he played bingo and talked.

Progress had made him prosperous. He could afford to enjoy his oldtime Cracker apprehensions.

Sanibel still had mosquitoes that command respect, but if visitors complained, Rutland happily reminded them that there were worse things than mosquitoes.

For him, Miami Beach was the prime example. "I've seen mosquitoes at Miami Beach as bad as any anywheres," he said. "I worked on a dredge down there once (when pioneer Carl Fisher was developing Miami Beach) when they was so bad they had to screen the boat so we could keep on working.

"There was only one pavilion there then. You could go on the beach anywhere. Now you go down there and you can't get on it anywhere. "It's gon' be the same way here."

If Rutland tended to exaggerate for emphasis, he nevertheless used truth in the mix. As a teenager, he did work for Fisher. And although Sanibel remains beautiful, motels and stores and condominiums — all necessary to accommodate the people who want to come here and make the oldtimers rich — are changing the nature of the island.

Rutland, however much he talked, fully understood what it meant at the bank. Some 30 years earlier, he had borrowed $1800 and bought his beautiful old house and acreage on Periwinkle Way. In 1973 he turned down an offer of $200,000 for it.

"I said, 'Mister, what in the hell am I going to do with $200,000?' The value's not there, to my notion," he said, drawing an oldfashioned distinction between value and price. "But these days, they say the value is what you can get."

Rutland was born in 1890 on the west side of Lake Apopka in central Florida. His father owned citrus groves, but the freezing winter of 1894-95 killed them. Rather than go in debt to try again, the elder Rutland moved to Sanibel to become a farmer.

"They was still homesteading land then, but it was all taken up," Rutland said. "So he worked on shares, raising tomatoes and peppers and egg plant. The owner furnished the land and fertilizer, and we did the work. We did pretty good in them days, but it wouldn't be much now.

"The end of the railroad was at Punta Gorda. They was a steamer that would leave Punta Gorda in the morning and one that would leave Fort Myers, and they would make that one trip a day. That's the way we shipped out."

Rutland quit school after the third grade. At age 12, he worked on a cattle boat running from Punta Rassa to Key West. Punta Rassa, where the present bridge to Sanibel touches the mainland, was then a major shipping point. Cattle were driven in herds across Florida to the boats.

"It was like out west. They was some fightin' and killin' going on all the time. I can remember when cattle walked up and down Front Street in Fort Myers. Get off the sidewalk and you were just as apt to step in a cattle pie."

After several trips to Key West, young Rutland hopped a schooner to Miami Beach, and it was then that he worked on one of Carl Fisher's dredge boats.

"That was the beginnin' of my runnin' around. I wasn't but about 14 but I was a big as I am now," he said.

He would drift away from Sanibel for a few weeks or a few months. He once followed the migrant trail with the fruit and vegetable crops, was a street car conductor in Tampa, worked in a saloon. "I've done anything everybody else has except kill somebody," he said. "Never done that."

Sanibel always was home. "Anything went wrong, I always came back here." In 1925, he came back to stay. His garage was built on the site where his parents first lived.

He solved his water problems a quarter-century ago by building two 10,000-gallon cisterns out of concrete block. When telephones were new, he had one of the first ever installed on Sanibel. Later he decided they were a nuisance, and would not tolerate one in the house.

In the good old days, before the bridge, he had a taxi business. "I had a couple trucks and Model T's. I used to get $15 to carry them drummers (salesmen) from the landing down there to Captiva and bring 'em back to catch it that afternoon. That was a lot of money in them days, but you had to know what you was doing to get it.''

Aside from how the fish were biting, Rutland in those years worried most about the future of Sanibel. He thought it grew with more speed than wisdom.

''Fella asked me the other day what I was going to do about it,'' he said. ''I told him I got 18 acres right here and I'm gon' move my house back in the middle, and tell 'em all to go to hell.''

Uncle Clarence has passed into history now, but so has the Sanibel that he knew.

Stuart

The Natural Order
Of Ernest Lyons

Ernest Lyons, a man who wore suspenders, long ago began discovering and writing about the laws of man and nature. He grew up in Stuart eating cabbage palms and swimming with alligators. He drifted down jungle rivers, roamed swamps and inlets, and decided that nothing natural was commonplace.

That probably was his first law. In later years — as so many seemed so certain that so much was ordinary — he encountered doubters, but that did not change his perception. He argued with questions that were answers.

"What's happened to awe?" he asked. To those who did not see the mystery in nature, he spoke of flowers that stared into the sun. He wanted to know, " What frailty is in us that we cannot ever look the sun in the eye?"

Lyons wrote like that, using small words to encircle large thoughts. The heavy gray mustache and black suspenders, hoisting a pair of black pants up around his white shirt, give him a Mark Twain look. Yet inside hid a modern man, a philosopher not swayed by the fashions of the day.

He would articulate his natural laws while sitting on a beach at low tide watching clams contest the issue of which could spit the farthest. The jump of mullet and the gate of a gopher were, to him, like apples falling on Sir Isaac Newton's head. Criminy. Eureka. In his mind, the laws emerge:

"Any man who would crank his lawnmower at 5:30 a.m. would shoplift.... In a small town, Big Brother is a gossipy Big Sister.... In Stuart, if you put on a coat you are going to church, a funeral or an

226

installation. Add a hat and you are going to New York.... Nothing is so completely gone as a storm that has passed or empires in which people have stopped believing.''

Hermits, poachers, moonshiners and bandits inspired him. Once he advocated a national campaign to save the quiet places, and he pre-selected them. "Make national shrines of every moonshine still in America," he said. The moonshiners, he argued, had more esthetic taste than anyone else. As proof, he offered to point out five examples in Martin County.

Nothing really confused Lyons, unless it was tourists and Yankees. "Millions come to Florida," he observed," and never see it. They are like motorized pellets in a glamourized pinball machine, hitting the flashing lights of widely publicized artificial attractions before bouncing out of the state and back home.''

After retiring from a half-century of newspapering (most of it at The Stuart News) and hunting and fishing, his quiet times came at his 1885 frame house that sat a block off the St. Lucie River. The living room was Stuart's first schoolhouse.

Lyons continues to find the world a remarkable place. Taking their ease in a comfortable, cypress-lined Florida room, he and wife Ezelle made it clear they had not lost their awe of Florida. They marveled at people the way they once marveled at the wild places and things. This inspired him, of course, to come up with another law: The more people, the less contact.

In the old days, when the trains stopped at Stuart to let off tourists, people here would go up and introduce themselves and offer help to get them settled. "People respected people," Lyons said.

"Now we go to supermarkets where there are 300 or 400 people and nobody knows anybody. When oldtimers run into each other, it's like a reunion. They hug each other and stop and talk as though they had been away for years.

"People arrive now and disappear into condominiums like cave dwellers and we never see them again. It happens with our own people as well as the newcomers," he said, emphasizing the possessive. "They go to live in a condominium and it's like they dropped into a black hole.''

The Lyons family moved to Stuart from Mississippi when Ernest was eight years old. In 1925 his father was one of 30 men to put up $1,000 each to lobby the Florida legislature to create Martin County. In 1931 Ernest went to work for The Stuart News as a reporter, and he retired in 1975 as editor. Collections of his columns became books entitled *My Florida* and *The Last Cracker Barrel.*

With his naturalist's eye for change, Lyons became intrigued by developments such as Stuart's plans to alter its Confusion Corner — a junction of five streets and a railroad, without a traffic light — because it was dangerous. "As a matter of fact, we have few accidents there," he said. It's a place which depends upon courtesy to succeed, and I think that's a pretty good demand to make. But they say that's not good enough any more."

He once suggested that Stuart change its slogan from *Sailfish Capital of the World* to *Stuart, Where Peace, Quiet and Natural Beauty Are More Important Than Money.* " I guess we oldtimers are walking along on the tail end of the parade these days," he said.

But he did not really believe that. You could not convince him that the rightness of courtesy among people and a respect for the mysteries of nature were matters of fashion. It is the natural order of things. He has watched too many clams squirt and mullet jump to be diverted. The parade, temporarily, is simply going the wrong way. When the error is discovered, there would be a turnabout, and Ernest Lyons would be out in front again. Suspenders may come back, too.

Oldsmar

The Odd Regrets
Of A Klansman

Sometimes, Bill Hendrix wished he had never joined the Ku Klux Klan. "I'd been a lot better off if I never got involved," he said. "Not out in the open anyway." He began as a wide-eyed young initiate in 1932 and rose to become a fiery national leader in the 1950s. At 68 he had backaches and emphysema and worked as as maintenance supervisor at an integrated housing project. That was in 1979.

Hendrix a tall, heavy fellow with thick gray hair and icy blue eyes, presented himself as a reasonable man preoccupied with a plan for retiring on five acres near the Suwannee River. But 21 years earlier a member of a Florida legislative committee investigating the KKK called him "one of the most dangerous men in the country."

Hendrix laughed about that. "There were times in public meetings we probably said a lot of things we shouldn't have, but I never hurt anybody," he said. With classic good-ole boy ease, he waxed righteous, confidential and ambivalent at the same time. He did not ever believe in white supremacy, he said, but he still advocated segregation. He never was prejudiced against Jews, he said, but his old KKK literature noted, "For white Christians only." Although he was the leader, he never had anything to do with the printing, he explained

In the 1950s, columnist Drew Pearson accused him of being involved in the bombing of a black schoolhouse in Clinton, Tenn. "I wasn't anywhere near Clinton at the time," Hendrix said. He sued Pearson for $1 million, but dropped the suit. "I didn't want to pursue it any further. Just not worth it. Besides, I kinda liked old

Drew," he explained. He put aside his affection for old Drew later to send out some postcards which federal officials said defamed Pearson. A judge fined him $700 and gave him a year's probation.

Hendrix boasted that he took the Klan out of the back-alleys and put it into the courthouses. He said he never profited from the Klan, never committed violence, never threatened or intimidated anyone and never burned a cross on anyone's lawn. "The only cross I ever burned was at a meeting. It was just a small cross," he said.

Rather than committing violence, Hendrix said that he actually had done a lot to prevent it. He told, as one example of how he worked, of a minister in St. Petersburg who had been sending buses out to bring black and white children together in church. Hendrix was working as a building contractor in Tallahassee at the time. Friends wrote him about it.

"I come down and saw it was a dangerous situation. They was fixing to blow the church up, these people here in St. Pete were. It wasn't the Klan at all." Hendrix went to the minister. "This fellow was so up in the air, you know, that I wasn't even on his level and I couldn't talk to him. I said OK, I'll be back." Hendrix went to Tallahassee, gave a new employee in the tax collector's office $7.50 and told her to type out an evangelist's license for him. She had not heard of that license, but he persuaded her.

"I came back down to St. Pete and said, now look, I'm a licensed evangelist. I wasn't on a level with you before but now I'm above you and I'm gon' talk to you. I said these people all disturbed about this thing and they fixing to really blow your church up. They want it stopped. That's all I was gon' tell you," Hendrix chuckled. "That stopped it for three, four years."

Hendrix spoke casually of days that most Americans consider shameful, of history so bizarre that many would like to dismiss it as a distortion. His stories reminded you that it was real, that it was not long ago, and even that strains of it persist. In 1978, the year before we talked, crosses had been burned in both north and south Florida. "They's still a lot of Klansmen around," Hendrix said. "They's four groups right around here and they even fight each other."

In 1953, Hendrix announced his resignation from the Klan, and recommended all Klan groups disband and disrobe because they were "causing disunity in the ranks of the white people." In 1960, he again announced his resignation, adding that the Klan could not legally stop integration. In a Klan news release then he said anyone advocating integration was saying, "God made a mistake," noting that one of the greatest of the Ten Commandments was "Thou Shalt Not Adulterate."

Hendrix said he ended his Klan organization in the early 1960s after taking a trip to Mississippi that forecast trouble. "Man, they were talking out there about killing people," he said. "Didn't make no bones about it. So I came on back and we had a meeting and just ordered it broke up, all our records destroyed, not keep a list of members or anything."

After 1954, Hendrix lived in Oldsmar, on the northern edge of Tampa Bay in Pinellas County, and remained relatively quiet until he decided to try to write a book to be entitled, *Thirty Years of Ku-Klucking.* For that, he began tidying up old stories and offering new ones.

At one time his Klan group had 15 different organizations. At various times he has belonged to the Southern-Northern Knights of the Ku Klux Klan, the National Christian Church, the Knights of the White Camellia, the Order of the Rattlesnake, the National Secret Service Agency, the Confederate Army, Bomb Buddies ("a civil defense group") and the White Brotherhood.

After the 1954 Supreme Court decision Hendrix suggested a solution to school integration. "Just give the white kids some baseball bats. . . ." He remembered one election day during the 1930s (when Florida had a poll tax), that he voted 13 times. He liked to tell of a campaign to put a ceiling of $85 on Florida welfare to raise "a million dollars" to send blacks North where welfare payments were more generous.

Hendrix knew the Floridians who supported the Klan secretly, and left him to handle the public thunder and lightning. There were state officials, well-known businessmen and politicians. "I got a good education out of the Klan and met a lot of good people," he said. Moments later, pondering a question about regrets, he added.

"I guess you could say I wish I'd never joined. Yeah, I guess you could say that."

He wanted to put as much of that as he could into a book, the conflicting emotions and stratagems of the public leader for a clandestine organization. "It's gon' be real interesting," he said. "If I really lied about it, you know, and told about bombings and crossburning and all like that, I think it'd sell more, but . . . .

Moore Haven

Moore Haven:
A Woman's Responsible

A woman put Moore Haven on the map, and neither fire, flood, hurricane, epidemic nor the misdeeds of men have been able to erase it.

Moore Haven sits astride U.S. 27 on the southwest side of Lake Okeechobee. Its citizens like to think of themselves as the strong ones who remained after the faint-hearted and weak-kneed had fled.

But until Marian Newhall Horwitz came along, Moore Haven was only a real estate developer's scheme. She turned it into a town with a special place in Florida history.

Horwitz pioneered women's equality in a day when it was not fashionable, and in some cases even dangerous. Because of her, women voted in Moore Haven three years before the 19th Amendment made women's suffrage a federal law.

She became the first mayor of Moore Haven, and perhaps the first woman mayor in the United States, in 1917. She was president of six businesses, including the first bank, organized a railroad and founded two other towns, nearby Newhall and Clewiston.

She was rich and pretty, came from a socially prominent Philadelphia family and during World War I national magazines dubbed her "The Duchess of Moore Haven."

For awhile, she was thought to be an angel. Later, there was a difference of opinion.

To understand better the heroic qualities of Horwitz, first consider the beginnings of Moore Haven. A Seattle developer named James Moore started things in 1915 when he bought 100,000 acres.

Moore gave the place his name, and a nationwide boomtime land sales promotion. Soon, dreamers from as far away as North Dakota had become Florida landowners.

That first year, Moore Haven had a scattering of frame buildings and about 400 residents, 99 per cent of them men. According to one well told story, one of the few women was an enterprising secretary who did not mind night work. She booked four dates an evening and you had to make reservations six weeks in advance.

By the time more families began arriving in 1916, Moore went broke. He sold out to another company, which split after two of its investors challenged sharp business practices.

Those two, John J. O'Brien and George Q. Horwitz, both of Philadelphia, formed a rival company. Horwitz died and his wife, Marian, visited Moore Haven to check the investment.

She arrived across the lake by steamboat from Palm Beach, and found a low-lying prairie village that had no paved highway and no railroad. But she took hold. By September, the town was incorporated and she was mayor.

Whatever came up, Horwitz appeared equal to it. During an epidemic of typhoid fever, when the town was quarantined, she organized the women to feed and care for the sufferers.

She imported black laborers for her farm operations, and was warned that there would be a strike and violence until they left. When the shooting started, she formed vigilante committees and stopped it.

Because of her prominence, and perhaps also because of the dismay of her Palm Beach friends who kept urging her to come home, Moore Haven began to get national attention for something other than its come-on advertising.

Articles in the Saturday Evening Post and the Literary Digest said she had given up a life of ease to "live as roughly and crudely as her ancestors of the Mayflower." They praised her as a "leader of a type of man who brooks leadership only from men more capable than they."

She married O'Brien, the Atlantic Coast Line railroad reached Moore Haven in 1918, and all seemed well. Then, slowly, the situation reversed. Neither historians nor oldtimers find any one cause.

Some cite the fact that she and O'Brien were rich and successful, and that he especially had a regal air about him that stirred resentment. Some say a woman running things bothered people. Ms. O'Brien drew criticism for riding her horse like a man, and he for wearing riding breeches and being Catholic.

The affair of the black laborers was not easily forgotten. The rivalry between the two land companies became surpassed by the rivalry among bootleggers after Prohibition became law, making the town doubly restive.

Additional resentment came after she founded the town of Newhall just northwest of Moore Haven with British families, some of them retired military officers, who smoked cigarets in holders and drank tea every afternoon at 4.

Nevertheless, the O'Briens forged ahead. They decided to establish another town 15 miles south at Sandpoint, to be called Clewiston after Tampa banker A. C. Clewis who helped finance it. They shifted their home and headquarters there and in 1921 completed the Moore Haven to Clewiston Railroad.

What finally finished them, though, was the weather. It had been dry for five years, and crops flourished. Then in May, 1922, it started raining and did not stop until August. Two more wet years followed.

Farm lands flooded, and crops ruined. Even the railroad could barely run. Businesses closed, and finally the banks in Moore Haven failed. The old resentment bubbled over.

One night a shot was fired into the O'Brien home, chipping a piece of glass that cut the Dutchess' scalp. Then someone burned their new home. In 1924, the height of the land boom elsewhere in Florida, the O'Briens packed up and left.

Only bad luck followed for Moore Haven. Hurricanes of 1926 and 1928 devastated the town. The full Depression came along. Its high hopes never materialized.

The remarkable Marian Newhall Horwitz O'Brien lived along the lake but seven years, from 1917 to 1924, but in Moore Haven one day there should be a monument to her.

She was modern a half-century before Florida was.

St. Augustine

St. Augustine:
Charlie and Big Red

Charlie Walker traded in nostalgia, not speed and comfort. The big St. Augustine tour buses honked and zoomed past, and the auto-trains snaked along with their loudspeakers going. Charlie only chattered away and his horse, Big Red, just trotted along pulling a buggy through the ancient city's narrow streets.

While St. Augustine traded on its magnificent history with all manner of modern convenience, Charlie Walker and other horse-and-buggy tour guides offered authentic samples of oldtime transportation.

The fringe-topped carriage bumped and creaked on the brick streets, and depended upon the Bay of Matanzas breezes for its air-conditioning, but with the clip-clop of Big Red's hooves and Walker's personal touch there was no way the buses and trains could match the ride in spirit.

Walker wore top hats he ordered from New York, his carriage rolled on rubber-tired wheels from Philadelphia, and Big Red ate hay from Georgia.

With all that, Charlie donned a bright green jacket, often complemented it with a yellow shirt and red tie, and further dazzled the tourists with big smiles and a courtly manner.

He worried little about the competition, even though the motorized tours offered more convenience and about the same tour at only slightly higher prices.

"The people that come to ride in these, they're going to ride in these," he said, making his case. "We have folks that take the train around and then come back and take the buggy. They want to ride in the buggy just for the experience of a buggy-ride."

Walker's daddy moved to St. Augustine from South Carolina in 1907 to work on Florida pioneer Henry M. Flagler's railroad. Charlie was six at the time, but he remembered seeing Flagler in those early years, and he remembered Flagler's funeral in 1913.

Walker, when I took a ride in his buggy in 1973, said he had owned a horse-and-rig for more than 30 years, but began to drive it himself only after retiring as a truck driver in 1965.

Local ordinances then limited the number of carriages to 39, only three of which (including Walker's) were independently owned. The others belonged to a tour company.

St. Augustine kept a close eye on the buggy operation. It issued permits for the drivers, based partly on their knowledge of the city's history; provided a station for them along the Bay on Avenida Menendez near the fort (Castillo de San Marcos); accorded special deference to carriages in traffic regulations; kept a public watering trough for the horses and insisted that the horse manure be cleaned off the streets twice a day.

"We got a man who does that," Walker said. "We follow the same route all the time and he just comes along behind us with a shovel. Course, out there where we're standing, if it happens there, we have to get a shovel and clean it up ourselves."

Walker always kept Big Red and one other horse at his home, outside St. Augustine. During the busy winter season, when he made the limit of six trips every day, Big Red worked alternating days with the other horse.

Because he had a barn, Walker beat the feed costs by driving a pickup truck to a friend's farm in Georgia, where he could buy hay cheap.

"You got to cut costs. You got to know how," he said. "That's one thing I like about St. Augustine. It's not a big-salaried town but it don't cost you much to live." Walker had four children, but he and his wife then lived alone.

In 1970, after the last blacksmith available to him left St. Augustine, Walker had to improvise carriage repairs or sent out of state for parts and service. A local upholstery shop kept the top and the seats in shape.

Walker was a St. Augustine promoter at heart. He did it with a casual air and an appealing, noncommercial manner.

"Giddap, Red," he said, over and over, occasionally flicking the horse lightly with a long whip as part of the show.

"Now this body of water you see on your right, that's Matanzas Bay. Giddap, giddap, Red." Lines of cars and buses and trains formed behind the carriage. Walker enunciated clearly, if exaggeratedly, and never stopped talking.

"That's the old Spanish fortress, right there. That's made of that old coquina rock. That's a beautiful old material...."

Then came the old schoolhouse, the old gates, sugar mill, the restoration area, the love tree (a palm growing out of an oak), the cemetery, churches, homes, the oldest house and all the other antiquities.

At intersections and on left turns, the gas-eating vehicles waited for Charlie and Big Red to trot by. Walker made sweeping gestures, and tipped his hat in apology as if the traffic jam were his fault alone.

"They haven't made a law on that, but most of the people will give the buggy the benefit of the doubt," he said. "We always have the right of way. Course, we got to be careful. Some of these people coming in here from out of town don't know about that."

Whatever the problems, and no matter how fancy the competition, horses and buggies survived on the St. Augustine scene. "We not be going out. Don't you worry about that," Charlie predicted. "We still gone be here right on."

Wakulla County

The Mother Hen of Wakulla County

High above the old 1893 courthouse in Wakulla County, there was a weathervane shaped like a mullet and it told you which way the wind blew. For about 15 critical years, anything else you needed to know, a salty lady named Elizabeth F. Smith could tell you.

She was the mother hen of Wakulla County, and she produced one of the most remarkable local publications — The Magnolia Monthly — that Florida ever saw. She wrote it all, and hand-cranked it out on a mimeograph machine in her home.

For Wakulla, and for all of Florida, it was a thing of value. She cast light on old Florida manners and customs. The Magnolia Monthly was brave, tender, angry, concerned, always interested and interesting. To receive it and read it was to get a family picture of, and to develop a family affection for, Wakulla.

No one and no situation was too high or too low, too old or too new, for The Magnolia Monthly and its delightfully frank opinions.

In 1965, when a local businessman complained because consolidation (and integration) would move the school's business away from him, Smith wondered sarcastically: "How smalltown can a man be? . . . Would he prefer that these kids not get an education so he can have the pleasure of helping to support them on welfare for the rest of their lives?"

When a Sopchoppy resident sent a message back to the county with his tax bill, The Magnolia Monthly revealed it: "Take it, hog," the man wrote.

About the late Ed Ball, Wakulla's most celebrated and powerful absentee landowner, the M-M commented while he was still alive

239

and active: "Ed would rather die rich than live rich."

After a 1968 wet-dry election: "The Dries won...and the active workers got together in the courthouse...and sang 'Praise God From Whom All Blessings Flow.' Out in the woods, the moonshiners echoed the refrain." (In 1975, Wakulla voted "wet.")

About changing times: "It's no longer considered necessary to go to church to get ahead in the world, unless one wants to be president."

On modern morals: "The last time I saw my mother...she was complaining about the scanty attire my 20-year-old niece was wearing on a date...I made the observation that morals weren't any better in my mother's time.... There was, for example, my great-aunt Libby.... (She) had a baby when she was 15 years old and I don't recall anyone ever coming around and claiming to be the father.... People in those times worked a lot harder, spent a lot less, and went to church more often, but their morals were just exactly the same as they are today...not very good."

Wakulla County, located in the Big Bend of Florida on the gulf coast south of Tallahassee, in those days had an estimated population of 10,500 — oldtime farmers, merchants and fishermen, commuters from Tallahassee, mobile home retirees, workers at the gunpowder plant. About two-thirds of the county was in the hands of wildlife preserves, national forests and pulpwood companies (principally Ed Ball's St. Joe Paper Co.).

Smith loved the charm of Wakulla's rural setting and the manners of the people but recognized that its best qualities could be accompanied by its worst — ignorance, inconvenience, corruption, sometimes violence.

"But this county's no more primitive or violent than any other in the Panhandle," she said. "All these people appreciate the fact that nobody else has ever written about them the way I do."

She opposed the Vietnam war, supported George McGovern for president, groused about environmental destruction, poked at Ed Ball, jibed at state politicians and regularly issued enlightened appraisals of north Florida. She became an authentic, if not typical, spokesman for a strain of Panhandle citizen not often noticed or examined in public print.

She chronicled vote-buying in politics, bizarre murder in the woods, skeletons in old closets, comings and goings at church, secretive misconduct, accidents, fires, the luck of beekeepers, the chilling escapades of hunters endangering people as much as bears and deer, politicans' folly, fights in the school cafeteria and achievements in the classroom.

The Magnolia Monthly never was profitable. The circulation never reached more than 280. It carried no advertisements and cost only $6 a year. But its influence and reputation far exceeded those apparent limits.

Her spicy comments and awesome accounts of history and folklore made the publication popular among those who would be insiders. When Reubin Askew was elected governor, she noted: "He was liberal enough for south Florida and pious enough for north Florida."

Among her subscribers were the New York City Public Library, two people in Alaska, politicans and fatcats, many city and university libraries across Florida.

She spared no one, not even herself. When doctors discovered her cancer, she had a mastectomy and then set her thoughts down about the whole thing: "When you find out you have cancer you go through various stages," she said. "The first one is fear that you are going to die.... The second stage is, 'Why me'.... The third stage is anger...."

She told of an encounter with her doctor. "Why does he have to take away a part of me where I have practically nothing and leave what I have a lot of to spare? Why don't women get cancer of the hips?"

Finally, in 1977, she had to give up The Magnolia Monthly. She called it the hardest thing she ever had to do. On the last page of the last issue, after rendering the usually gossipy items, she added matter of factly:

"The editor regrets that continuing bad health has caused serious problems... and no one else has ever done the work or knows how to handle any of the typing and mimeographing problems.... Please accept my regrets for such an abrupt ending...."

In the old courthouse which had the mullet weathervane atop it, they set aside a room for The Magnolia Monthly's archives. It is the Elizabeth F. Smith Room, a memorial. The mother hen was gone. But like all mothers, she left us something of value.

Everglades City ★

Jimmie Robinson And Her Boys

Jimmie Robinson was talking about her boys, the commercial fishermen of Everglades City and Chokoloskee. They were her boys, all 228 of them. Maybe outsiders saw them as a pack of hard-drinking, tough-talking primitives, but not Mrs. Jimmie. The men of her family had been Florida fishermen for four generations, and she knew their side of it.

"See, we're looked down on, for some reason," she said. "You have to understand we've always been pushed down. We've never bothered anybody but we've been pushed down. It makes you mad. It does something to you. They tell stories and make us look terrible.

"We're not this bad a people. We just want to fish and tend to our business and be left alone. They have lied to us, harassed us, done things to us and the fishermens drew back. We're not gon' take it anymore.

"They call my boys drunks, but we don't get any drunker than that congressman or that senator that I go up there to Tallahassee and have that dinner for every year. They get out there on the floor and fall, they get so drunk. No difference." She hesitated. "Well, I haven't seen 'em fall, but I've seen things worse than falling, and I'm not saying what."

The year was 1981. Jimmie Robinson, gray-haired at 61 and a little heavy with the years, impressed a stranger as a plain-speaking, stouthearted woman who would fight for those she loved. These included her husband, who harvested stone crabs for a living, her son, her daughter and her rambunctious boys. She knew the trials and troubles of their mamas and daddies and she knew theirs. She

243

avoided talk about how the fishermen's growing resentment against their treatment made them even more vulnerable to the temptations of drug smuggling.

Mrs. Robinson described the struggle between the commercial fishermen and the Everglades National park as class discrimination: The government kicking around a small group of disadvantaged citizens not able to squawk as loudly as the recreational fishermen, a larger group who had the tide with them.

"We live just like other people," she said. "When we have money, we eat steak just as big as anybody. If we don't we eat fish and grits. We want for our kids the same things other people want. Some kind of a chance. We want 'em to be hard-working, and they're trying to put 'em on welfare."

In 1980, the federal government announced that after 1985, no further commercial fishing would be permitted in park waters. It advised fishermen to sell their boats and find other employment. Officials cited declining fish populations and the need "to reallocate a diminishing resource" among user groups. For Mrs. Robinson, it was the second act of a long-running nightmare.

About 30 years ago, the park condemned and bought her father's fish house at Flamingo, on the southern tip of Florida, now the park's main entrance. Everglades City is the western entrance. At that time, and later, there were promises that park waters never would be closed to commercial fishing. Those promises were being cited now. The fishermen did not care that conditions governing that pledge have changed. To them, it remained simple: a broken promise.

"The boys don't know anything else," she said. "You can't take someone that has been taught from the time he was born to pull a mullet net, and put him in a city. The problem for us is survival. The way it looks to us, they don't want to just put us out of the park. They want to put us out of Florida."

Mrs. Robinson was a central figure in forming the Organized Fishermen of Florida in 1968. The organization, which had 1,500 members statewide, took the park issue to the courts.

"The boys can get real upset and do things they're not supposed to. They get teed off, and they'll cuss a little bit, but they can't help it," she continued. "They try. When I tell 'em they have to act certain ways when they go to certain places, they listen. There was a time the parks people didn't want to meet with us. They said the last time they came over here there was a big argument and almost a fight. Well, the fishermens would have beat 'em up. The man called the fishermens a liar. They don't like that.

"I got the boys together and told 'em, 'Now, when you go over there if you get too loud or start saying too much, I'm gonna hold my hand up and that means for you to hush. If you cuss these people out, really too bad, you'll get in trouble. You're not going to show yourself, cause this is what they want you to do. They want you to really show yourself, so they can tell about it. Well, you're not gonna do it.' And they didn't do it.

"When we have meetings now, I have prayer and I say, 'Boys, stand,' and about 40 of them old hardheaded fishermen out there, they'll stand up. The next minute they might be saying something I don't want to hear, but they stand for the prayer."

The Everglades City area had an unusual overdose of federal government in the 1970s and 1980s. New regulations for the Everglades National park and huge land acquisitions to complete the Big Cypress National Preserve increased isolaton of the tiny communities of Ochopee, Chokoloskee Island and Everglades City and altered (some would say, threatened) their futures. The 1980 census, for example, showed Everglades City with 350 residents (a spokesman at City Hall said this was low, and offered an estimate of 680, explaining that a lot of residents had refused to return the census questionnaire), compared with 462 in 1970. Enrollment at Everglades City High School dwindled to 79, making it the smallest high school in Florida.

"People are moving down here so fast," Jimmie Robinson said, shaking her head. "We didn't destroy those estuaries. What happened to the fish is not our fault. All those condos and causeways, that dredging and filling, all those people, that's what's happened to 'em. But they blame us. Now all those people in those condos will be able to fish in the park but we won't. My son won't. Is that fair?"

It is not, but it is a correct public marketplace decision to preserve the park's resources for the use of the greatest number of people for the longest time possible. When government makes order out of millions of lives, sometimes it must do things like that.

Except, when we shift focus from the millions to the individuals — to Jimmie Robinson's boys, the cussing, bleeding, bewildered commercial fishermen — we understand that being right is not always something to celebrate.

La Belle

La Belle: Grandma Forrey

It was December, and warm in La Belle, but Grandma Forrey was chopping pecans to put in the fruitcakes she made for her family at Christmas, and talking.

"I give one to all of 'em, but none of 'em don't care too much about it any more except Ella," she said, spiking a paring knife into the bowl and capturing a pecan meat against the blade with her thumb. "Ella needs to be eating cake. She's too thin. She used to be stout.

"Used to make cakes for Christmas and all the birthdays, too, but I quit that. Got to be too many. Four daughters, 11 grandchildren, 14 great-grandchildren, and one great-great-grandchild. That's just too many.

"I was born right around the corner by the Baptist Church 84 years ago. You know when that was? 1891. Raised right here. Raised my own family over here on this other corner.

"All of 'em lived right around here for a long time. In 15 minutes they could all be right here at this table. I wrote my cousin a postcard the other day and I told her I didn't know anybody more blessed. That's all you can call it. Blessed."

If you could have sat at Grandma Forrey's table, as I did that December day in 1975, she would have put you in a Christmas mood. Within minutes she told me about her family, the history of La Belle, recommended the chicken and roll dumplings at Flora and Ella's restaurant and supplied recipes.

All the while she smiled as though she had a beautiful secret. Flora and Ella were two of her daughters, and she liked to go down to the restaurant and sit at one of the tables and talk. One of her great-granddaughters waited on tables.

"This is a family affair," Grandma said. "We cook and sew and mind babies, and just whatever is needed. You know, I had four fine son-in-laws. They did a lot. Two of 'em's dead now."

Her family, the Pooles, moved from Georgia during the 1880s, when La Belle (27 miles east of Fort Myers on SR 80) was just a pretty spot in the woods that overlooked a winding, tree-shrouded Caloosahatchee River.

By 1883, the river had been deepened from Fort Myers to La Belle and a canal dredged east to Lake Okeechobee. About 1910 the government began dredging again to make the river deeper and wider (a procedure that has been repeated often enough since to make it broad and almost straight).

"One Sunday when we were girls," said Grandma, "some of us decided to go down to the dredge and pick out a boyfriend. I got the captain."

Melville E. Forrey, the lucky captain, was from Iowa. He had come to Florida as a soldier during the Spanish-American War, and decided to make it home. He tried raising tomatoes, but gave it up for the dredge boat.

With Corine Poole (later to be Grandma) at his side, he settled down. That was about the time (1911) La Belle organized as a town so that it could make laws to keep hogs and cows off the streets, and so that it could control the working dogs (every family had dogs to help with the cows, to hunt deer, chase raccoons, etc.). Forrey opened a general merchandise store, handling everything from bear traps to silk hose.

To bring government closer to home, he and six other men had a four-year fight to make La Belle the seat of a new county. They succeeded in 1923, and it was named for pioneer Francis A. Hendry (Hendry himself had named La Belle for his two daughters, Laura and Belle).

A year after the 1926 hurricane, Forrey died. In April, 1928, the store burned. That fall, another hurricane hit. By then Florida was in the grip of a Depression.

Using insurance money, and letting customers pay off their old grocery bills with labor, Grandma and Flora and Ella and their husbands (the sisters married the Burchard brothers) rebuilt. In

1933, they branched from a grocery store into a meat market and restaurant.

Using Grandma's recipes, and with all the family rallying to help as needed, Flora and Ella's place became the pride of La Belle. It was a diversified place — a coffee shop, as well as restaurant, sundries store, Western Union and Trailways Bus Stop — but the main business was food cooked the oldfashioned way.

Almost everything else had changed since Grandma was a girl. The river, wider, deeper, straighter, is not as pretty. There are more people, and different kinds, and more keep coming.

"The river used to be so crooked and nice with those trees hanging over it," she said, "but we still like it."

People have different ideas about what's important, too. They have made an art of using things, but forgetting how to create them. They eat, but do not cook. "Don't nobody hardly come along that knows how to cook," Grandma said. "If you get somebody to cook, you've got to teach 'em yourself."

Least changed may be the oldtimers like Grandma. When she talked, the river seemed as beautiful as ever and the old ways seemed rich and alive again. The black-eyed peas, served in a bowl with onions and rice and cornbread on the side, were ageless, classic.

"Now I like peas and fresh snaps," she said. "What you do is cook 'em down real good and...."

Florida grew great with people like Grandma Forrey, and it misses them.

Okeechobee

Okeechobee: Uncle Will on Women and Hell

Will Addison, who was born in 1880, sat in a wooden rocker puffing a corncob pipe and philosophizing about how the world was going to hell.

Addison listened to the traffic roaring down U.S. 441 between him and Lake Okeechobee. Posted near the front door, painted red, was a sign warning tourists to stay out of his orange grove: "Pick at your own risk." There were huge banana trees in the backyard, and a broad, cattle-filled pasture across a fence beyond. The smell of citrus blooms filled the air.

Addison grumbled that in his first 95 years of life, almost every occupation he tried in some way had been either denied him or made unprofitable by the tides of progress.

Once he sold egret plumes and hunted alligators, and that was outlawed. Once he raised cattle on the open range, but a fence law and slaughter regulations complicated that for him.

Once he fished Lake Okeechobee with giant trotlines. Once he could build his own house with pine logs taken from the woods, but now that would be stealing.

He complained he could no longer make money growing oranges because the law would not let him sell directly to truckers. All fruit had to go to a packing house before shipping.

When Frederick William Addison, known around Okeechobee City as Uncle Will, complained that life was "a mess" he included all these things and more.

"They even changed dinner and supper to lunch and dinner," he said, marveling at man's ability to complicate the simple. "And

250

they say 'root' (route) when they mean 'rout'."

Women did not escape his expert criticism, either. He had four wives, and offered a rare word of caution for lightheaded young men who may dare to rush in where he so often has tread.

"Yeah, I had four of 'em," he said, like a golfer recounting four putts that rimmed the cup. "I didn't get a wife every time I married. I just got a woman.

"If you get a good woman, a good woman is the best thing on earth. But if you get an old mean one...." He shook his head, emphasizing the gamble. "If you get an old mean one, she's the meanest thing on earth."

Addison had one wife who died, one whose family he thought shared too fully his worldly goods, one he thought did not stay home enough, and one who had a keen eye for where he stood in the actuarial charts.

"This one would have been all right, but I had a little money and they (the in-laws) thought we ought to live with them, and I just ought to let them use my stuff as theirs, and they separated us.

"This other one left me. I took her back once. She come back and I said if you do this again, you're going to do like the turkey gobbler when he left the tall pine, you'll flipflop and you're long gone. I proved it to her.

"This other one, I was here by myself and lonesome and I found out I was hooked, the next day," he said. They quarreled about his property and whether her name should be on the deed. While away on a visit, the issue came up one last time.

"She put in on me and I said, 'Let me tell you something. I told you once that I am not agonna do that.' And I said, 'Furthermore, if you don't shet your mouth I'm going back home.'"

He took on the last one at age 88, and at 95 — the year I talked with him — he carefully had weighed the matter and decided that four was enough. "I wouldn't marry nary another 'un," he said.

Addison called himself "a fullblooded Cracker." He was a tall, thin, always active man with an owlish view of life to the end.

His grandfather left South Carolina before the Civil War and moved to DeSoto County (southwest Florida, near Arcadia), where he became a cattleman. His family once tried to drive 2,700 head of cattle across Indian trails toward Fort Lauderdale, where they were to be shipped to Cuba. That was decades before the diking of Lake Okeechobee. A storm blew up, flooding all the low lands, and all but 300 of the cattle drowned.

"Maw said after that water went down there was a lot of their cows that had got in a fork of a tree and they was just hanging up there. It was terrible," he remembered.

Addison's parents pioneered a community in Allapattah Flats about 15 miles northeast of Okeechobee. When Western Union put a line through, the place was called Addison. Later, the name was changed to Bluefield.

"I ain't got much education," Uncle Will said. "I just got through the Fourth Reader. I went to school in Fort Pierce and I went to school some in Fort Drum. My mother, she teached me some.

"Course, she didn't have too much education, but I tell you, I don't believe a fella needs too much education if he's got brains."

He said there once were alligators everywhere in the area. "A six-foot gator brought 65 cents. A seven-foot one brought 85 cents, and a five-foot one brought 45 cents and anything under that brought 20 cents or 10 cents."

Addison said he never ate alligators, just sold them. "I won't eat a coon (raccoon) either, or a possum. I had an uncle that said he wouldn't eat anything a dog wouldn't eat. I wouldn't, either.

"These plume birds, the women dressed their hats with 'em in them days, you know, and people hunted 'em. Them big white plumes, people would get a dollar apiece for them. Egret plumes. They was curled up and they was beautiful. Sometimes they might get a dollar and a half apiece.

"I seen my Daddy bring two corn sacks full, and he'd take one on the front of his saddle and tie one up behind and go to Kissimmee and sell 'em. He got paid in silver dollars. Have you ever seen those 25-pound sacks they used to load (gun) shells in? He had two or three of them big old shot sacks full of silver dollars."

Addison's father paid a man $100 to build the pine log house where they lived. "I wish I had a house like that today. I'd rather have a log house than any house I know," he said, rambling through history. "We couldn't get kerosene then. I held my mother a light a many a night while she was cooking. Them lightwood splinters, you know, tar'd drop out of them onto my feet."

The chimney of the log house was fashioned from mixed moss and clay applied to a wood frame. "You got to wet it (the clay), to make it stick good, and then you daub it. Then it'd dry. If you didn't daub it good it wouldn't stand because the fire would burn them sticks away."

For supplies, the Addisons travelled by ox-cart either to Fort Pierce or to Basinger, where the Kissimmee River flows into Lake Okeechobee. Ocean-going schooners called at Fort Pierce with supplies, and steamboats came down the Kissimmee with goods from the railroad.

"It'd take a little over a day to go to Fort Pierce. We'd get to Ten-Mile Creek, that was 20 miles from home, and camp there that night. Next day we'd go into Fort Pierce and do our shopping, and come back to Ten-Mile that night. It'd take about three days to make the trip, with oxen, depending on how much water there was. Sometimes you'd run up to the axle of the wagon. Dry weather you could make it quicker.

"When the flats was full of water it'd be better for us to go to Basinger. It was a little farther, about 35 miles, but you could order by mail and meet the steamboat when it came bringing the stuff."

Addison moved to Okeechobee about 1907. "Old man Peter Raulerson and his son Lewis lived on one side of Taylor Creek and Judge (H.H.) Hancock lived on the other side, and that was all the people there were here in them days," he said.

He worried that too many people had found out about Okeechobee. "It's gonna make a regular Miami," he said. "I go out to my mailbox and I have to stand and wait and wait until I can get across the road. Then I get across and want to come back and there's more waiting."

For Uncle Will Addison, pedigree Cracker who bridged Florida history, it was a perfect example of how the world was going to hell.

North Ft. Myers

Frog Smith: Authentic Cracker

A sensitive biographer could make a tragedy of E. A. Smith's
life: How a boy of 12 went to work in a sawmill to support the family
because his stepdaddy was lazy; how he labored from sunrise to
sunset for only pennies a day; how jobs petered out in the Depression and he fed his four children by hunting frogs in swamps at
night; how some fellows demeaned him by calling him Frog.

All of it is true. The skilled biographer could make Smith a mirror of early 20th-Century inhumanity to the working man and point
out how his exploitation inevitably led to the rise of social legislation and to the organization of labor unions, relieving these
burdens and liberating the worker for a better life. It could be
socially powerful.

Trouble is, old Frog would say it ain't so. He revelled in the
adversity of his youth and declared that life was never sweeter. At
82 (in 1979) he politely said yessir and nosir to his juniors, who
know so little. To him the old life was fine and funny and he never
tired of telling its tales.

"I'm a pretty good egg but I've been sat on too long," he said,
beginning to call up his favorite one-liners. "The way to get even
for the Civil War is to marry your daughter to a Yankee.... Moonshine'll kill you but sometimes it takes nigh on to 100 years.... I
growed up in Georgia until I thought I knowed it all and then I went
to work, at age 12....

"They say you ought not eat pork because it has worms and it'll
kill you but I've never swallowed a worm yet that my tapeworm
couldn't lick.... Man's the most vain animal there is, except one —
woman.... A man asked me if I was a Democrat or a Repubican
and I told him that from what I've been called I must be a

Republican.... He asked me what I'd be if I wasn't a Cracker and I said ashamed."

Frog had been a sawmill worker, a yardsweeper, a blacksmith, a machinist, an oiler, a steam locomotive operator, a lumber inspector, a harmonica player and an alligator hunter, in addition to his frog enterprises. For him, every skinned knuckle and busted rib and sprung muscle added a touch of wisdom and a new story. He was an evangelist for hard times.

"Appetites? I knowed a fellow once that could eat a chitterling five miles long, with a loaf of bread for every milepost.... A man complained that some of the sausage stuffed in a chitterling wasn't all natural hogmeat, but I told him it was better than what come in there original.... Dad wore a mustache to brush the dirt off his feet when he put his foot in his mouth.... That fellow was so thin that if he'd a had a tapeworm you coulda read the inches on it...."

Frog was authentic Cracker. He was born in Pinebloom, Ga., in 1896, and as a boy moved to the piney woods of North Florida to work. He lived in nearly every part of the state. In 1950, already acknowledged among his friends as a master storyteller, he branched out. He wrote a letter to The Tampa Tribune telling an unlikely tale of how his family came to Florida. The Tribune published it, and Frog Smith was elevated to forklorist.

With that, Frog eased into a role as one of Florida's all-time characters. He has been at it ever since, peddling his stories in all directions, to magazines and newspapers, on television, on stages, around campfires and in classrooms. For 25 years, he was a featured storyteller at the annual Florida Folk Festival in White Springs.

During the Bicentennial year, 1976, he performed in Washington at the invitation of The Smithsonian Institution. Tape recordings of his stories and some of his primitively styled paintings of sawmills are part of the Smithsonian's offerings on American folklore.

Frog lived in a small house on Mariana Avenue in North Fort Myers. Two half-buried tires marked the driveway. When the dog barked, a short, restless man with close-cropped gray hair would meet you at the carport, adjusting his glasses and telling stories compulsively. Sometimes he repeated himself, but in a man who has had two wives, 14 grandchildren and eight great-grandchildren, no one minded. As he talked, he energized. In his backyard shop, where memorabilia surrounded a typewriter and a fan held back the heat, he tried to type as fast as the stories occurred to him.

Raising an outrageous caution to the unwary, he grandly labeled his stories nonfiction (a stork dropped him in the Okefenokee Swamp, for example, and a tumble-bug rolled him up to his Mama's house and she took him in), but he nevertheless seriously questioned whether modern convenience and comfort improved either the quality or the happiness of lives. That conviction anchored his farm-fresh humor with more than just nostalgia. Of his two self-published collections of stories (*Crackers and Swamp Cabbage, Frog Smith's Scrapbook*) he said, "If you find anything in here that your better judgment won't let you believe, just tear the page out and smell it."

Frog simply thought the old days were better. He was a rare piece of the Florida heritage, museum perfect and worthy of study before the formulas for living in adversity — and liking it — were forgotten. "I'd go to work at 5:30 a.m., get off at 6 p.m., and still feel good enough to take my shotgun down to the swamp and kill enough squirrels for next day's lunch — but we called it dinner. Fella goes to work at 9 now, piddles around all day, gets off at 5 and he's wore out. Things are more modern now, there's shorter work hours and more pleasure, we get more time and more pay, but they don't mean nothing," he said.

Frog was raised in a time when anything worthwhile required sweat and patience and probably pain. He floundered in leisure, and doubted easy comfort. Hard times and the Depression built his character and nearly a half-century has passed since there has been any mass production of it to compare. That was how he explained it, anyway.

The best thing to do was to remember, and to enjoy. The 'instant' age? "That just don't fit my britches."

Reflections

The Travels, The Search

My friends envy me the travelling life as a good one, and I tell them they are right, which is true. But my truth is not their truth. They imagine quaint villages, ease aplenty and the stimulation of distinctive strangers. They do not realize that quaint is kin to peculiar, that fickle ease keeps company with both monotony and anxiety, that distinctive includes oddball. There is more in the mix than they suppose.

My wife, Gloria, and I were travelling south, watching the gas gauge, and reached Fort Pierce on a late afternoon in February. The first gas station was closed, the second had only oil and air, the third told us about a place in Stuart. There, we waited in line one hour and 20 minutes for a fill-up which permitted us to proceed to the second issue: a room for the night.

None was available. The manager of one chain advised us there was nothing to the south, and we would have to drive 90 miles north for a guaranteed vacancy. "If you feel lucky," he advised, "drive down U.S. 1 and check all the Mom-and-Pop places. That's what everybody else is doing."

Racing for a room became a contest: motel roulette. Cars were competing for position, guessing whether the first lighted motel would be a left or a right turn. Two, three would wheel up to the office, one behind the other. But we soon discovered that was no good. Nobody had more than one room available. The smart ones sacrificed early chances in order to move to the head of the line.

By 8 p.m., the game had carried us far south. We had the lead position on a seedy, poorly lighted stretch of highway. A sign loomed: Vacancy, all rooms $21. We wheeled into the dark, as an arrow indicated, and captured the prize — one ratty little room for $50 (never mind the sign), equipped with roaches, thin walls and little signs inked on the wall advising you how the curtain should hang in the shower and indicating which volume position on the TV was too loud. For dinner, we had a quarter-pounder and for entertainment we rested from the 12-hour endurance race. Quaint.

In Fort Lauderdale, once, I choked on a piece of steak and wound up in the hospital. In Pensacola, with sleet beating on the room windows, our neighbors spent the night shouting and arguing with men who threatened to break down the door and commit murder. In Lake Placid we had a flat tire, in Okeechobee a generator belt broke, in Brooksville the air-conditioner quit.

It goes on. Over the years we have gathered no moss but plenty of humility, abundant awareness of the necessity to make do. We have learned to live with dry throats and a yearning for rest stops. Gloria, who shares the driving and the work, once fumed for an hour while I sought a clean-looking filling station for her. She rushed in and I, waiting, fell asleep in the car. Nearly an hour later she returned, angry. A misfortune with the restroom door had locked her inside, and I had abandoned her. An attendant finally heard her pounding on the door, yelling for help.

We live by search. Where have we not been lately? Who have we missed? We comb the map, go to the places, seek out the situations, look for the people who reflect importantly, interestingly or entertainingly in the mosaic of Florida. Through letters, conversations, encounters, we hear about names and learn about human entanglements. Sometimes we call ahead, but not often. We go and search, and wait and wait and wait. We want to find people and things as they are, not as they would pretend to be.

We find heroes and clowns and philosophers among a stable of wonderfully varied Floridians, most of them familiarly flawed and ennobled by contradictory character streaks that entwine about consuming ambitions and fears that never will be realized. We see our country, our state, ourselves in them.

In Inverness, a kind motel manager placed a soft, dry towel by the door so that we might use it to wipe the morning dew off our car windows. In Haines City, when we did the same thing, the manager demanded we buy the towel.

We find serious men in out-of-the-way places crusading for the environment and warning of coming disasters while equally serious other men curse the artificial restraints that inhibit the use of property, create scarcity and drive prices up. Oddly, population fastens and grows upon population like oysters upon oysters, and leaves vast tracts barely touched.

The tourist flits through it all, barely seeing. He darts at the simple appeal of the immensely complex Disney World, at the fantasyland of hotels on the ocean, at the souvenir shops laden with imported goods, at the tacky little road attractions that make him laugh while being gulled. Near Leesburg, there was an attraction called Big Sam, world's biggest bull. It was. But Big Sam died, or something, and was reincarnated as the world's largest horse. A touch of white paint on the road signs showing a silhouette of the old Big Sam now leaves new Big Sam, world's largest horse, with a bizarre, faint under-image of old Sam's horns and male weapon. Tourists care not.

The travels take us from Big Sam to Gov. Graham, and from a rat-hole to a highrise, and it is, just as my friends say, the good life. Not so romantic as they think, nor so easy, nor so carefree, but nevertheless good. That is our truth.

Looking For
Modern Scarecrows

The decline of the scarecrow has been a sad thing. There was wit and mystery as well as practicality about the scarecrow. Old clothes stuffed with straw and strung upon crossed poles became the spirit of the master, unblinking, uncomplaining, homely enough to be loved easily and without complication.

The scarecrow was a comic talisman of serious purpose. Not only did it frighten off crows and other pests, but it put a stamp of personality and ownership upon the land. It stood as a retaliation of wit to the wild, a proof that reason too was a weapon.

Rarely do you see those fine figures posted across the agricultural fields of Florida anymore. Where scarecrows are needed, artistry has been replaced by trinketry. Rather than an imposing scarecrow flapping a black sleeve in the wind, there are whirling reflectors and mirrors, noisemakers, spiritless gadgetry that has no humor and no mystery. For most of us, they are meaningless.

One reason is that our bogeymen have changed. When real scarecrows did sentinel duty, there were a lot of small farms and every house had a garden. The scarecrow fit those times. Things are different now. The real bogeymen to most of us are no longer simple, well defined things of the country. They are more scary, more unreal, more urban, and they may fly at us out of the clear sky as well as the dark night. They come as unpredictable and uncontrollable changes in life, and often we cannot identify their forms until they are upon us.

Maybe they come because seductive drugs besiege our frailties with the colors and flavors of candy, or out of the crime that attacks in ordinarily safe places and often hides behind deceptively young faces, or in bewildering shortages of necessities in the land of plenty.

Against these, none of the old scarecrows works. Neither straw-stuffed effigies nor computers nor Rube Goldberg mechanics control these bogeymen because beyond their physical impact there is this problem of what they do to the spirit. They reduce our potential.

"There is a difference in our human outlook, depending upon whether we have been born upon level plains, where one step reasonably leads to another, or whether, by contrast, we have spent our lives amidst glacial crevasses and precipitous descents," wrote Loren Eiseley. The difference now is that we do not have that psychological separation. The plains and the crevasses are interspersed. We cannot with any certainty know whether two tiptoe steps might be followed by the need to leap across a chasm. The bogeymen refuse to conform to familiar pattern.

What we need are new scarecrows, tailored to fit the times, and they must have in them enough mystery and practicality to rearm this dimension of the mind that is being battered and abused so impersonally.

I thought about this the other day as I thought I saw a bogeyman sweeping in my direction. A machine started clearing some undeveloped land across the lake from where we live. It looked very much like a crow. I watched the thing, worried.

But as the thing grew it proved to be not a bulldozer but a small tractor, not invaders of some sort but a young family, excited and enthusiastic over a new homesite. They cut grass and cleared brush and exuded a joy. Among them were discovery and hope. This was no crow. This was a beginning of particular significance for those strangers, and for me it drove away a false bogeyman.

But there was in this a hint of what the new scarecrows should be. They should have the capacity to put unreal fears into perspective through renewal of faith in the survival of normality. They should call up a proper inventory and cataloguing of the human stock so that its better qualities will not be forgotten.

The new scarecrows would not dismember the bogeymen, for these new crows appear unassailable by individuals, but they would dispel the dispirited reaction to them. They would remind us how to tolerate knaves and fools, even when they are ourselves, to adjust to them, not to let them swell out of proportion. It helps if we do not mistake a couple of pairs of crows for the Four Horsemen of the Apocalypse.

William Alexander Percy, a patrician planter's son, in effect suggested the dirt garden as a scarecrow in the 1940s, long before the bogeymen took on their present dimensions. He observed in that day "the intolerable serenity and conceit" of the gardener who planted seeds and pulled weeds and believed so firmly in the mystery of the life process that when the vegetables and flowers miraculously emerged he took on "the air of the Lord God after He did it in seven days." What a perfect modern scarecrow.

The reward of a garden (or even potted plants on the patio) is that it is a dirt-rooted, breathing, hurting, real arena where you can observe and learn from things which do not have the ability to press an accelerator or pull a trigger or waft acid into the air but still they flower and perform essential functions. It exercises faith and confidence. Gardens are little patches of life where the struggles for sunlight and nutrition are no less desperate than ours, yet nearly always the mystery succeeds. When there is weeding and watering and fertilizing, when the climate is right, the magic works. Always, there is renewal.

The garden breaks down the rat mazes we forge for ourselves, where our bewilderment creates spooks and crows, with compelling example. There is drama in the struggle, humor and good cheer in the blossom, triumph in the fruiting, understanding in the determined cycles.

We all need scarecrows again, talismen of our own making that reaffirm our ability to endure and prevail. Maybe the garden has not the romance of the old clothes stuffed with straw, but in whatever form — a pot, a planter, a plot — it stakes out a dwelling as a place where the spirit and the imagination resist those lousy crows. It is late October again, almost Halloween, and time to plant.

Lost: A Sense of Place

It has been a peculiar summer. Early one morning, I saw a rabbit swimming in the lake, and that confirmed it. Rather than romping through the briar bushes, or burrowing in a comfortable warren, he was taking a casual swim. This clearly was a very modern, reckless rabbit. He had no sense of place whatsoever.

It seems to be the way of this July, and I am beginning to wonder if there is more. Alignments have been jarred a tiny bit awry, I notice, not quite enough to be called crazy, but out of place. The winter was historically cold, the summer is historically hot, the rainy season historically dry. Something is afoot. "Things are in the saddle, and ride mankind," Emerson said. There is a definite trend but, so far, peculiar remains the apt word.

Look around at the little things, the small indicators. The rabbit has not been alone. For example, I saw two long and skinny black snakes, normally secretive and private creatures that panic when approached, coiled into a throbbing slip-knot on a stump. They did not break their concentration even when I walked close enough to be suspected as a voyeur.

A large owl, which usually hoots only after midnight and never before had shown his face, one afternoon took a stroll on the beach in full light. He drank water and browsed, hooted magnificently, and ignored the fact that nature had ruled he should avoid daylight and public places.

Here in North Central Florida, among the sand hills around Melrose, the lakes have dipped to record lows and the St. Johns River not far away runs so slowly it really only walks. A short drive to the south, the ground has collapsed in several places and insurance men talk about selling you protection against loss of earth. It is strange.

All of this, and more, bumps and distorts our sense of place.

Have you noticed the other things? Sense of place is not confined to geography alone. There was a time when a man was embarrassed by being ugly; now some consider it a prized attribute, a quality suggesting honesty. Other frailties are celebrated as well. We sing about short people, encourage the bald to let their heads hang out, believe lefthanders have superior perspective, hail symptoms of ignorance as distinctive culture to be preserved.

There is a theory now that a lot of people voted for President Reagan because they did not think he would do the things he promised. The other recent Presidents never did. Now, it turns out that he acts the way he talked. They are disappointed.

You see? Almost nothing hangs right. Rabbits go swimming and snakes and owls and people have jumped their tracks. This thing no longer can be quarantined to California. The subtle crazies are loose, altering natural habitats, and there might be consequences. When that rabbit went into the water, for example, he lost his natural cover. When he came out, two dogs ambushed him and ate him.

In Florida, the rabbit has a lot of company. So many new people arrive so fast, to a strange environment rapidly becoming even stranger, that for them there is almost no sense of place at all. Perimeters fly off on tangents and behavioral rudders flutter. The audio and the video are not only out of sync, but out of the box. Who can tell what might happen next?

A sense of place involves knowing where you most naturally belong, and why. It is recognizing the environment whose rewards and risks are large enough reasonably to accommodate your abilities and hopes without undue jeopardy. It is not so confining as it is reassuring. You may outgrow it but you always want to be able to go back if you need to, because this is the place that nurtured you and somehow it renourishes the strengths that have been used up. Without a way to find it again, the seasons of life lose the beginning cycle. Somehow, it must be recreated.

"Each man goes home before he dies," said the naturalist philosopher Loren Eiseley. Actually, it seems to me each may go home figuratively before he really lives, seeking confirmation that sustains and identifies him.

An intelligent fellow I know, who understood all this very well, wanted to cement his new marriage by having it formalized in a setting that always would be there. He was looking for an adoptive beginning. He wanted a physical setting to which he could return years later and experience the same surroundings. He hoped they would help him renew the mental framework of his wedding day. He looked around Florida, and finally chose a wildlife sanctuary. He was married there, gambling that this prop would keep the circle intact.

The bridegroom knew the kind of magnetic force that origin can exert toward reforming elements in disarray. Poets and philosophers have fed on this idea: that lives revolve in cycles, that they can be freshened and stabilized by returning to familiar touchstones, whether physical symbols or beliefs.

"Woe unto him that join house to house, that lay field to field, till there be no place," said the Biblical Isaiah.

The rabbit did all this, stirred all these thoughts. I knew he should not have been out there swimming in the lake, but he had lost his sense of place. In Florida, it is getting harder and harder to retain it. Poor old rabbit; poor old us.

The Mystery, The Celebration

Environmentalists generally are a pretty glum bunch. Hardly ever will you meet a happy environmentalist. It is due to environmental hydrophobia, an infectious madness that causes the victim to see things that others do not see.

Aldo Leopold explained it best 30 years ago and it still is true. One of the penalties for being an environmentalist is the realization that we live in a wounded world, but nobody else seems to see it.

As Leopold put it in his classic book of essays entitled *A Sand County Almanac,* the environmentalist either has to harden his shell and make believe that the damage being done is none of his business, or he must act the part of the doctor who sees the mark of death upon a community and delivers the death message. He has a right to be unhappy.

There are many reasons why people ignore environmental degradation. Some of it is reluctance to face the truth. Some of it is simply ignorance. Some think nature will repair itself. Some of it comes from a perception of economic necessity — a belief that cannibalizing the environment is the only way to keep the cash registers ringing.

Some of it also is because a few of our leaders and politicians insist on pretending an optimism that the rest of us would be eager to adopt if we could understand that there is a foundation for it beyond a hunch that some day soon human nature will change and science will pass miracles we have not yet imagined.

But there is another central reason, I think. In urban lives today, we have placed too many things between us and nature. We lose touch with the wind and the dirt; we are shielded from the rain, from the full brunt of the heat and the cold. Once, the weather so touched us that it determined our daily routines; now it barely influences them.

Vital relationships are being obscured. The mystery that is in the land, in the living, growing things, is being denied us more and more. The sense of place, of a dynamic connection between each of us and the earth is being interfered with.

We fail to get the renourishment that comes from being in close touch with things natural, from being acutely aware of the relationships between people, the seasons, the land, wildlife. It becomes a problem of the spirit that reduces our potential, our view of what is possible.

These may seem like inconsequential things, but I think they affect us powerfully. For example, if we paid attention in November, we would notice the coming of the Florida fall. By enchantingly varied degrees, it moves down the peninsula. The thunderstorms begin to fade. The hot summer eases. By December, even in South Florida, we begin to realize that a great, sweet change is sweeping over the land again.

It is a marvel. Nobody can tax it, or sell it, or claim credit for it. The seasons run perfectly, without excuses, without sly increases in cost, without artfully hedged promises. Obviously, something more than human is involved. Any cynic can see that.

This sense of mystery that we should get from nature puts a celebration into life. It imparts a certain quality available nowhere else. It elevates reality and brings a fleeting perception that there really are things that have meaning that cannot be computed, things that lead us to flirt with a wisdom that is beyond full grasp.

Every now and then, just for a moment or two, we are seized and shaken by this insight. Too briefly, there is a flash of revelation how crowd psychology imposes standards and goals upon many of us that we really would not choose if we gave it careful and independent thought.

These are some of the ways that we are being robbed when we let something completely block out the natural things. If something wipes them out of our lives entirely, it is too easy for the mind to become calloused, to give up and go along.

Economics always sets the physical limits of what can be done with our lives, but Leopold's line of thinking persuades us that economical considerations should not be the only ones that have validity. There are other factors that count. In our private lives we put certain interests above economic arguments.

In serious matters of health, for example, we do whatever is necessary. Cost is not a factor. For family, children, church, personal satisfactions, we do a lot of things which, although limited by economics, are not solely determined by the dollars involved.

Because in Florida there are good and sound and compelling economic reasons for getting angry about environmental degradation, many have turned away from those other arguments of spirit and health. They should not.

Conservationists should not let the spoilers, who have only economic arguments, deny their cause that full range of other things in our lives that are just as basic and that give us more meaningful dimensions.

In Florida, environmental concern is growing, but the problems are growing faster. J. Frank Dobie provided poetic perspective when he wrote, "What is the spirit, the tempo, the rhythm of this plot of earth to which we belong?...Often it seems that the essential spirit has been run over and killed. But nature...cannot be betrayed by man; in the long run, man can only betray himself...."

Put more simply, you ought to worry about the natural things that are being blocked out of your life. They are the ones that make all the difference.

A Cry, A Speech,
A Chuckle, A Buzz

Midnight, the poet said, shakes memory the way a madman shakes a dead geranium. Out of it fall little pieces. Some of them come as flashbacks, and for me they lack sound. Nobody speaks the lines. The old times are like silent movies, where the characters make gestures and mouth something unheard, and so they are vague, unsatisfying things.

The imagination intervenes. The place is not always certain, the colors not always true, the shapes blurred. They come out of an old lens that has lost its sharp definitions.

But that does not happen with sounds. The memory of a sound has a completeness of its own. There will be a picture, too, but the picture will be only scenery and staging. Sound will dominate.

Sound has the deeper dimension. It calls upon a greater range of recollection. It has point and precision. It came from somewhere or something that had meaning to you.

Consider. What has been the sound that comes most to your memory? An acorn rattling down a tin roof on a dark night? The bawl of a baby? The crack of lightning in a thunderstorm?

The choice is difficult, and the answers tentative. The explosion of guns? A plea for help? A whisper? The clink of coins in your first pay envelope? A touching prayer in an old farmhouse?

All these have been significant, memorable sounds. Choosing among them slights a hundred special things of the heart and the mind.

When the madman shakes the dead geranium at midnight, I hear four distinct, haunting sounds. Each time, I want to hear them again. I want to hear something more that will help me understand them better. Somehow my mind at rest has decided these have an importance that my mind at work has not grasped. I have written of these before, but the list and the conviction grow.

I hear one small and fleeting cry; one speech that stirred my sense of patriotism as no other has since; the odd chuckle of a doctor preparing to wield a saw and scalpel; and, finally, the buzz of a fly on a quiet afternoon.

The first came at the end of a family gathering many years ago. I had to leave early to catch a plane to go far away, it seemed to them and to me, and so my farewell had the attention and the thoughts of all.

It was cold, and in that crowd of embraces and handshakes, somehow my little brother got squeezed out. I did not see him, and thought perhaps he was preoccupied with a game or a television show, and I understood.

But as the driver pulled the car away, I heard my brother calling my name. He was waving, and he obviously thought I had overlooked him. On his face was a hurt look, and his cry sounded like a boy lost.

Then I was gone, and could not turn back. But I kept hearing him call, over and over, for years after and somehow that scene began to represent in my memory the many things of value that I discovered too late.

When John F. Kennedy spoke his first words to the nation as president, his manner and message gave me a sense of pride in nationality that never has seemed quite so grand again. What happened later, good and bad, sometimes disillusioning and sometimes fulfilling, has no bearing on the memory of that sound.

President Kennedy seemed a young courageous figure and he lit up the nation with a kind of spiritual power. His words — at that time — represented to me the best in America.

The presidents since then have seemed to me but politicians. The simple explanation could be maturity on my part, using greater experience and greater knowledge and detecting the human flaws. Or, it could be frailty on theirs. But that is the truth of it for me.

''. . . The torch has been passed to a new generation of Americans

...." Kennedy said that day. But, it seems to me now, the torch never really passed. It shone and moved forward briefly, perhaps for the full thousand days, but then somebody carted it off to a political museum.

The doctor's chuckle was the last thing I heard as I waited to be wheeled into the operating room, fading fast, the pill and the shot working splendidly. The lights were bright, the stretcher rolled and my imagination was full of great drama. Then, the doctor chuckled. That was the last sound I heard. I wondered just what the hell was so funny.

The fly is an altogether different memory. I heard it as a boy lying on a pile of freshly picked cotton; I heard it as a university freshman while sitting at a desk in an absolute panic over the deadline for a weekly English theme; I hear it now, in the yard, during the quiet times, when I am puzzling over why something grows or does not grow because of or regardless of my supervision. It always reminds me of those other days, when a different age made me a different person. I like to remember what my worries and my hopes were then. It is amusing, healthy medicine.

The fly buzzes when it is warm, absolutely still, and issues the kind of sound that a mind might make if it had a motor that needed a touch of oil. I am convinced now that it did need a touch of oil.

That tiny, persistent sound had the value of suggesting a detached viewpoint, a separated appraiser of my circumstances, one from the fly that was objective and nonthreatening and totally lacking in drama. The fly represented my personal historian, telling an ordinary and relaxed story.

The sounds that count, at least for me, have not been so much the mileposts passed as the values discovered, indicating that the more important things all along were not the ones I noticed most.

The sounds tell me that. I listen, shake the dead geranium again and again, hoping that I can master their messages this time. But I am never sure that I do.

Brooksville

Turning Us Into Turkeys

Steve Fickett, a wildlife biologist and sometimes philosopher, had a way of explaining things. The deer and the turkey and the quail will survive the foreseeable future, he says, because there is a master plan for them. While he talks, the imagination develops its own perspective.

Wildlife has been set aside, protected. When food becomes scarce, the state rolls out tractors and plants gardens for them, or puts out feeders, or control-burns the underbrush so that the natural food will come back and flourish.

Whatever gets out of balance is put back into balance. If a predator becomes too great a danger, then a hunting season can be opened a crack, or the predator's hide can be approved for commercial use, or maybe even a bounty can be offered. When the predator is brought under control, another regulatory button is pushed and it may push his life methodically along.

For the wildlife, there is a kind of security plan. There are problems, but mostly it works. "Florida has more deer right now than it had in the days of the Indians," Fickett said, clinching his point.

The major enemy of wildlife is urbanization but some of the bigdomes have sat down and quite objectively, quite precisely and dispassionately, figured out the best ways to keep "useful" wildlife from being too distressed by it. They figure out how, and then they do it. How lucky can a turkey get?

Not every creature fits under this little blanket. Some of them do not have attractive hides or meat and some of them, the panther and the bear for example, do not really observe the conventions and so their future is not so secure. They tend to be too wild, too magnificently independent to be really "useful." The key to their ruination is that they create fear in humans; people will go out and shoot every one of them, and brag if they can get the last one. They are vulnerable because they simply insist upon being unorthodox.

On the other hand, nobody is afraid of a deer or a quail or a turkey and so they are protected. The regulations say they may be shot only in season, and only so many each season, and the results are monitored and the regulations then adjusted to insure that wildlife enrollment in the managed forests stays even or grows.

It is enough to make a human wonder. Should we be envious? Where is the dispassionately administered master plan for us? Although there may be disturbing aspects of *1984* in the question, some South Floridians will tell you that 1981 was not so calming, either. There has been little relief from the predators, no restricted seasons and no limiting licenses, no etiquette at all in the disruption.

The managed wildlife areas are protected from excess by scientific control of the numbers, much like open-air zoos where licensed hunters become the instruments to trim population until it matches the habitat and food and space, allowing the system to function again.

The deer and the turkey and the quail think they are free (in the book, *1984*, the Ministry of Truth sloganized, "Freedom Is Slavery") but their hard bargain is to provide a quota of victims from the zoo, supplying meat and sport so that the rest may live like Bambi.

Do not blame Fickett for these radical ruminations. He is the kind of man who would not use the word *zoo* in polite company. He does not dabble in politics. He is a naturalist of rare breadth, a lifetime hunter and a lifetime birdwatcher and an ardent conservationist who devoutly believes the three are complementary. Few others in Florida bridge the range of environmentalist considerations that Fickett, a father of six, does.

Not only is he one of the Florida Game and Freshwater Fish Commission professionals, but a member of the board of directors of the Florida Audubon Society, president of the Florida chapter of The Nature Conservancy and a member of the national and Florida wildlife federations.

In the cypress-lined living room of his home in Brooksville, a West Central Florida city of 6,000, 59-year-old Fickett explains the broad principles of conservation. He stresses the value of adaptability in wildlife, points out the mortality rate of the animals which inspire fear, emphasizes the contribution to beauty and balance made by every tiny throb of life.

He explains that the Audubon Society and hunters are allies, keeping an eye and friendly checkrein on each other, together battling to preserve the natural state and outdoors heritage of Florida. He is a believer in many camps.

But, as he talks, the maverick mind wanders off to another plane. What is more fearful than a panther? The smashing of a door at night, an armed stranger in the shopping center, a car that deliberately pulls too close in the next traffic lane?

It has been a long time since we were pioneers banding together to meet a threat from the wild. The frontier has been turned inside out. Now the wild is a meat and sport market; people have become the threat and the prey. It takes a reversal in thinking to handle that.

Impatient bigdomes are being tempted toward futuristic computations of the best ways to relieve the new stresses on the system. There is a tendency to think of human-life management areas. Match the people to the resources. Rather than scaling expectations to realities, set a reasonable quota of sacrifice — to inflation, to pollution, to security, to all of it — and select the victims.

The numbers would make sense, but little else. The life style would revert to sophisticated primitivism. But to those seeking shelter from horror there is attraction in this idea of being managed. If we reach that point, the *1984* slogans begin to make fearful sense. "Freedom Is Slavery," and vice-versa.

Yet, these will be the arguments of the future. Already they have begun. In troubled times, the wildlife example is appealing. We should give it some thought. They would make things right by turning us all into turkeys.

Putting Humanity In The Ink

When my hair gets long, it curves out and up on the sides, giving my head the striking look of a shiny soup bowl planted bottoms-up in a field of stale carrot curls. Sometimes, when I am absorbed in my work, it gets that way before I notice.

A young neighbor who infiltrated the yard saw me in that condition and inquired how my head got that way. In the absence of a good explanation from me, he concluded that it was a birth defect.

But, he suggested that I might be able to make a bad situation more tolerable if I went out and got a haircut, and if I found myself a steady job.

That is the way it is with newspapermen. There are critics everywhere. Hardly anyone understands them. Not even other newspapermen always understand. For example, I never understood James Gordon Bennett Sr., 19th Century publisher of The New York Herald, whom angry readers horsewhipped in the streets six times. I always wondered why, after the second time, he did not stay off the streets.

Where newspapermen are concerned, wonder comes naturally. Yet, in fact, newspapering is a noble calling. I selected the word *noble* carefully. Except for the ministry, possibly, I can think of few other pursuits that embody greater opportunity to wreak well-being upon the land.

Anyway, wandering around Florida as I do, it has been natural to wonder about newspapers. I search them for information about what life is like in Florida, and it is frustrating.

In some towns, I am struck with wonder whether there be any ordinary folk living there. I hope for the appearance in print of a regular human being, but everybody is either a commissioner or an offi-

277

cer or a board member, or something of that sort. I do not see a mention of a plain person anywhere. It is incredible to realize how many invisible people there must be in Florida.

Furthermore, I get the feeling that none of these titled creatures ever does anything that you and I do. Rather than worrying and making mistakes and arguing and balancing joy and despair, instead they are always charging or defending or planning or announcing. They never seem to have stomach aches or car trouble. It gets dull.

I wish for that compelling drama of the normal life to be more completely told. I am not talking about soap opera stuff, but just a little of the normal lather that accompanies staying alive.

I long for the scent of human flavor to come wafting off the pages. I worry that newspapers are being turned out in hypnotic trances, by a fast-paced scanning process that settles only on the automatic feeds from government structures, on the easy targets, the friction-causing events, the bizarre, the appealing peculiarities that have no significance.

I wonder at how the news can become so ritualized that the compelling nature of it is lost. It is surprising how every new development can be shaped into the cliche of a familiar pattern because there is not time to explore its individuality. Must news be factory-stamped so that most of it smacks of something that has been heard before? Must it be buried in irrelevant detail?

This is all a personal grumble, of course. The newspapers could make things more convenient for me, if they just would. It would be nice, for example, to find more of them which understand that these days it takes more courage to praise than to criticize. There are so many knaves in the world that, on percentage, you rarely come up with a bad average by steadily criticizing. Later on, if the subject of the criticism improves, the writer can take credit for it. Praise, however, has fewer targets. Furthermore, praise is open-ended and risky. Tomorrow, a praiser might be exposed as gullible.

When this human dimension is missing, I wonder how the citizens know what is the reality of their communities. They cannot see enough of the common links. They miss the comfort and security of knowing that everybody else is troubled and entrapped, too.

Sociologists call that alienation. Edward C. Banfield in his book titled *The Unheavenly City* said that comfort, convenience, amenity and business advantage alone are not enough. He was talking about cities, but it applies to newspapers, too.

· "...If some real disaster impends...it is not because parking spaces are hard to find, because architecture is bad, because department store sales are declining, or even because taxes are rising," Banfield wrote. He said the real need is "giving greater scope and expression to that which is distinctly human."

How strange that illuminating and emphasizing the human dimension, that gift of glory and debility that we all share, would be so hard to do. The good newspapers know all about this and they try very hard, and occasionally succeed. The titled creatures give them hell for imperfection, but a lot of us just wonder. Ministers are luckier than newspapermen. Almost nobody expects all of them both to have a full head of hair and to get every blessed one of us into heaven.

In the Human Library, A Treasure

A good way to sort out the realities in your life, to test your courage and to clear your head of all but the important things, is to visit someone you love in a nursing home.

When a fine old lady, a gracious woman and teller of witty tales who always had the faculty of reducing life's anxieties to amusing denominators, wheels in with an apprehensive look on her face, that is a time of truth.

To a boy, she had seemed a rock-solid guarantee that the world was a safe place for those who had the grit to live "right." In a wheelchair, frail and uncertain, she was an acknowledgment that wind and time can wear away even the rock of Gibraltar.

When her apprehension turned to delight, to such delight that she cried — just because a once-young rascal paid her a visit — that was an immeasurable reward, but it included a bill that all receive but few ever realistically anticipate — the accounting of age.

An inevitable summing up takes place. The elaborate facades we erect and the hollow things we endlessly pursue turn to trinketry. We are left, for better or worse, to deal with the kind of human being we have turned out to be.

The elderly are such a human treasure, but only for the brave and the thoughtful. Not everyone can stand the truth, but many can. Perfection is for them not to whimper, and for us not to turn away, for both of us instead to salute that vintage essence remaining. Courage, the stoutest kind, makes the difference between gold and horror.

The late years, when the distorting emotions have been tamed and the false ambitions have been unmasked, might be the best perch of all for understanding the ant-trails that make up a life. There is immeasurable privilege and value in being able to share a clear-eyed view from that perch.

A friend once asked me why I bothered to write about older people. "Are that many people really interested?" he asked. I thought he revealed something significant about himself, not only shallowness but fear, a refusal to accept the risk of understanding. He has rendered a verdict on old age that is a needless self-punishment. Why should anyone be embarrassed or ashamed of growing old? The difficulties are enough without adding guilt.

In almost any other field, intelligence demands we consult the full range of previous experience. We turn to those who have done it before us, to the library where catalogued references explain the detailed probabilities. Somehow, that same dispassionate search is not so popular with the aging process. Many will consult the figures involving pensions and insurance, but avoid studying the equivalent in actuarial curves for flesh and feelings.

To me, the elderly are like a human library. They are the experienced ones, the experts. They have gone ahead of us, and they have a more realistic grasp on our chronological frailties than we have of theirs.

In a library, I always have the feeling that only thin barriers separate me from discoveries of great personal value. That prospect brings a sense of exhilaration. There, it is possible to shed one more burden of ignorance and it is possible to replace it with a useful, satisfying idea.

In any library not all the volumes are good ones but all nevertheless represent one person's struggle and conclusions. Even those that fail objectively can give us fine suggestions about the process and how it led to what final chapter. The volumes are there, like so many experiments or trial balloons, whose results we may study for our own purpose.

Those who think that age alone determines human value practice prejudice of the most self-deceptive sort. Eighty-year-old bores probably also were bores at 30 and at 50; at 80, at least, they have justifiable excuses. Have you ever had someone look at you, and estimate you to have no redeeming qualties, because of factors that do not reflect quality? It is not a nice feeling. Height, facial arrangement, color are matters of contour and light, not merit. So it is with age.

Alex Haley, the author of *Roots,* once said that grandparents sprinkle stardust on the lives of children. The elderly have that capacity for us all. "My son, he owns this company," the elderly woman in the commercial says, and the stranger cringes on the bench next to her. From an elderly stranger, a friendly gesture might be interpreted as witless pride when it is only simple impatience with artificial barriers to comforting small talk.

Today, I myself am impatient, as you can see. The kind, wise, understanding old lady who contributed good things to my life is in a wheelchair and a nursing home and it angers me to consider that some therefore would dismiss her as without interest or value.

They do violence to a kind of sweetness that comes not from innocence, but from something far more laudable. It involves the imperfections of experience, retrospection and selfless bravery of the highest sort.

Today, I celebrate the lasting gift to my consciousness of a visit to a nursing home.

Here's to wrinkles.

Remembering When I Was Rich

I have been rich several times, but it never lasted. Rich is a condition roughly the opposite of indigestion: quite noticeable, seemingly without end until there is a burp or something, and then it is gone. You must work to bring it on again.

A feeling of rich means you have not lifted yourself to the rim of your nutshell and peered over to see that your boundaries are Lilliputian. Once you see, there should be a certain poverty forever because you cannot know and understand and have impact upon it all. To be rich, you must like your nutshell, must be able, as Shakespeare said to settle in comfortably and dream yourself to be king of infinite space.

My first notable feeling of being rich came in my Saturday matinee days, when *The Shadow* ruled the screen for several Saturdays consecutively. That was when good guys had control. The Mafia and the bureaucrats, to mention two current dread enemies, would not stand up to righteous genius. Now, I wonder whether the brotherhood of each is not dispirited at the lack of challenge. Morale surely must be low.

In memory, rich first came to me fleetingly in a large jar of olives, clandestinely purchased in protest against dinner table cautions that olives should be eaten in ones and twos because in great numbers they cause distress. I skipped the Saturday morning popcorn and invested in olives to be eaten in the dark. That was rich. It gave me a bellyache.

I was rich again the first time my paycheck hit $100 a week. From Monday until Wednesday, anything was possible. My nutshell had the proportions of the Grand Canyon and was swelling. By Thursday, doubts began. By Friday, rich was gone again and my suspicions of it became more or less permanent.

There were other memorable occasions, all picayune, and the pattern never changed. Rich was the top of the hill and when I reached it, the vantage point revealed another hill. Rich was edible, enjoyable, soul-satisfying but too quickly gone. It wore out, gave out, used up and the brief euphoria was gone, often with a burp.

That was not real rich, of course. There was a time, once upon a time, when real rich existed and had permanence, but nearly all of that is gone now. It meant style and class as well as money, and if a Depression or unwise investment spree flattened the accounts, real rich was not lost. Style and class remained. Inevitably, the cream would rise and float the accounts again.

No more. Cream has been discredited; it means cholesterol. Class has become anti-democratic; it smacks of prejudice. Rich has lost its non-financial standing, that aura of thoroughbred inevitability. Rich, now, particularly among the young, tends to mean you found a gimmick or a hustle that clicked. It is less a confirmation of class than a trick, and you must bleed it hard and fast before the world catches on and spoils the illusion with a faddish rush to copy.

Time has proved wry old W. C. Fields wrong; you *can* cheat an honest man if he is greedy; the one you cannot cheat is the unambitious man. Lack of ambition has become today's great defense. It is a different kind of rich, a reverse rich made popular by the dropouts of the late 1960s who stole the idea from Socrates, who said, "He is richest who is content with the least." Others have beaten the thought to death for years. Andrew Carnegie once felt so burdened by wealth and public perceptions of the wealthy that he predicted, "Public sentiment will come to be that the man who dies rich, dies disgraced." What he did not count on was that after Watergate and a few other revulsions neither disgrace nor rich would be a distinction.

It is now hard to tell, for example, how much money a man has simply by how much he spends. The well-off try to hide it from criminals by living simply, aping the great defense. The fabled food-stamp Cadillacs may raise the blood pressures of the tax-beleaguered wealthy, but it is a lifestyle approach that runs all through a society reveling in its uncertainties by spending to the hilt because inflation decreases the value of debts and savings.

Unless you are poor, it is hard to feel rich any more. The rich are still different from you and me, but it is because they sweat more. The poor things are handcuffed to their gold ingots, trusting neither banks nor investments and certainly not relatives. They see burglars and swindlers at their bedroom windows, welfare cheaters parking their Caddies overtime in the town square. Everybody else is getting away with something; what once was a clear field has become fiercely competitive. They scheme to protect themselves. Tension makes them no better than poor.

Philosophers have diddled with the rich for centuries. Francis Bacon said wealth is to virtue what baggage is to an army: an impediment. "If thou art rich," said Shakespeare, "Thou art poor. For, like an ass, whose back with ingots bows, thou bearest thy heavy burden but a journey, and death unloads thee."

Of them all, though, I savor the prayer of the *Fiddler on the Roof,* who acknowledged poor and rich, and asked for a choice. He observed that it was not a disgrace to be poor but it was no honor, either. The Fiddler put it perfectly for all poor men. Lord, his prayer queried, would it spoil some vast and cosmic plan, if I could be a miserable rich man?

Fashion: Not Funny

Fashion is no joke, but it has the ingredients: impracticality, posturing, naive mimicry, primitive inclination toward colorful imagery and bright trinkets. If our pants were not so tight, we would laugh. But that is, or was yesterday, fashion.

Fashion preys on an ambivalent urge to be different and popular and first, all at once. Then, do something else, to emphasize the difference between sheep and chic. Curiously, most of us admire this trickery, pay homage by adorning ourselves with its fodder: pleats, cuffs, beads, feathers, ruffles.

We even alter our bodies. We have tried to exhale ourselves thin, like Twiggy, or to inhale ourselves into pneumatic magnificence, like Dolly. We have tried to be slim and graceful, like Fred Astaire, and to be winningly ugly, like Willie Nelson. The contortions would make Darwin give up genealogy.

Following fashion is like volunteering for a plague of the hives. As it moves across the country, we blossom with chameleonic colors, a warp of lines.

Fashion works only because our response times differ. The hives' blossoms appear in staggered season, creating an appearance of progress. Were everyone to bloom at once, there would be no mystique. The secret would be as apparent as the nose on the face of the emperor who wore no clothes.

But only the very young, the very old and the prideful eccentric can get away with ignoring fashion. Crackers suggest immunity comes through honesty. They repeat a fine old story about the fashionable woman who approached a small boy one Sunday morning in front of the church. "Sonny," she said, twisting about toward the entrance, "is mass out?" The boy looked at her steadily, from bottom to top.

286

"No, ma'am," he said helpfully, "but I think your hat's on backwards."

There is a disinclination among Crackers to look foolish deliberately. On the other hand some city folk, the Cookies, take pride in being insincerely silly as an entertainment. When a Cracker appears foolish, he really is; he is not kidding. With a Cookie, you never can be sure.

That has a significant effect on the progression of fashion through the countryside. It explains why new styles take hold in the country last, and hang on there longest. The Cracker gets into the new foolishness only after he is convinced it has ceased being foolish; by that time, a true Cookie has lost interest. He has spotted another Judas-bloom that might make him admirable. Should he stick it in his hair, behind his ear, or just where?

The peculiarities of fashion reinforce rural suspicions of the city. James Dickey illustrated that with the tale of the Cracker buying a new suit, and worried about the fit. The salesman assured him it was perfect and showed him how to angle his arms to make the sleeves right, how to crook his shoulders to correct the neckline, how to hitch his legs to adjust the pants. As the fellow walked awkwardly and painfully down the street, his friends assumed he had been stricken with arthritis. "But don't that new suit fit him good," one said. That is fashion.

The remarkable thing is that we continue to coddle its tricks and changes. Hems go up, down, skirts change to pants, pants legs taper and then billow. Shoes take on high heels, low heels, holes, pointed toes, blunted toes. Ties go wide, then narrow. Shirts form-fit, hang out, tuck in, sprout animal decals supposed to denote class. Collars point, button-down, flange, roll. Suits demand trim lapels, then broad ones; padded shoulders, then natural ones. None of these necessarily relates to quality or comfort or fit. It is fashion.

A minor infection of practicality threatened fashion when jeans became so popular, but commercial nourishment soon over-powered it. Jeans were simple, comfortable, long-wearing, classic. Crackers who had taken a lifetime to graduate from bib overalls to what they called dungarees found themselves briefly ahead of the Cookie. Dungarees actually were jeans, and many already had nice fades and patches. But the Judas-bloom moved on.

That brief dalliance with practicality was like the Detroit auto-makers' early passes at the small car. It soon progressed into the equivalent of tailfins and chrome strips. Tiny fanny-flaps began to establish distinctions irrelevant to function, followed by stitched patterns around the pockets and down the legs. Some were embroidered. Some had simulated cuffs. Some turned to pastel colors.

This was a small advance in candor. Staring at a woman's bottom was no longer an insult, but a complimentary investigation of her fanny-flap. It was so Roman, so fashionable.

It goes on forever, these hives, this chasing of chic, this instinct to disguise rather than to reveal natural individuality. It is a societal witch-dance which we must accept, else be considered peculiar. No-body wants a cynic at the seance.

What woman can be expected to stand plain when all the others fancy up so prettily with holes punched in their ears from which trinkets can dangle, red on their lips, a lacquer erection for their hair, hose that neither hide nor protect, mascara making bulls eyes of girl eyes? What sort of man, what manner of clod, would not camouflage his chin, his stomach, his aroma in the latest clever way?

If beauty really has something to do with truth, there is something wrong here. If it is in the eye of the beholder, mine eye swarms with gnats. But it cannot be, of course. That would suggest conspiracy, a massive joke being perpetrated upon us. No. There is nothing funny about it. It is fashion.

Southerners: Skinned Again

A long time ago, my grandmother made a solemn request. Before she died, just once, she wanted to see the ocean. The family took the frail old lady to the beach, and let her walk out on the sand. She trembled in the breeze and stared intensely across the waves at the horizon.

"Hmph," she said, disappointed. "It's not as big as I thought it'd be."

Southerners, you see, tend to be thoughtful and different people, neither easily impressed nor quickly explained. What Coleridge said about poetry — that it gives most pleasure when only generally and not perfectly understood — can be said about them, too. They need appreciation, not definition.

The collective Southern mind historically has been different. The Southerner, elaborately courteous and persistently clever, with an exaggerated sense of what is proper, long ago established a style that flourished in a thicket of contradictions. He only lacked a romantic nationality which would permit his quirks to be celebrated.

When Jimmy Carter was elected President, there was a brief period when it appeared this quaint, baffling creature — the Southerner — and his region might be considered as much innocent as backward; as not just relatively poor and undeveloped, but beautifully untouched and ripe; not merely ugly in prejudice but blindly clinging to self-defeating customs.

Briefly, there seemed a chance that the humanity of Southerners, their sensitivity to slight, their mysterious ability to be proud though humble, might be hailed for promise rather than dismissed as absurd.

The redneck had a fleeting chance for rescue. He might have

become a symbol of honest toil rather than bigotry, for there could have been sympathy for his tragedy in shouldering the wrong yoke and nurturing the wrong seeds. The Confederate flag might have been able to rest easily as a historical banner and not have to continue suffering the rot of being identified with that obnoxious streak in the regional family.

Southern writers might have been able to shed their sackcloth and spit out the ashes and write of something more positive than their region's lonely communion with sin and defeat, something other than the viral weed of mythology that debilitated the honest and encouraged the dishonest, burdened the wronged and bolstered the wrong.

But that brief time slipped away into the old misunderstandings, and the easy cliches came back. Faddists moved from the jokes about accents and fried chicken and refrigerators on the White House porch to deeper prejudices which doubted substance that had different form.

They missed the Southern technique of orchestrated indirection. Southerners reserve a portion of their thoughts for themselves alone. They keep mental bankbooks, deposits of secrets. In their own time and way they deal out those coins carefully and obliquely.

For example, there was the Southerner who tired of hearing a friend boast about frequent bathing. It was an awkward thing. The Southerner did not wish to offend the friend, but he wanted to end the crude boasting. Finally, he advised, "I wouldn't tell that if I were you, about all that bathing. You ought not to let on to strangers that you get so dirty."

There is a certain wry rhythm and upside-down truth in the use of indirection. Opposing politicians lather up and say indirection indicates indecision. Newsmen complain that it is hard to fit into a brief sentence. But to a Southerner steeped in its uses, indirection can issue truth without bite. It can be both stunning and beautiful. It uses a smile instead of a sneer.

There were the three farmers who sat in the barn passing a fruit jar of moonshine among themselves. The first two tipped the jar more frequently than the other, and soon began to boast of their financial worth. With each drink they became richer. The third one finally broke in. "Y'all lemme have that fruit jar," he said. "You gettin' ahead of me. I ain't got my house paid off yet."

Look past the behavioral trivia which are foisted off as the truth about the South. Accents and fried chicken and peculiar pride are only the trappings. What is different about the Southerner is his vision of life, his courtesy, his humanity, and that certain woodsy spin on his approach to problems, the indirections that leave you blinking until the truth dawns.

Southerners ride uneasy. They are neither appreciated nor defined properly, and it has been thus for 200 years. Even Thomas Jefferson criticized them. He said they were unstable and unjust, a Virginian offering his own example of the nimble, indefinable Southern mind.

Still, attempts at definition lamely go on. The dispassionate attitude of the detractors reminds us of Lincoln's story about the boy who skinned eels. When asked if it was not cruel to hurt the eels that way, he replied: "It don't hurt them so much. It's been goin' on for a long time. They're used to it."

Southerners, too.

Cowed at Christmas

The other day as we drove to town, we saw a cow, with only minor flourish, giving birth in a pasture just across the fence. A little calf popped out, shivering, shaking off its wrappings.

The vulnerability of that little bit of veal was overwhelming. It landed without hands in a chilly world that loves hamburgers. Yet, it seemed quite happy to be there beside its big, warm Mama.

If the future had limits, the choices left — which clump of grass to munch, which teat to suck, whether to switch its tail in anticipation of the flies or only after they bite — must have seemed heady self-determination.

We proceeded to town on a mission to generate the Christmas spirit. The crisp weather helped, but the calf that defied inevitability did the most. The symbolism could have been better only if the calf too had appreciated the wisdom and courage involved in not letting risks spoil the happy pursuit of ideal.

We were going shopping, the conventional way to elevate the season's cheer. We would buy the usual trappings: the decorations that advertise sentiment, the cards that signal a time of goodwill as though it were a temporary ceasefire, the presents that threaten with calculation.

The tale of the calf came as counterpoint to all this. And at first we told it only to close friends, thinking that others might not tolerate us in something so trivial. But it got such surprising reception that we later tried it on any who would listen.

There was no punchline to the story, no neat message, and not any really new information. It was just a quiet little page of life. Still, most seemed to like the details of a newborn calf testing its legs on a cool morning, leaning anxiously against its protective Mama, gazing fearfully around a large and strange pasture. Somehow, so innocent and fragile a tale encouraged friends to make similarly tentative expressions.

We realized with some surprise, after we thought about it for awhile, that many people find it difficult to express their positive thoughts. It is not quite as acceptable as being critical. Some of us wear cool masks, trying so hard to be laid-back and safe that we smother spontaneity. We struggle to cover instincts that might reveal us as trusting, and therefore naive. If we succeed, it leaves us with such smooth surfaces that we hardly know each other at all.

To praise, to care, to confess the struggle against shortcomings, to commit ourselves to an idea or a person or a job — all of these — become speculative risks. We like others to take them, but we shy from the vulnerability. We have become reluctant to be courageous except defensively.

Anyway, the tale of the calf eased us into the Christmas season with cynicism in retreat. Though to some we might seem Pollyan-naish, no vampires or swamp salesmen have gotten us yet. We are discovering the outlines of a secret majority: closet good people, hiding behind those cool masks but eager to come out as soon as they find it is safe.

But unless we make a conscious effort, when our feet hurt or strangers snarl or a mugger threatens or we check the actuarial charts, all those good intentions shrink into new fears. Because of what we know, it is difficult to sustain an overview of life that per-mits us the calf's equanimity.

During the Christmas season, I look for help. Sometimes a memory works. Once during the holidays, I stood in line at the old Miami airport on 36th Street waiting to catch a midnight plane. There were maybe 10 people ahead of me when an announcement came that there were two planes loading at the same time for my destination. I could board either. I walked 50 years farther, and was seated immediately. I was the only passenger. The other plane crashed at the Jacksonville airport, killing everyone, while my plane circled. Remembering that gives me a nice, positive perspec-tive on the holidays.

But that memory grows old. And I always search for fresh evidence that will grind away cynicism. Maybe I only invent what I need. A cow immodestly performs just as I drive by, and in a little calf I see a parable around which the mind can rally. I share it with you as a Christmas wish that need not be only seasonal: Be merry. It is a good risk.

New Year's: Pianissimo

The trouble with New Year's Eve is that it tends to focus on the night, not on the last chances of the day, raising odds that when the first of the New Year blooms full, it may not be a thing suitable for trumpets.

As a veteran sinner and experienced repentant, I spend the day grumbling, anticipating and dreading, while I go through the ritual of shucking the trimmings off the Christmas tree. Will I disappoint myself again and have a helluva good time tonight? Mine enemy grows older, not wiser.

Things are quiet around the house — just the warm sounds of a popping fire, small scratching noises where tree limbs touch the roof and in the kitchen the faint bubble and aroma of hash. The bareboned hull of a turkey sits on a counter, not a giblet of meat left, better used than the year.

Dismantling Christmas and making ready to compromise the New Year, all in one day, seem indecent. We should be making resolutions and turning over new leaves, but instead we denude the tree, boxing up little angels and shepherds on beds of cotton, turning off the glow in a shining star, stowing Santa away under old clothes in the closet.

We inter the symbols of man's best reason to hope, at a time of beginning, and we have the feeling that there ought to be a better way to do this.

The little wire and plastic tree that we bought two years ago serves the day and the mood. During the holidays it did not dry out and shed fragrant needles or show bare limbs, but it nevertheless performed. As long as it had tinsel on it and tiny bulbs that glittered and glowed it was a model of festive efficiency.

But as we strip it down, the realities show and the disguise falls. The trunk has metal fatigue from too much bending to pedestrian whim, the green paint peels, the plastic rips, and all its pretensions seem tawdry.

We do not really like the artificial tree, but we will save it as carefully as the angels and shepherds and probably piece it back together next year when we resurrect all of them. It is convenient.

Since the little pretender has no cycle of life, it has no death, either. It does not brown and wither either with inspirational grace or demoralizing panic. Rather than the value-enhancing frailty that is the price of being alive, it has a cheerless but handy constancy. The contrast makes a blessing of mortality.

Still, we think of the night, distracted by unreality and tinsel. Before the bulldozer-sized task of clearing away the residue of a year, and preserving the substance, we pick away with a trowel. We are preoccupied with old goals unmet, letting new ones get a long lead on us. We stare long at the fireplace, where oak logs burn in hours the energy it took years to accumulate. The fire has the significance of sacrifice.

Once we finish the ritual of shucking the tree, we pull out the wire limbs and lay them side by side with the metal trunk in a cardboard box. There is a temptation to throw a blanket over it, or at least the little rug we always use under the tree, but what for? Why waste tenderness on a manufacturer's tool, even one that has an instruction sheet for assembling the Christmas spirit? No one, or no thing, feels good if it cannot also feel bad.

Mark Twain once made a wicked point out of that in a speech to insurance men, pointing out the nobler aspect of their business, how it literally lifts people from poverty. "In all my experience of life, I have seen nothing so seraphic as the look that comes into a freshly mutilated man's face as he feels in his breast pocket with his remaining hand and finds his ticket (policy) all right," Twain said.

By now the hands of the clock should begin to fall toward sundown and soon start rising toward night, and my grumbling ruminations can lighten, for the circuitous rationalization has been made: without the night ahead, tomorrow would not have dimension, not have the remorse so necessary to firing and tempering a righteous will for the New Year. Of course it is better this way. Of course.

Whoopee again, until tomorrow. Then, violins only, please, and pianissimo.

Home

Melrose

Melrose: The Life

To appreciate the vintage beauty of Melrose, you must stay for awhile, get to know how its past and present have met. A visitor may see its umbrella of huge oaks, quaint buildings and rural lifestyle, and misread the message.

You mistake the special grace of the Melrose life if you call it just a sleepy little village perched along the shores of Lake Sante Fe in north central Florida.

Melrose roots go deep, and most of the 300 residents find a certain satisfaction in that. "But what do you *DO* here?" a stranger will ask.

For business, Melrose offers services to the thousand or so lake homes scattered throughout the area, and to the weekenders who come to fish and play. "For entertainment, we gossip," said one lady, smiling. "That's the main activity."

More accurately, Melrose lives depend more on individual talents and initiatives than on commercial or business stimulation. Life is more positive than defensive. That becomes part of the identity that Melrose bestows. There is something extra here. Strangers, please do not crowd.

Main Street probably was first traveled by Indians, maybe several thousand years ago. The Spanish came along late in the 16th century and turned the Indian path into an East-West trail.

In 1834, the U.S. Congress approved a grant of $20,000 to convert the trail into a wagon road between St. Augustine and Tallahassee. John Bellamy subcontracted to do most of the work and the road was named for him.

North Central Florida became cotton plantation country. A burying ground was established in the 1840s near present-day Melrose. The Civil War ended the plantations and for 12 tumultuous years afterward — during the period called Reconstruction — there was uncertainty and depression. When that settled, the glory days of Melrose began.

Henry Flagler had not yet begun to unreel his railroad-hotel development magic. Hamilton Disston had not yet bought four million acres of south Florida for 25 cents an acre. Steamboats were Florida's principal means of transportation.

That year, 1877, the town of Melrose was laid out for one mile along Bellamy Road. Orange groves dotted the shores of nearby Lake Sante Fe and a canal company dug a two-mile waterway to link Melrose via three lakes to the narrowgauge railroad lines at Waldo, making the shipment of citrus easier and more profitable.

For nearly 20 years, Melrose boomed. Beautiful houses went up on Melrose Bay. New residents as well as seasonal visitors came. Town population reached about 1,000.

The golden days slacked off when Henry Flagler's (and Henry Plant's) railroads diverted business from the steamboats and shifted growth to new areas of Florida. They ended with two successive hard freezes during the winters of 1894-95 and 1895-96. Citrus trees died and growers moved south.

Since then, Melrose has changed its mind about what sort of town it wishes to be. In 1901 it incorporated, but about 10 years later it unincorporated and has remained so.

The town takes care of itself voluntarily through the churches, the Melrose Woman's Club (organized in 1890), the Volunteer Fire Department and civic clubs.

Most of those who claim Melrose residency actually live out in the woods and on the lakes. Within a 25-mile radius, there are 70 lakes and most are ringed with houses. We moved into one of them in 1974, part of the backward pioneer movement, the migration from the city to country.

Our house faces northeast, and the sun reaches us each morning by climbing over a hill of pines and live oaks and shooting across the lake. By the time it has made the water glow pink, the silhouette of the shore has turned into trees and tall grasses and the sun beams into our bedroom window.

Short of a honeymoon caress, there may be no more gentle, beautiful way to wake up. There's not a sound, just a gradual awareness that night has passed.

Living in rural north Florida has been a revelation and an education to us. We discovered, as we got settled, that the backward pioneer was a familiar figure in the area. A man who fled Miami put up our new fence; a refugee from Jacksonville laid in a new ceiling; the television repairman was from Hialeah; the service man for the air-conditioner and heater had moved here from Hollywood; the service station owner migrated here from Homestead; nearby were commuters to Gainesville (25 miles west) and retirees from everywhere.

We have become addicted to the serene setting, though other backward pioneers have built new houses on the lake since we moved in. We have noticed that they arrive excited and noisy, but after a few weeks begin to blend into the woods just like the rest of us.

During warm weather, we swim in the clear lake waters each day. The beach is sandy and white. There are bream, catfish, bass, alligators, coots, turtles and a variety of birdlife, including a tame egret called Biddy that comes to the backdoor and begs food.

In the woods we have seen possum, raccoons, rabbits, deer, fox squirrels and have heard strange noises that we fearfully identify as a wild caterwhompus.

Sandhill cranes nest on a prairie nearby, and we have seen them perform their strange waltz and at night have heard their startling whoops. Other cranes, egrets and herons patrol the lake. Occasionally a covey of quail skitters across the yard to peck at cracked corn fallen from the birdfeeder, whistling a musical bobwhite to spread the news.

We find it a place where each day has a value of its own, not like the others, and the splendid feeling has not diminished. Even local history seem appropriate. Our land was part of 76 acres granted to a freed slave named Nelson Mason during Reconstruction Days by President Ulysses S. Grant. The symbolism is powerful.

There are days so still, so beautiful, that we can be startled by the sound of an acorn falling on the tin roof of the carport and rattling to the ground. We can hear black bass chasing the bream in the lake shallows. The call of a chuck-will's-widow, or the hoot of an owl, is the siren of the woods.

This is the kind of Florida that is fast slipping away from the mass of Floridians. Under the pressure of such backward pioneers as we, it will not last many more years. This is the Florida that is as elusive as a wild thing, which keeps retreating from the crowds until it can retreat no more. Too soon we may be able to find only small, sensitized patches of it behind clicking turnstiles and in air-conditioned museums. Monotoned guides will tell us how it once was.

But for now, we enjoy what we have, its value enhanced by the sure knowledge of its frailty. There is, about it all, a certain touch of the genuine, the real, a feeling of truth in life. When the black, black night falls, and the neighbors' lights shine comfortingly across the lake, we sit on the front porch or walk along the lake and breathe the sweet night air, and remind ourselves that tomorrow we do not have to go home. We are there.

Biddy: At Bottom A Glow

My friend Biddy celebrates Christmas in the most spectacular way. Late in the fall, her tail feathers grow long and lacy. In the morning sun they create a diaphanous glow, like a halo, around her bottom as she prepares for the mating season.

In a lot of my friends, this might seem tacky, too gaudy, too heavy on the makeup and perhaps a shade too suggestive. This does not happen with Biddy. She has an extraordinary sense of taste, knowing just how much she can doll up without smirching the dignity and true beauty of her season.

Biddy is simply an old-fashioned lady who refuses to cater to whimsical changes of fashion. She has been doing this all her life. By Christmas, she is the glorious female, poised, graceful, classically beautiful. She is almost perfect.

She has only one real problem, just one tiny flaw in her superb manners. As the feathers spread and bewitch us, as the heat grows inside her, she gets a powerful appetite. She cannot get enough to eat. It is not altogether becoming the way she stands at the back-door pleading for another bite, gulping it down and immediately resuming the plea. Actually, it is less a plea than a demand. Biddy has a strong personality.

Her season and our holidays arrive together. As our Christmas tree and wreaths and spirits go up, her long, yellow bill takes on a slightly orange tinge. A little green patch appears on it, a nagging, defining beauty spot. But the way she carries it off is inspirational.

Biddy has been part of our household for several years now. She is a Great Egret, with the emphasis on great. Most of the year, she has the stern, skeptical air of an old maid aunt. As December rolls around, though, we see that she is in her way a liberated woman, free and listening attentively to the beat and call of her heart. It puts an air of celebration into our Christmases.

Until you know her well, it would be easy to mistake her for the other Great Egrets who sometime visit our rustic house in the woods of North Central Florida. Since she adopted us, her compellingly real appreciation of the life processes, her practicality and patience, have revealed her individuality to us.

Like the others, she stands about 3 feet tall, virginally (deceptively) white. Most of her height is in the long graceful neck and the skinny legs that look as though they have been sheathed in shiny black leotards. As she walks across the yard she picks up those long toes with the deliberate, finger-dripping motion of a fine pianist.

Her wings spread out about 4½ feet. When other egrets find it curious that she lives at our house and come to investigate why, she drives them off by lurching at them and beating her wings, frightening them off with aggressive cries. Biddy is animal royalty, a loner, and will not tolerate poachers and pretenders.

At times, as many as three Great Egrets have congregated at our back porch, and briefly we have been confused which one is ours. Biddy identifies herself with the kind of quiet John Wayne aggression that builds slowly and then explodes. The other egrets flee.

As grateful as we are, we are not entirely sure why Biddy so honors us. She just began to hang around. One day several summers ago, while my father was visiting, sitting out on the dock fishing for bream, he playfully tossed her a small fish. She finically picked it off the sand, washed it in the lake, swallowed it down, and in effect asked for another. She has been here ever since, except on the occasions when she takes maternity leave.

For a long while, my wife Gloria fished for Biddy, selecting small catches and saving fish for her. Biddy always swallows fish head-first, so that the fins do not stick her in the neck. But finally, it was impossible to fish often enough and fast enough to keep her in the style she demanded.

Gloria experimented with a few other morsels from the refrigerator, without success, and then one day hit upon fish-sized strips of beef kidney. Biddy likes these. It is possible that she prefers them. She should. They now cost 89 cents per pound and in her most feathery days she can eat a pound easily if we do not limit her.

We think that Biddy probably first struck up a relationship with a neighbor of ours on the next lake, the late Howard Bishop, who was a fisherman of some renown around here. Howard was only a part-time resident, however, and it appears that our steady offering of beef kidneys alienated her affections. Howard was happy with the arrangement, though. In effect, he willed Biddy to us. He had worried that she might have given up fishing for herself and that she had become too trusting of strangers. Biddy has been our god-mother ever since.

During the years, we have shared the kinds of experiences that cement relationships. During summers, Biddy walks around on the roof, roosts there at night, and some mornings will peer over the eaves into our bedroom to inquire how long before breakfast. During the day, if we do not appear at the back door on schedule, she stalks around the house, looking in the windows until she finds us. When she fixes that stare on me, patiently prepared to wait for hours if necessary, I have learned that I might as well get up from the desk and go feed her.

Once, we saved her from an eagle that hovered around the house, trying to grab her. She was really scared. Another time, we discouraged her from trying to eat a snake about 6 feet long. It was not difficult to do. I think she understood the problem. Once, she walked into the open kitchen door, and had a confrontation with our dog who considered this an intolerable affront (they usually ignore each other, sharing the backporch).

All these things have made Biddy important to us, especially at Christmas when she is so extraordinarily lovely. She accents the season. We do not know how long she may live (one ornithologist advised that with luck she might have a lifespan of 20 to 25 years), but we hope that it is a long time. At this season, the glow of her bottom is irreplaceable.

Neighbors: They Do Exist

There was a time, just after we moved out into the woods near Melrose to live, when our only neighbors were a raccoon, a possum and a standoffish alligator. We caught glimpses of humans speeding past our fence, heads bowed to the challenge of the two-rut road.

The possum and the raccoon were not bad neighbors at all. The possum was a fat little fellow with long, thick whiskers and the thoughtful expression of an editor eating dill pickles. He usually paid a sociable call about dark, nibbled around the dog bowl and ambled off in his miniature elephant gait.

The raccoon kept later hours. He came like a bandit, or a reporter, testing garbage lids, investigating porch trails and frequently kicking over a can just to let us know he could.

The alligator hung back, snappish, lying in the water off the beach and peering across his nose at us in a clear complaint against mixed neighborhoods.

We noticed quickly that the nights get darker out in the woods than they do in the cities. They were so dark that it seemed somebody had switched off civilization. One little yellow light shone across the weedy lake from a house on the far shore, and we held it as proof that the final plug had not been pulled, that somewhere the traffic was screeching and honking.

So, under those circumstances, the raccoon and the possum and even the alligator had star ranking as neighbors. But that was before we got to know the Sunshine Boys, plus Aunt Ernestine and Uncle Jim, the Bishop clan, the praying Simpsons and a few others. These are real neighbors.

In Miami, where we lived for so many years, a neighbor was

someone who lived next door. Years might pass with only a wave and a hello and maybe not even that. But here in the north Florida woods, around Lake Mason and Long Pond and Cue Lake, neighbors have a status that gives them a kind of family lien on you. There is a certain mutual responsibility that exists.

For us it was a remarkable thing, discovering this old-fashioned neighbor business, as soul-refreshing as our first sight of deer cantering through the forest.

It's hard to remember who came calling first. One day Luke McDowall walked up to the door and said hello. Next thing he was bringing us squash or a mess of bream (cleaned) and telling us to come on over to his place at Long Pond and his Ethel would feed us some stone crabs they had caught at Cedar Key.

Then Sonny Hulett called and said he wanted to come over for a minute. He rolled up in his pickup, asked where would I like him to plant this grapevine he had for me, and proceeded to put it into the ground with proper portions of clay and leaves and fertilizer. Pretty soon we went over to his place at Cue Lake and he and Olive were feeding us quail and doves and sending us home with a package of venison steaks.

Various members of the Bishop clan met us at the mailbox and before long we were on their active party list. The brothers Donald and Howard, with their wives Millie and Rodney, have put in probably a half-century of time in these woods and they can tell the finest tales without lying you ever heard. Howard tamed an egret which we adopted, and nearby Gainesville named a school for him.

Uncle Jim and Aunt Ernestine, the Roberts, weekended in the old farmhouse closest to us and they shepherded us through such crises as snakes and freezes. Aunt Ernestine makes cornbread and turnip greens and spare ribs that would, as the folks around here like to say, make you fight your Grandma for a second helping. Uncle Jim, a quiet man, can spot a neighbor's hurt with an eagle eye. On more than one cold day when my bones ached, I have seen him walk across the yard without a word and do chores that seemed too much for me.

The Simpsons, old family friends, bring wood and vegetables and check our mail and mother-hen us and when we need it, which is often, go down to that friendly fundamentalist church of theirs and bow their heads in our behalf.

Before all this, we have little to offer but gratitude. Not often do they seem to need anything, and so we stay continually in their debt and looking for a way to repay. The effect is beneficial, and humbling. It tends to make us nicer people and in time we ourselves may be fit neighbors.

Over the course of four years living here in the woods east of Gainesville, we have seen Luke and Sonny develop into the Sunshine Boys, inseparable fishing and sightseeing buddies who keep a quarrel going for their own and their neighbors' amusement. Luke likes a crowd. He gets what he calls "cabin fever" if he goes too long without socializing. Sonny can spend days daubing and planting in his garden without getting restless. When Sonny declines a fishing trip or a party, Luke grumbles and fumes. Their act plays well.

"I never saw a man like that in my life," Luke will say. "Gets out there in the dirt and fools around, just daydreaming you know, doesn't even know what he's doing." He looks at Sonny, who does not answer, and continues, "I never saw a man like fertilizer so much," Luke laughed. "He loves fertilizer."

Sonny does not answer. "Did you hear me, Sonny? I said you loved fertilizer." Luke grumbles some more and goes on talking. When he finally wears down, Sonny looks at him. "Did you say something to me, Luke?" Luke shakes his head. Sonny smiles.

All of them have made us appreciate good neighbors now as an asset that enhances home and life and peace of mind. Maybe it is age, but we like to think it is discovery. We have often talked with regret about not getting to know our neighbors better when we lived in Miami, and how much we missed. Maybe we simply were not good neighbors ourselves. But we prefer to believe that the interdependence of life in the country made neighboring easier.

One day we had what we must call our all-time most surprising visit from a neighbor, and it erased those self-doubts. When Gloria walked up to the mailbox to get the noon mail, a car was waiting under the shade of a big live oak. The couple inside called to her, and she brought them down to the house to see me.

They had been our neighbors in Miami. In seven years living across the street from them, we had waved and nodded but never visited. Now they, after reading some accounts of our life in the country, had driven to see us. It was a gesture we treasure, but we still wonder how urban inhibitions were enough to deter it but a gap of 350 miles and rural isolation did not.

On dark nights here in the woods, we think about that. We are often alone, but never lonely. The Sunshine Boys and the others are a half-mile or more away, too far even to see their lights. But neighbors, we have learned, need not be near to be close.

Summers: For Snakes and Guests

One summer day in Melrose a visitor rolled his car down our rocky driveway, got out complaining of the heat and promptly received a cool greeting. A snake fell on him.

A little black snake dropped off the overhanging branches of a live oak tree, brushed his shoulders, hit the ground and scrambled to get away into the bushes.

The fellow stood there with a stunned look and shivered. He did not stay long, and we have seen little of him since.

At our house, snakes and guests gather with greatest frequency during the summer heat.

They wage a struggle for rights of encroachment around the lake and in the woods. Yet they are frightened warriors, full of bluff and belligerent postures and remarkable reverse speed.

We have a certain fondness for each and so do not take sides, except to try to keep anyone from getting hurt. We can see both points of view. For us, it depends on the individual snake or guest. Some are poison, and we naturally tend to like them less.

Up here among the low sandhills and lakes of north central Florida, when the Crackers sit around at night and spin horror tales, they speak more often of snakes and company than ghosts and bogeymen.

The scare quotient between them is closer than you first might think. Hardly anyone ever gets bitten by a snake but guests on vacation, especially relatives, rarely miss. Their bites might not put you in the hospital, but they surely will make you humble at the bank.

During the winter, the horror stories dwell on guests. Not all of it is negative. There is genuine admiration, too. A kind of competition occurs in which a man takes pride in boasting of having hosted the most awesome guests.

The ranking yarn-spinners borrow from the well-developed skills of the fisherman whose big one got away. They apply reverse spin and come up with sketches about company that arrives without warning and rarely departs without postponement.

Like the ones who got away, the ones who come to stay become fabled: great mouths that can open and close over food and never stop talking, the incredible stamina of one who can sleep until noon even when you arrange for a neighbor to keep the telephone ringing, the prim couple who would not throw trash on a highway but primly litter the living room while chuckling about the casual customs of country folk.

Summers, when the visitors are here, the horror stories switch to snakes mostly. I prefer to think that this simply illustrates old-fashioned Cracker courtesy at work, but some of the more worldly woods folk say that it is even more old-fashioned than that. Courtesy, they smile and declare, never mothered a snake scare.

Let me give you a sample. At an early summer gathering, after a few relatives have opened visitor season, the conversation will turn to coral snakes. Everybody knows the coral snake is pretty and that his bite has been known to kill in as little as 20 minutes.

To say the countryside crawls with coral snakes, without adding detail, has a scare quotient that without embellishment can empty a guest bedroom overnight. But the Crackers are more stylish than that. They want you to understand completely, and so they tell you that coral snakes have small mouths and small teeth and lethargic temperaments and so are remote threats to a careful person outdoors.

What the coral snake really likes to do, they will add, is snuggle up to a sleeping person and search out soft, easily mouthed bits of flesh. A coral snake, they say, loves to teeth on the sheath of skin between a man's fingers or toes, or whatever is available. The bite may cause little discomfort, like a minor scratch, and the venom itself may not be initially painful. Why, they say, it might not even wake you up.

When a stranger has absorbed those possibilities, they deliver the clincher. One couple recalls with sweet simplicity the night they returned to their woodsy home, tired and sleepy, and as they prepared for bed discovered a little candy-striped black-nosed coral snake curling among their covers. Then everybody usually says goodnight.

Folksy conversation like that gets a stranger's attention. Often it is followed, or continued at a later date, with the terrors of diamondback rattlesnakes with their powerful bite and shocking strike and the aggressive cottonmouth moccasins which can bite underwater as well as on land.

Strangely, all of this is true, but none of it has real impact until a visitor sees — or feels — the snake itself. For example, the fellow who felt the black snake drop across his shoulders never was in danger, but the suggestion was powerful.

· We do not join in that stranger-baiting, of course, here at our little woods house. We like company and try to put them at ease. We keep a snake handbook on display and when a new visitor comes, all we do is explain the need for caution and relate the mild encounters we have had.

None of them have been bad. We have killed only nine coral snakes in our front or back yards, one rattlesnake near our grape vines, and two suspected (but unconfirmed) cottonmouths in the grass. Of course, we have seen many other snakes, presumed to be harmless: in the kitchen window (outside the screen), on the back porch, on the front stoop, in the palm tree by the front walk, by the pumphouse, by the dock, by the workshop, in the lake.

To dissolve all fears, we often take visitors to see some oldtimers who have a quaint old farmhouse and who scoff at snake fears. They feel perfectly safe because they have a pet pine snake which they keep under their house to chase the strange snakes away. They swear it works.

Anyway, here it is summertime, the visiting season. Y'all come. Do not worry about the campfire stories. The really frightening ones are told only in winter.

Live Oaks:
Lessons And Examples

Nobody can appreciate the toughness of a live oak tree like a man with a cold fireplace and a dull axe on an icy day. Chopping a live oak log is one of those jobs you do not relish until you have finished. In retrospect, it seems noble and character building.

As mean work, it compares to saving money: you had best be patient, and chip away a little at the time. That way, the hands may sting a little, but the bones and muscles will stay in place.

Around Melrose, live oak is appreciated for its admirably stubborn character. When the wood dries, it hardens and resists flame. Naturally, some people think it too much trouble.

But your axe will do its work if you do, and the woodbox will stack up full. Before you lay the sticks across the fireplace andirons, in a ritual paying homage to nature's reluctant sacrifice, a small prayer might not hurt.

Wood of less stern character goes on the bottom, in poetic priority. First, put on fat pine splinters which will take the match quickly, then twigs to feed the flame, followed by soft pieces of water oak. Finally, it is time to lay on the regal live oak.

With live oak logs, you do not have to trot back and forth to the woodbox. They fight the good fight for hours, and you have plenty time to sit in the big rocking chair and reflect on the years it took to accumulate the energy that warms you.

While the pleasant-smelling woodsmoke curls up the chimney in a sign of surrender, you can enjoy the satisfaction of a conquered chore.

All of it has logical sequence. The live oak has made you sweat and wonder at its strength, has made you speculate about its character. The fire comes as a small victory, giving a winter day depth and charm.

When we went visiting, there was ice on the ground but we entered a house that was warm from unseen flames. City folks have it easy.

In the den was a fireplace, and the fellow who lived there went over and cranked a valve. Yellow flames sprang up and licked at logs that would never burn. The man cranked the valve again, adjusting the flame just right, and stepped back to admire his work. He thought it looked so real. In a moment everyone turned away. There was no need to stare at anything so trivial.

The crank of a valve had opened a gas jet and a pilot light made it flame over phony logs in a fireplace that had no chimney and needed none.

The fire had no purpose in an already warm house, except as decoration. There were no logs to cut, no ashes to haul away, no woodsmoke to smell, just a valve to crank on and off.

The live oak is a beautiful, tough old tree. It stays green through every winter until it dies, shedding a few leaves, but never giving up. After death, it leaves logs packed granite-hard with energy.

A man who takes the trouble to build a live oak fire on an icy day gets a bonus lesson in logic, a stiff exam on the natural order of things, a wedge of understanding about the building of values. You cannot do it with the crank of a valve.

Once, during a summer storm, we heard a single, clean explosion outside. We looked and there were splinters of wood scattered about the yard.

One of our prize live oaks had been hit and it still stood, gnarled and bent, unchanged except for a fresh wound — neat as a surgical incision — that began at the topmost branch and spiralled to the ground.

We walked around it again and again, marvelling at the awesome power that could twist the rock-hard trunk, and wondered whether even so strong a tree as this could live.

Oldtimers told us that it would not, that it might take a year or more, but it would die. They said the magnificent old live oak was in a death struggle. For awhile, we went out every day to monitor the signs. But after six months, except for that one awful scar down the trunk, there were few. A scattering of leaves turned brown, but that was all.

Once, in the days of wooden ships, the government held Florida's live oak forests in reserve for naval construction. In the 1800s New England seafaring men favored it and sent cutters, called Live Oakers, to Florida to harvest this reliable wood. Now the trees are scattered, more valued for their shade than their substance. They are relics, survivors of another age, like sailing masters and blacksmiths and hand craftsmen.

Knowing all this, we feel a kinship with our stricken but surviving live oak. We notice things now that we overlooked before, special marks of character, knobs and blemishes and distinctions.

Our ancient and wounded friend has awful posture. Off an uneven trunk, a dozen crooked limbs extend far out and then curl upward in tortured thrusts. The tree looks like a tough old arthritic frozen in place as he jerked and strained to straighten up. Despite all that, it reaches a height of at least 60 feet, and casts a shade far wider. It was the first to take that lightning bolt because it was the tallest. The message is clear.

For us the live oak is the noblest tree in our woods — not as elegant as the pine, which stands arrow-straight and somewhat arrogant; not as graceful as the palm; not as pretty as the perfumed magnolia, the maker of myths; but more worthy than them all.

It makes beauty from imperfection, builds strength from flaw. Even in a death struggle, there was uncomplaining style and commitment. We cherish our scarred tree. We do not really need the shade, and we certainly could use a fresh supply of that splendid firewood, but more than anything else we need the example.

The Wonderful Impossibilities
of Spring

The other day we noticed that one of the duck decoys on our lake had a friend, a little coot that kept swimming chummily about, and we knew spring was here. In spring everything alive in these woods gets notions, not always practical ones.

Another day a hawk swooped down, grabbed a clawhold, and almost pulled decoy and anchor and all into the air before letting go. He did not give up easily, either. He circled and tried again before deciding that this was more than a heavy meal.

Spring does that, and for me that makes it the proper start of the year, no matter what the calendar and tradition say. Spring makes a perfect beginning. It nearly always goads me, too, into ambition beyond my capacity.

Nearly always I get an irresistible urge to plant another tree. It seems an appropriate evolution of the young man's fancy, and less taxing, but there remain complications. My yen is for another orange tree, even though I know that for oranges this lake region of north central Florida is on the outer edge of possibility.

The past two winters burned my other little orange trees, and stunted their growth, because I did not cover them properly during hard freezes. It is not an easy thing to do. When the wind blows and the temperatures drop into the 20's, you must go out in the dark and tie old sheets over a bunch of little trees. Next morning, when the sun comes out, you must remove the sheets.

There are lot of other trees that do not mind the winter, but the chemistry is between me and the orange tree. The dogwood, for example, has lovely white blooms and shade but bears no fruit and it strips stark naked of leaves in the winter. The sight of it worsens my chill factor by five degrees. Azalea bushes stay green and bloom royally and briefly in early spring but bear no fruit. A pecan tree yields a harvest, but also strips in winter. The orange stays green, blossoms and bears golden fruit. There really is no comparison.

Usually we discover spring during the daily walk to the mailbox. To get our mail we follow a scenic two-rut trail a quarter-mile through the woods, going past a tumbled-down fence and a broken wagon wheel and a dead pine tree.

There, at what we call Three Points, two double-rut roads meet the big road in a mingle of virginal, rust-colored sand. They form a triangle bordered by the row of mailboxes, sitting like one-legged tin soldier war veterans whose wounds still show.

During winter, the neighbors dash up in cars, roll windows down, shout hellos in puffs of frosty breath and empty their mailboxes as though it were a holdup. Usually it is the opposite. We go there looking for envelopes full of cheer, and most often find junk and demands.

But one day in late February or early March there comes a change. On the walk through the woods, there spring will be, bringing that impossibly ambitious resolution and optimism. All around us trees and bushes browned by winter take the risk of greening again.

The neighbors begin wandering through the woods, some even jogging, and stop to talk about the relief of a winter passed. They open their mailboxes and joke about the same junk that three weeks earlier had depressed them.

Most of the year, Gloria and I argue over who gets to walk to the mailbox every day, and she graciously lets me lose except in spring. I try harder then, and so I get to make the walk, and I find myself making all these spring resolutions.

Padding along in the sand, occasionally poking a stick to move a snake sunning himself in my path, watching my Collie chase squirrels he knows he cannot catch, I am caught up in this Pollyanna mood. I resolve again to be better than I am. I vow once more to sort out as carefully as I can where meaning and value separate from custom and cost, and not to get them confused. I know that it is impossible, that I will not make it stick, but it is spring and I am moved to try. Should I let a coot and a hawk be more enterprising?

It does not take long to become uncomfortable over such thoughts. Things too sweet and too heavy have a way of not agreeing with me. I remind myself that ambition need not be impossible, that things of value cannot be measured by difficulty alone.

Armed with this home-brew wisdom, I pledge to keep our rustic little home and woodsy acreage in its natural state. I will not let the demands of conformity push me into cutting back the wild growth or try to force what's here into any kind of artificial pattern. I will respect the quail and the raccoons and the possums and certain snakes (not to mention the coot and the hawk) and maintain a haven for them around the edges of my own little haven. In this resolution I am being a naturalist, a man of temperance, a disciplinarian and yet a realist. At the height of spring intoxication, I need this one reachable dream to keep my balance.

Otherwise, spring romps. The coot tries to love a wooden duck, and the hawk tries to eat one. I try to nurture little orange trees in a climate too cold for them, and reaffirm ideals beyond my nature, all the while pledging to be practical.

Spring demands these impossible ambitions. They are the beginning of a new cycle, the bargaining for a fresh contract, and negotiations should start high.

We Do Not Care To Talk
About Lightning

One night we heard lightning strike in the woods not far from our house. Days later, we found a great oak popped open like an over-cooked weiner, the bushy crown torn off, pieces of wood flesh explosively scattered.

The tree became a curiosity and more. All the neighbors went to see it. We gathered and fingered the tears in the trunk, remembering how axes bounced off this same wood and how it could make chain saws smoke and strain and turn dull.

We would stand back and stare at the stone-hard oak, stunned at how the rough bark was blasted away, the grain ripped and cauterized by a familiar force, lightning. The evidence was too powerful for digestion. Reality dimmed and mystery flirted.

On such evidence, in ancient times, mythology began. Where truth seemed inadequate, superstitions explained. The oak in those days was known as the tree most often struck by lightning, and it was assumed therefore that a sky-god loved it most and descended periodically to consume it. Stricken trees sometimes were fenced as places of glory. Anyone hit personally by the sky-god, in an awesome application of love, was buried on the spot to commemorate the significant honor.

Now we know at least a little about how lightning generates out of the air, that it involves pent-up electricity that follows a jump-pause pattern searching for other electrical fields through the clouds and to the ground. Intelligence dismisses the sky-god, but the temptation that created him remains.

Even though scientists can tell us why lightning strikes and under what conditions, we still do not know exactly when or exactly where or exactly what we can do about it. The truth still seems too much.

With summer, the thunder starts rumbling across the low sand-hills and lakes near Melrose in north central Florida and lightning season begins. Soon it will be snapping right into our little house in the woods. Occasionally, a ball of fire will pingpong across the living room and vanish with a loud pop.

We retreat to the farthest wall from the big windows overlooking the lake, and sit in the dark transfixed by the notion that while the electricity we buy has fizzled out, the stuff is running wild through the air all around us with enough force to broil anything it caresses.

The feeling is, if you can remember it, like sitting in a horror show at age 10, wide-eyed and sensitive to imminent disaster. The windows flash blindlingly white and then go black, making afterglow halos and changing familiar forms and shapes into threatening images.

When the telephone rings, we do not answer, for lightning plays along the telephone lines and rattles the bells and in a fit of temper it has been known to blast a phone right out of the wall. Light bulbs pop, appliances smoke and birds stop whistling.

We reside in that patch across middle Florida known as Lightning Alley, the most active lightning region in the United States. Between May and October, we average about 100 thunderstorms. Florida has the highest lightning death rate in the nation, and the Alley leads Florida. The sky-god loves us.

We have heard all the advice: stay indoors, avoid machines, move away from windows and fireplaces, keep off the lake and in the open stay away from trees. If suddenly you feel a sensation like your hair standing on end, do not lie down but drop to your knees and be thankful that you make such a small and insignificant target.

When you have survived, you may become expansive and philosophical about truth so overpowering that it produces a kind of lie. You can ponder, for instance, about historians who can tell us why the Vietnam war occurred despite common logic against it; why the incredible web of Watergate should have been a predictable consequence of the trends in political practice; why only involuntarily will we conserve energy even though we know the supply is finite;

why, despite all these apparent lessons, bad history can repeat itself just as lightning can strike twice in the same place.

We walk out into the woods and look at that giant old wounded oak, and we speculate about everything except that the next lightning strike might hit us. Oddly, we do not mind speculating about being bitten by a snake, perhaps because statistics tell us that in Florida lightning strikes far more people than snakes bite.

Scientists who somehow count these things say that lightning strikes the earth 8 million times a day. Our Lightning Alley gets more than its fair share. Whether we install surge controls on the power lines or offer up a fresh young oak to the sky-god, it still comes every summer and scares the hell out of us.

Neither modern logic nor ancient superstition helps, and so we just do not care to talk about it.

Fall: The Gentlest Season

Summer is a lazy cat in a laid-back world, and fall wakes him up. The first chills of October dry the sweat and bring a sweet, natural high that lasts until December makes fog of your breath.

Fall has a wild recipe, a mix of unresisted temptations and accepted realities. It draws a little from spring, turning the fancies of the old, too, to things basic. It borrows some from the full moon, when seeing shadows at night encourages madness. It takes dashes of truth and desperation from old heads who believe nothing is free or forever.

In Florida, fall passes with different gaits. In the south, according to an old expression, it might occur one Tuesday. But that is deceptive, for much of the winter in South Florida has the magic of fall in it. Here where I live, in the lakes area of the north-central highlands around Melrose, it takes several weeks for fall to amble by and during that time things happen.

We first noticed probable signs of fall sprayed across a yellow road sign. Some young fellows of high spirits and good upbringing had tried to cut loose their inhibitions, but only partially succeeded. Apparently unwilling to use four-letter vulgarity, they sought to shock by writing in big letters: "SEX."

A neighbor of more mature years opened her refrigerator the other day to find a rattlesnake coiled on a shelf — skinned, cleaned, dressed and ready to eat. Her son had killed it and prepared it, and then found the only way he could fit the meat into the refrigerator was by coiling it. The rattler got the last kill — family appetites.

Our actuarial calculations are upset. A car hit and killed a young deer on our dirt road. But a tiny crippled quail, part of a 14-bird covey that supped last spring below our birdfeeder, beat the odds.

He hopped along like a rear scout who needed crutches, and we had marked him as an early victim of predators. But this fall, with hunters' guns sounding in the distance, he boldly limped up to the feeder. Trailing the master at a respectful distance was a mate.

Fog hovers over the lake each morning and crows sit on the beach and caw loudly while the sun slowly burns the day clear. Color begins to show in the leaves of the dogwoods and for the next two months, other trees will copy. Acorns shower down at night, rattling across the tin roof of the carport with a startling loudness, and the squirrels give up digging into the flower box on the front porch for the feast in the yard. Lake dwellers begin to gather wood and sit before lighted fireplaces with neighbors they have seen little since last winter. Summers are full of guests and gardens and chores.

I crack a window, letting in just enough of the breeze to cool the office while I work, and the clack of the typewriter brings a pileated woodpecker. He answers me, pecking away at oak trees. It is a peculiar communication, but the only birdcall I can make.

Our pet egret, Biddy, confirmed our suspicions that she has been sharing us with friends. One day recently she ate, flew to the marsh and another egret came to take her place for a backporch handout while Biddy watched. We estimate that we may be feeding as many as four egrets regularly, and that may not be the end. A great blue heron has begun to stand around in the grass observing the egrets, trying to decide whether to risk it.

This season took on an extra touch of class when a bald eagle, the first we have seen here, chased a hawk across the front of our house. When the hawk dropped a snake from its claws, the eagle swooped down to grab it off the ground and wheel away. Even the high and the mighty get down to basics.

A grandmother chose this season to be fitted with a new pacemaker. When the doctor told her romance could reenter her life, she smiled big but asked whether that meant she could eat sausage again. One granddad got a new pair of cataract glasses and his wife said she was so glad because now he could see well enough to bait his fish hook. But the first thing he focussed on was a television show starring Charo.

Fall is like that here, the release from summer that mixes a ration of the unexpected with the commonplace to give life one more twist before winter comes. In Florida, it is an underrated season.

Your Florida Scrapbook

Paste Additional Al Burt Columns Here

Other Popular Books In The Florida Collection
Published By Florida Classics Library

JONATHAN DICKINSON'S JOURNAL or God's Protecting Providence, A True Story of Shipwreck and Torture on the Florida Coast in 1696

FLORIDA'S GOLDEN GALLEONS, The Search For The 1715 Spanish Treasure Fleet, by Robert F. Burgess and Carl J. Clausen

BATTLE OF PENSACOLA — Spain's Final Triumph Over Great Britain in The Gulf of Mexico by Dr. N. Orwin Rush

THE OTHER FLORIDA, by Gloria Jahoda, The "other" Florida is north and west, another country altogether.

MY FLORIDA, by Ernest Lyons, Humorous and philosophical sketches of life in Florida from 1915 to the present.

THE LAST CRACKER BARREL, by Ernest Lyons, Additional essays by the former editor of the Stuart (Fla.) News.

FLORIDAYS, by Don Blanding, Pictures and Poetry from a "House In A Hammock" now available for the first time in paperback.

THE CAVE DIVERS, by Robert F. Burgess, A history of diving in Florida's caves and sinkholes and the historic artifacts they have yielded.

THEY FOUND TREASURE, by Robert F. Burgess, Accounts of dives to famous wrecks many of which are located in Florida waters.